THE GROWTH OF FREEDOM IN EDUCATION

THE GROWTH OF
FREEDOM IN EDUCATION

A Critical Interpretation of
some Historical Views

By
W. J. McCALLISTER

VOLUME I

KENNIKAT PRESS
Port Washington, N. Y./London

THE GROWTH OF FREEDOM IN EDUCATION

First published in 1931
Reissued in 1971 by Kennikat Press
Library of Congress Catalog Card No: 73-115324
ISBN 0-8046-1115-7

Manufactured by Taylor Publishing Company   Dallas, Texas

PREFACE

FREEDOM is one of the educational topics which may be expected to arouse the interest of the general reader. Everyone is inclined to pass judgment upon the adequacy of his education and to be critical of those who have attempted to educate him. No discussion is more likely to arouse the deeper memories of youth. If it is voted dull or wearisome the fault is not in the subject. Whatever may be the appeal of the present book its author must confess that one of his aims was to gain the ear of some whose interest in education is general rather than professional.

The book has grown out of lectures to students preparing for the teaching profession. It is not a text-book of history. It is not intended to be a substitute for the study of the writers who are reviewed in its pages. It hopes to give to the course in the history of education a measure of unity and to do something to connect it with the general theory and practice of education. Too often the history of education is suspended in the mid-air of professional studies, or is forced to yield place to the more pressing claims of practical training. Yet history is the natural means of co-ordinating theory and practice, and no firm or sure grasp of either is possible without it. The book may suggest *one* way in which the three aspects may be interwoven.

The author gratefully acknowledges the help of two of his own teachers—Professor C. W. Valentine of the University of Birmingham who suggested the importance of a book on the subject, and Professor John Laird of the University of Aberdeen whose lectures on the philosophical aspects of freedom stimulated his further study of its meaning in education. He also desires to thank his friend, Rev. Cassells Cordner, M.A., and his former colleague, Miss F. E. Simms, M.A., for assistance in preparing the book for the Press.

QUEEN'S UNIVERSITY, BELFAST
November, 1930.

CONTENTS

CHAPTER   PAGE

I. INTRODUCTION - - - - - - - -   I

Definition of freedom necessary—It underlies all forms of
education—Extreme statements of freedom—Analysis of
the educative process—Freedom and self-education—
Freedom and cosmic education—Connection of freedom
with progress—Freedom and the young pupil—Historical
survey of its meanings an aid to its definition—Its main
functions in the history of education.

II. PLATO'S FREEDOM THROUGH CONTROL - - - -   18

The Greek view of freedom—Socrates states the real start-
ing-point of education—His scepticism—Plato and state
control—Freedom dependent on knowledge—The case for
obedience to the laws—Plato's theory of play—The data
and functions of education in the *Republic*—Two fundamental qualities or tendencies in all education—Their
functions in the various stages of education—Does reason
spring out of ' gentleness ' ?—The continuity of the Platonic theory—Two types of educational adjustment—The
aim of these adjustments and their relation to the laws—
The definition of justice—the principle of non-interference
—Relation of these ideas to freedom—Plato's early and
later views—Summary.

III. ARISTOTLE'S FREEDOM THROUGH THE MEAN - -   50

Aristotle's view of ' completeness '—Its relation to freedom in education—Freedom is not equality—It is not a
principle of ruling and being ruled in turn—His view of
the Soul and particularly of Reason—The relation of
Reason to the Passions—Aristotle's recognition of the
emotions and passions.—Happiness to be found in the
Mean—The psychological and ethical implications of the
Mean—Relation to freedom—Summary.

IV. FREEDOM AND THE ἐγκύκλιος παιδεία - - - -   61

Modifications of the Platonic scheme of studies—The
Sophists—The conception of a ' general ' education—The
history of the ' liberal arts ' the early history of freedom—
Cicero's *doctus orator*—Seneca's criticism of the liberal arts
—Quintilian's training of the orator—Plutarch's practical
view of philosophy. The contributions of these writers to
the practical work of teaching—Why the early idea of the
' liberal arts ' failed to give freedom in the schools.

V. CHRISTIANITY AND FREEDOM - - - - -   78

The conflict of polytheism and monotheism—The Christian Schools and ' pagan studies '—Christ's teaching and

vii

CHAPTER   PAGE

freedom—Clement's *Pedagogue* and *Stromata*—Tertullian's
views—The *Panegyric* of Gregory Thaumaturgus—Origen
as a teacher—Gregory's view of freedom—Jerome's *Letter
to Laeta*—St. Augustine's view of disciplinary studies—
General summary.

VI. FREEDOM IN THE MIDDLE AGES   -   -   -   -   99

The Middle Ages a period of educational consolidation—
The Church as Educator—Education through ' occupations ' in the monasteries—The Royal School of Alcuin—
Rhabanus Maurus and the monastic course of studies—The
monastic view of discipline and supervision—Attempts in
the Middle Ages to make lessons interesting—Aelfric's
Grammar and *Colloquy*—Neckam's *De Utensilibus* and
similar works in the thirteenth century—New forms of
education—The Middle Ages an anticipation of Rousseau's
' negative education.'

VII. FREEDOM AND HUMANISM -   -   -   -   -   -   119

The new forces of the Renaissance—Vergerius' idea of
liberal studies—His appeal to the best human interests—
Erasmus and choice of subjects—Following Nature—The
right relation of teacher to pupil—Pleasurable methods
of teaching—Vives and the experimental attitude—His
psychological point of view—Cardinal Sadoleto's two
types of habit—His analysis of shame—Its relation to
freedom—Practical attempts to give greater freedom in
linguistic studies—Influence of the religious movements—
Luther—The Jesuit view of freedom—The works of Castiglione, Ascham, Elyot, and Mulcaster—Huarte's ' *Tryal of
Wits* '—The Grammar School and freedom—Rabelais, a
critic of the old and the new education.

VIII. MONTAIGNE'S FREEDOM THROUGH MILD SEVERITY   -   148

Montaigne's scepticism—His view of the relation of
teacher to pupil—Not an extreme advocate of individual-
ism—His main idea the reference of all things to the self—
Faguet's criticism—Montaigne's advocacy of a ' sweet-
severe mildness.'

IX. FREEDOM AND REALISM -   -   -   -   -   -   158

The idea of *directness*—Its presentation in Bacon and
Descartes—Its embodiment in the Port Royal Schools—
Fénelon's idea of teaching under the appearance of liberty
—Milton and the Puritan point of view—Hezekiah Wood-
ward's conception of free culture—Sir William Petty's
Advice to Samuel Hartlib—John Dury's *Reformed School*—
The conditioning factors of the teacher's work—Comenius
and pansophy as a form of freedom—Formal Training and
freedom in the works of Comenius.

CHAPTER   PAGE

X. LOCKE'S FREEDOM FOR 'INDIFFERENT ACTIONS'   180

Locke's view of liberty as indifferency—Freedom as ability
to do what one wills—Locke's criticism of education from
this point of view—Two partially conflicting ideas in his
writings—Their synthesis is liberty—Liberty the secret of
education—Reasoning with children—Disciplinary values
—Locke and Formal Training—His views of liberty.

XI. WATTS' APPEAL TO REASON - - - - -   195

The Pietist movement—The Dissenting Academies—
Watts' *Essay on the Freedom of Will in God and in Creatures*—Liberty of voluntariness and of indifference—Freedom through the appeal to judgment—Freedom of Understanding and of Will—Freedom and *Religious Instruction*—
The proper degrees of Liberty and Restraint exemplified
in the education of Eugenio and Phronissa—Watts and
Formal Training.

XII. A SATIRICAL VIEW OF FREEDOM - - - -   212

Two ways of expounding the value of freedom found in the
educational writings of de Crousaz—Freedom in education
as it appears to the worldly-wise—Reference to the teaching of Religion and the Classics.

XIII. A FREE ACADEMY - - - - - - -   219

Fordyce anticipates the *Emile*—An eighteenth century
Socrates—The discussion of the Academy on Freedom in
Education—Summary.

XIV. ROUSSEAU'S 'WELL-REGULATED LIBERTY' - - -   227

Rousseau's plagiarisms—The criticisms of Formey and
Dom Cajot—What is borrowed and what is original in
Emile—The work a pictorial representation of liberty—
Its three main features—(1) An active view of Nature
(2) A scientific determination of the course of studies—
(3) Freedom as the guiding principle of education—Over-
emphasis of the physical and the social environment—The
three stages of Emile's education—Is *Emile* the negation of
liberty? The account of Rousseau's own education in the
Confessions—His view of freedom in the *Contrat Social*—
Well-regulated liberty a system of controls without the
appearance of authority—Errors of *Emile* with regard to
reason, society, the method of discovery in education,
moral training and the imagination—Permanent contribution of Rousseau to the problem of freedom.

XV. EVALUATIONS OF 'WELL-REGULATED LIBERTY' - -   250

Basedow's Philanthropinum—Priestley's criticisms of
Rousseau's method of teaching religion—His use of Hart-
ley's doctrine of Association—David Williams' tests of
Rousseau's theories—Freedom through the study of edu-

CHAPTER   PAGE

cational exponents of freedom—The Edgeworths and
Thomas Day—Contributions of *Practical Education* to
several aspects of freedom—Godwin's challenge of John
Brown's *Thoughts on Civil Liberty*—Godwin reinforces the
appeal to reason—A new view of juvenile education—The
plea for the giving of genuine liberty to the child—Freedom
in education not incompatible with determination—
Summary.

XVI. KANT'S FREEDOM THROUGH OBEDIENCE - - - 271

Influence of *Emile*—Freedom and Restraint—The Prin-
ciple of Non-Interference—The pupil's self-activity—
Maxims and Laws—The good Will—The appeal to Reason
—Obedience to the Moral Law—Its internal nature.

XVII. PESTALOZZI'S ANSCHAUUNGS-PRINZIP - - - - 280

Pestalozzi one of the early experimenters in the field of
freedom—Empirical synthesis of freedom and obedience—
His philosophy—Denial of freedom to the young child—
The spirit of his work—The *Anschauungs-Prinzip*—a prin-
ciple of directness—The three main ideas of the principle—
Early and later views of obedience—Summary.

XVIII. FICHTE'S FREEDOM THROUGH THE 'INSTINCT OF RESPECT' 295

Fichte's restricted view of freedom—Appeal to the pupil's
altruistic tendencies—Liberation of creative activity—
Segregation of the pupil—The instinct of respect—Its
main implications stated—Criticism.

XIX. HEGEL'S FREEDOM THROUGH 'SELF-ESTRANGEMENT' - 304

The history of freedom the history of humanity—Freedom
as the reconciliation of opposites—View of the adolescent
period—Self-estrangement through the study of the
Classics—Classics and 'useful' studies—Hegel's view of
Individuality—Criticism.

XX. FROEBEL'S 'THIRD TERM' - - - - - - 313

The Divine nature in the child—Double aspect of all experience—Internal and external forces in education—The
child's self-activity—His helplessness—Development the
result of reconciliation through the link of mediation—The
third term of Froebel: Its advantages and limitations.

XXI. HERBART'S 'INNER FREEDOM' - - - - - 324

Herbart a philosophical exponent of freedom—His pedagogical views of freedom empirical—Freedom and the
pupil's capacity for cultivation—Freedom and government—The teacher's forecast of the child's future values—
Inner freedom a relationship between Insight and Will—
The *Gedankenkreis*—The unified life as the expression of
freedom.

CHAPTER   PAGE

XXII. FREEDOM THROUGH SELF-DIRECTION - - - - 331

Experimental methods of exploring the meaning of liberty
—David Manson's Play School—His system of landlords
and tenants—Methods of discipline—The Hazlewood ex-
periment in self-government by pupils—Freedom as a
Partnership between teacher and pupil—School-Courts—
Critics of the Hills' experiment.

XXIII. WYSE'S FREEDOM AS A MEANS TO PERFECTION - - 347

National Education as a means to progress—The idea of
Perfection—Education as Preparation—The appeal to the
whole self—The use of the emotions in education—The
union of intellectual and practical activities—The working
out of these ideas through good methods of teaching—The
individual appeal in education—The rights of the child as
sacred—Freedom through good methods.

XXIV. MILL'S FREEDOM FOR INDIVIDUALITY - - - 360

Mill's exclusion of children from the privileges of liberty—
His arguments for the liberty of the adult—Do they apply
to education ? Two views of the self in Mill's *Essay*—The
influence of Robert Owen and Josiah Warren upon Mill's
views—The communistic experiments of New Harmony
and Modern Times—Owen's and Warren's views of freedom in education.

XXV. SPENCER'S ' NON-COERCIVE EDUCATION ' - - - 369

Spencer's views compared with Rousseau's—His advocacy
of an active course of culture—of the method of discovery
—of moral education—of freedom—Freedom without infringing the freedom of others—Applicability to education
—The affective aspects of education—The doctrine of
interest—The views in *Social Statics*—Spencer's plea for
the rights of children—His educational theory the reflex
of his own early education—His prescription of science—
His view of classical literature.

XXVI. TOLSTOY'S CONCEPT OF ' NON-INTERFERENCE ' - - 384

Tolstoy's early ideas of education and progress—All compulsion arbitrary—His school at Yasnáya Polyána—Freedom to transmit knowledge the main concern of the teacher
—Tolstoy's methods—The theory of non-interference
tested by his own records—Later views—The relation of
teacher to pupil to be natural—The method to be non-
coercive—Closing years—Education based on religion—
Suggestion the main force in the teacher's art—Liberty to
study or not to study—Teaching as an educational osmosis
—Concrete pictures of the free pupil, and of the art of
teaching.

CHAPTER   PAGE

XXVII. MONTESSORI'S BIOLOGICAL CONCEPT OF LIBERTY - 403

The fundamental principles of Montessori's works—The
influence of Sergi, Séguin, Itard and Pereire on Montessori's views—Séguin's conception of freedom—Montessori's
first work an extension of Séguin's experiments—Comparison of the early Montessori method with Séguin's
education of idiots—Transference to normal children—
The didactic apparatus—Auto-education—Biological and
social aims weakly interwoven in Montessori's exposition—
Freedom and its ' intuitive quid '—Does the apparatus give
freedom to teacher and to pupil ?—Its control (1) of the
child's general activity (2) of his imagination—Value of
some of the main ideas of the Montessori Method—Polarization of attention—Critical evaluation of one of the early
exercises—Summary.

XXVIII. PROFESSOR DEWEY'S FREEDOM THROUGH CO-OPERATION 432

The pragmatic point of view in education—Freedom in its
internal and external aspects—Freedom as social guidance
that expresses the individual's mental attitude—How
social guidance is made effective in school-work—Two
views of society considered—Their difficulties for education—Criticism of the value of social guidance for (1) the
development of meaning, (2) the attainment of certain and
exact knowledge, (3) the transfer of learning from school
to social life, (4) the promotion of discovery, (5) the
attainment of clear moral ideas—Criticism of Professor
Dewey's general contribution to freedom.

XXIX. FREEDOM AND THE UNCONSCIOUS -   -   -   - 462

Repression hitherto assumed to be an efficient force in
education—The teaching of the new psychology—Freud's
view of the Unconscious—The ego- and sex-instincts—
Pleasure and Reality Principles—General conception of
instinct—The possibility of sublimation—Adler's theories
stated—The pupil's feeling of inferiority—Criticism of
Adler's main principles—Jung's view of the Unconscious—
Psychical inheritance—The tendency towards the higher
life of the race—Conflict within the personality—Jung's
study of the neurosis—Its relation to freedom in education
—Sublimation as the finding of a common element—The
psychology of the Unconscious reinforces the arguments of
the previous chapters.

XXX. FREEDOM FOR CREATIVE ACTIVITY -   -   -   - 487

The creative aspects of freedom—Professor Gentile's
statement and resolution of the antimony of education—
Realistic and idealistic conceptions of culture—The educator as a realist—Sir Percy Nunn's view of freedom as a
universal ideal—His view of hormic activity—His conception of self-assertion—Self-submission as a co-ordinate
tendency—The rôle of self-submission in education—Why
it is often overlooked—Summary.

CHAPTER   PAGE
XXXI. THE PUPIL'S REACTION TO FREEDOM - - -   506

The pupil's view of freedom the subject of investigation—
Experiments in various Play Schools—The Caldecott
Community—The application of Play Methods to teaching
—The Class-Room Republic—Individual Methods—School-
government—Remedial and Reformatory Methods—
Professor Collings' inquiry into the results of a curriculum
selected directly from the purposes of pupils—An inquiry
into the right amount of freedom and guidance in school-
work—Summary.

XXXII. CONCLUSION - - - - - - - - 537

Three main conclusions—Increase in the content of education associated with greater measures of freedom—Un-
attained aspects of liberty the mainspring of progress—
Five stages in the evolution of freedom—The individual's
conception of freedom likely to be arbitrary—A moment of
freedom exemplified in Dr. Montessori's ' polarization of
attention '—Two types of relevancy—The general idea of
the at-one-ness of the self with some objects—The *maintenance* of a relevant value the minimum characteristic of
freedom—The quest for freedom—*Intensification* and *reinforcement* of relevancy through communal activities—
Methods of increasing the relevancy of school-work—Some
values demand an almost complete freedom—The *determination* of relevancy—Conflict of values—The function
of self-submission—The indolent self, the playful self, the
delinquent self—Their relation to freedom—Force not
necessarily incompatible with freedom—The active self—
Freedom as the balancing of self-assertive and self-sub-
missive tendencies—The teacher's functions—Past difficulties to be solved by experimental study of the pupil's
reaction to a full educational environment—Tests of a full
environment—Continuity of growth—The teacher's aloofness often wrongly stated—Freedom as the highest value,
common to teacher and pupil—Definition—Some of the
consequences of making freedom the central concept of
education.

BIBLIOGRAPHY - - - - - - - - - 566

INDEX - - - - - - - - - - - 581

CHAPTER I

INTRODUCTION

EDUCATIONAL theory seems at the moment to have reached the second of the three evolutionary stages through which, as Herbert Spencer and others think, all bodies of knowledge are destined to pass. The first stage—the dogmatism of the ignorant—is not a thing entirely of the past : the final phase—the unanimity of the wise—is scarcely in sight. A faith strong enough to evoke the healthy scepticism of inquiring minds is its prevailing temper. Hence the lack of reverence for the nebulous fringes which, like halos, envelop most of the popular expressions of educational aims, and hence the effort to trim and fit ideas woven from the rough warp and woof of everyday speech into the sober habiliments of a logically consistent body of truth.

None of its watchwords reveals more clearly the retrospective and prospective stages than the term freedom. Freedom gives a challenge to dogmatism and by the very piquancy of its vagueness invites the first step towards unanimity—careful definition. For although no other term is more widely used in current educational discussion, and none seems to designate with such alluring facility the peculiar tincture of reform that most readily flows from the pen of the individual writer, no adequate presentation of its essential meaning for practical schemes of education has hitherto been undertaken. Too often it is a mere cloak for the advocacy of partially conflicting and largely misleading ideas, associated with its use in popular speech, poetry, rhetoric, or politics, and pressed into the service of education where it is sure of a sympathetic and even deferential reception. So great have been its abuses in the realm of politics that one writer rejects it as ' useless in science,' [1] and banishes it to ' rhetoric and poetry where it belongs.' But

[1] J. R. Seeley, *Introduction to Political Science*, p. 104.

although in education, as in politics, it often stands for ' this and at the same time a hundred things totally different ' [1] it is, as we shall attempt to show in the following pages, a fundamental and necessary concept for a science of education, and for the practice of education a term which, when carefully defined, may give point, direction and force to every detail and perspective of the process—a term, in short, so central for education that if it be denied or banished it will re-affirm its necessary presence in the very act of denial and banishment.

No doubt it often seems that actual teaching has little or no place for freedom. It may therefore not be amiss to consider some of the main forms of the teacher's art which seem to exclude its operation, and to attempt to find reasons for its apparent exclusion. Even if this method of exposition runs the risk of anticipating or stating rather dogmatically some of the conclusions reached in subsequent chapters it may have the advantage of acquainting the reader with the assumptions, in respect of the meaning of education, that underlie the criticism of other views of freedom soon to be stated and considered.

It has to be remembered, in the first place, that the term ' teaching ' is applied to a very wide range of activities. Professor Graham Wallas urges that the whole race is, and must be, a race of ' unqualified ' teachers. 'We could not continue to exist in our present numbers, unless mothers taught their babies from the moment of birth, unless brothers and sisters, and husbands and wives, and neighbours and friends, taught each other. Every employer and foreman, every housekeeping woman, every writer, thinker, artist, preacher, politician, doctor and policeman spends most of his time in teaching. In newspaper offices, theatres, cinemas, debating societies, Government departments, churches and chapels, libraries, ships, barracks, and factories much more effective intellectual stimulus and instruction may be going on than in the brick and stone buildings which are called schools and colleges.' [2] The man in the street is, then, for the nonce at least, a teacher : in popular opinion teaching includes the designs of a Fagin as well as the aims of a St. Francis of Assisi. It is equally tolerant of the methods of a Tolstoy who would make his pupils submit

[1] J. R. Seeley, *Introduction to Political Science*, p. 104.
[2] *Our Social Heritage*, p. 145.

to no form of compulsion save that which comes from their own impressionable natures,[1] and of a Trollope who required his son to repeat, almost in babyhood, the rules of Latin grammar at six o'clock in the morning, the son dutifully inclining his head while repeating his task, so that the father might easily pull the boy's hair without stopping his shaving operations.[2]

If we examine the list of teachers suggested by Professor Graham Wallas (retaining Fagin and Mr. Trollope as limiting types of the ' whole race of unqualified teachers ') we shall find it difficult to state any common and desirable quality of the activities in which, as teachers, they indulge. Fagin's lessons can scarcely be called ' instruction ' in the usual sense of the term, even though some of his pupils seem to have been intellectually stimulated, and we can scarcely agree that Mr. Trollope's stimulus was primarily intellectual. Teaching seems, in fact, to be applicable (1) (as in Fagin's school) to the skilful presentation of wrong activities for selfish ends, (2) (as in Mr. Trollope's lessons) to the faulty presentation of right activities for unselfish ends, and (3) (as in the whole race of unqualified teachers) to presentations, skilful or unskilful, of things right or wrong, for ends selfish or unselfish. In characterizing the activities as right or wrong, in distinguishing degrees of skill, and in attributing motives for undertaking the office of a teacher we are, it would seem, assigning qualities that are mere accidents of the term. In popular thought teaching is not to be positively defined by reference to what, or how, or why we teach. It seems to stand for the influencing of any person whom we are able to influence by any method of influence that we can devise. To say this, is to say that the teacher, and the teacher alone, is the arbiter of the process and to agree that he should be granted complete freedom of action. He is, therefore, consciously or unconsciously animated by a concept of almost complete personal freedom.

There are obvious dangers, as well as crudities of expression, in popular conceptions of teaching. It is true that the activities of Fagins may be checkmated by the lessons of the policeman, the teaching of the church supplemented by the

---

[1] Cf. Tolstoy, *Pedagogical Articles* : The School at Yasnáya Polyána (vol. iv of complete works translated by Wiener), p. 229.

[2] Cf. Anthony Trollope, *An Autobiography*, pp. 13-14.

presentations of the cinema or the theatre, the *obiter dicta* of one politician nullified by the terminological inexactitudes of another, and thus the cancelling of opposing views may permit society to live and thrive in spite, rather than because, of the intellectual stimulus and instruction of its 'unqualified teachers.' But within the special agencies of education (and particularly in those established or controlled by the state) some semblance of unity must be preserved. Checks to the complete freedom of the unqualified teacher, and a refinement of the concept of freedom, become necessary.

Even in the sphere of the qualified teacher, freedom often seems to be excluded from the teacher's art. But the reasons for exclusion are now very different. The 'unqualified' teacher (as we have seen) represents no one but himself ; the educator is primarily a representative, or even a servant, of some social group within the state, or, it may be, of the state itself. The more strongly he feels himself attached to his social environment and the more earnestly he strives to assimilate its point of view, its habits, customs, and ideals, the more completely he will give himself to the task of presenting and focusing these communal activities and aspirations. His aim, in general, coincides with d'Holbach's—to cause men to contract early, that is to say when their organs are very flexible, the habits, the opinions and the modes of life adopted by the society in which they will live.[1] In practice, however, he has to transmit qualities characteristic of a social group to an individual who as yet does not possess them, an individual who does possess, however, a peculiar flexibility or capacity for their acquirement. The task of 'causing' the pupil to acquire the social graces is soon found to be an exceedingly difficult one. With the appearance of difficulties come differentiations of procedure, three of which may be briefly considered.

The obvious way of meeting the difficulty of those who will *not* 'contract the habits and opinions of the social group' is to merge the freedom both of teacher and taught in the group itself, and by attempting to inculcate a zealous loyalty to the aims and habits of society to induce obedience to them. Too often the obedience is half-hearted and the appeal to loyalty is unintelligible to the pupil: what seem to the educator satis-

---

[1] Cf. *Système de la Nature* (1770), c. 14, pp. 290 ff.

fying aims and ideals worthy of reverence are for the pupil nothing more than the husk of convention or the patter of outworn creeds. Some form of compulsion usually follows. It is the setting of social aims and requirements on a pedestal that leads Tolstoy to define education as the ' tendency to a moral despotism raised to a principle,' [1] to argue that it cannot be put ' at the base of intelligent human activity,' that, therefore, it cannot be given the rank of a science, and that, in short, it is merely an expression of the ' tendency of one man to make another just like himself.' This transference of the freedom enjoyed personally by the ' unqualified ' teacher to the impersonal region of communal values means the abrogation of education as a science, the elevation of social habits and ideals to a position which history shows they have little hope of maintaining, and the inculcation of a loyalty which is likely to be strained and evanescent.

Another solution attempts to abandon the reference to social values and to elevate as a new principle of ' despotism ' the mental attitudes and disciplines associated with the studies in which the values are embodied. Arithmetic, for example, is no longer to be studied because of any value it may have for military manœuvres,[2] but because of the discipline it affords in reasoning, in abstraction and so forth. The undergoing of this discipline, however distasteful it is at the moment, is in some obscure manner believed to produce a mental flexibility that will in the future be advantageous to the individual and profitable to society. Again the solution is only partial, unless it can explain why mental agility should be increased by mental gymnastics which engender attitudes of dissatisfaction and distaste. With its failures, however, we are not at the moment concerned : our task is merely to point out that a type of freedom to be enjoyed at some future date is the directive influence in the educative process. It may be, like many things of the future, an illusory freedom, but it is a directive concept of education.

Another way of meeting the difficulty is so similar to the last that the two are often joined together in practice. It bravely meets the *impasse* of the pupil's hostility by setting up

---

[1] *Pedagogical Articles*, p. 110.
[2] As in Plato, *Republic*, vii. 525.

a new kind of freedom—the kind that can be enjoyed only by conquering distasteful tasks. As one Head of a school puts it : ' There is too much sloppy food in the educational nurseries of to-day : a little grit would help our mental digestion.' But while it is the mark of a coward to shirk inevitable difficulties, it is only a fool who makes needless difficulties, and it is only a foolish teacher who will increase the normal difficulties of the educative process, or speak as if he believed that the value of education is solely conditioned by its difficulty. But, again, our main point is to show that the compulsion of distasteful tasks really aims at the freedom that comes through facing and mastering them. In actual life the result may often be the retreat, not the triumphal advance, of the pupil, but in the mind of the educator a concept of freedom is a directive factor.

In the above cursory review we have seen the main burden of the concept of freedom pass from the shoulders of the teacher to the aims and values of the social group, and from those of the group to those of the person educated, or, more precisely, to values attached to some phase or portion of his life. We have still to consider the limiting view (such as that of Tolstoy) which emphasizes the freedom of the pupil here and now. Later we shall discuss the types of education known as self and cosmic education.

The remarks of a distinguished literary critic not only state the extreme case for the pupil's present freedom, but also clearly show that without a moderated concept of freedom it is impossible to admit the claim of education to be a science. The indictment is not despotism but something more serious : ' In all education as, perhaps in everything human, there is involved a fundamental contradiction from which there is no escape. We teach to write, and every style which is not original is no style ; we teach to think, and every thought got from another person is not a thought but a formula, . . . we teach to feel, and every borrowed feeling is an affectation, a hypocrisy ; we teach to will, and to will through obedience is an abdication of the will. By its own definition, then, teaching thwarts its own aims.' [1]

[1] Faguet on Rousseau's ' *Émile*,' *Études Littéraires* (Dix-huitième siècle, 2ᵉ Éd. p. 360).

The argument here is the direct antithesis of that which is supposed to justify the position of the ' unqualified teacher.' There all influence is held to be legitimate : here no influence is healthful. The one sets up an ideal of complete freedom for the thought, the feeling and the endeavour of the individual teacher. The other exalts a conception of freedom for the thought and endeavour of the individual pupil which would leave him (and us) totally uninfluenced by the eloquence of a M. Faguet, and would make every attempt to influence our fellows a tyranny and every opening of the gates of our minds to another a surrender of a free man's rights and a reversion to the instincts of a slave. Surely receptivity to influence instead of being the inevitably evil result of education is rather the very condition of its being. For, as one writer puts it : ' A willingness to know, a readiness to listen, a desire to be convinced, an attitude of candour, an honesty of the intellect— these things are wrought into the fibres of the *developed* mind.' [1]

Somewhere between the despotism denounced by Tolstoy and the extreme freedom demanded by Faguet there is a *via media* that will resolve the inherent contradictions of current forms of education ; a concept that will regulate the barren and mischievous tendency of making the pupil in our own image, and reveal the hollowness of the types of education that profess to attain some good end by means opposed and contradictory to it. When this elusive middle term is found there will be no need for the statement of a further aim for the educative process. It will have no aim outside itself. The aim of education is simply more education.

We are now in a position to state the fundamental factors in education. From the term we exclude all forms of teaching which do not connect the thing taught, whatever it may be, (1) with the social, or communal, or human ideals that sustain and preserve it, and (2) with the life aspirations of the pupil. If we use the general term ' individual value ' for any tendency, endeavour, or aspect of life that the pupil desires to express more fully, and ' communal value ' for any corresponding tendency, endeavour or aspect of life maintained and preserved by the community of which the pupil forms part, or by that wider fellowship that knows no distinction of Jew or Gentile,

[1] Horne, *Philosophy of Education*, p. 228. (*Italics* mine.)

bond or free, then we may say that the fundamental factors in any moment of a truly educative process are (1) an individual value that seeks a fuller contact with (2) nature itself, or with some communal value, which is in some respects fuller, more satisfying, more suggestive than the individual value, and (3) a principle of freedom that makes the union of these two values more vital and secure. Where the two are in vital *rapport* we have freedom in education, whether the value presented to the pupil is a philosophical view of the universe, or a ' little unpretending rill,' or the record of man's thoughts and achievement, and whether it is presented through an educator alive to the meaning of freedom, or by an ' unqualified ' teacher whose lessons happen to embody the conditions of liberty.

Education is possible without the active services of a *personal* educator. But the absence of the educator only means that personal agency is in the background. In any really educative situation we breathe the atmosphere of human aspiration and from it there is no escape. It would seem, nevertheless, that the limiting forms of self-education and cosmic education do not require a principle of freedom. These we must examine briefly.

Self-education need not detain us. It is not so much the education of the self by the self as the education of the self by external agencies and means that are self-chosen. It is sometimes held (as, for instance, in the pages of Herbert Spencer) to be the type of education *par excellence*, and the view is likely to gain support when it is contrasted with coercive and compulsory methods of teaching. A comparison of self-education with the general view adumbrated above is, however, simply the contrast of an activity guided solely by the individual's choice of educative material with a process animated by a concept representative of both the individual and the social values that underlie it. It may appear to beg the question if we assume the possibility of an educator (or a science of education) gauging more accurately than the person educated the materials needed for his education. But we take it for granted that the educator will determine his pedagogical activities by a principle of freedom defined partly, at least, in the light of the pupil's manifestations. There must therefore be some place for self-education within the scope of an education based on a concept of freedom. There may even be a very considerable importance assigned to those limiting forms of it which involve little reference to values external to the self. But to admit these facts is not to admit that self-education does not require a guiding principle of freedom. For if there is any truth in Tolstoy's idea of a tendency to make others like ourselves there must be some truth also in the tendency to continue to make ourselves like ourselves. This may be even more baneful than the tendency to which Tolstoy draws our attention, for we are likely to resist domination of the self by others and not so likely to perceive that of the self by the self. And it must be remembered that even if self-education and creative activity work on the highest levels of life and bring the deepest sense of freedom we may not be justified in taking them as models of all forms of the educative process. They may be as unrepresentative of it as they are of life as a whole.

Our argument up to this point has assumed the existence of communal values and the idea of progress. We have spoken of human aspirations not only as common values of a particular social group but also as forces that persist from generation to generation and influence the outlook and the effort of groups widely separated in time and space. It is well to remember, however, that human values persist only through their affirmation by individuals, and that few, if any, are so perfect or final that their content or mode of expression may hope to remain long embedded in congealed formulae of custom, habit, morality or religion. They have a life of their own—or rather a continuous rebirth in new forms. They are perpetually re-fertilized by the variations of human expression. If they are imposed rigidly on individuals they may become the bonds and fetters of the more sensitive souls. Men like Tolstoy, keenly aware of the complacency and hypocrisy of the forms of so-called progress, dare to question this tyranny of the past, to re-assert the worth of individual adventure, and even to challenge the things for which others profess themselves ready to die. In all ages there have been men valiant enough to sacrifice even life itself so that something greater than individual existence might be assured of life. What are we to make of these apparent contradictions of human existence?

Have our apparently fortuitous contacts with Nature any educative influence ? Do the hard facts of life—world-wide unrest, nature ' red in tooth and claw,' human beings puny and helpless before natural forces that in a few minutes may annihilate a race or a continent—harmonize with the ideas of cosmic education, progress and freedom ?

Our answers to these questions will depend on our personal outlook on life. We may believe with Mr. Bertrand Russell that ' all the labours of the ages, all the devotion, all the inspiration, all the noonday brightness of human genius, are destined to extinction in the vast death of the solar system,' [1] and yet find in this ' firm foundation of unyielding despair ' the basis of a *free* man's worship, and the sustenance of those hopes and fears that make up the flimsy tissue of his brief life. Or, on the other hand, we may argue, as another great thinker does,[2] that a power that waited four hundred million years for the appearance of man upon a planet which can still look forward to millions of years of habitable temperature may yet accomplish much through a race of beings that has learnt to co-operate consciously in the management of things. With him we may say :

' Hope is in the air, we can co-operate in the Divine plan, we can help and stimulate each other. Weak and erring mortals as we are, yet we feel within us infinite possibilities. The future lies large and splendid before us, both before the race and before individuals too. The frustrated struggle of our earth life is not for ever. Progress is possible both for the individual and the race and the ultimate Destiny of man is so lofty that in the long last we shall look back upon all this travail, this long effort to bring to birth a truly Divine race, and be satisfied that all the intermediate stages, all its imperfections, its terrible trials and griefs, are stages inevitable towards the attainment of the main result—the attainment of perfection not by compulsion but by free will.'

If we take this view from the mountain-top we shall regard all education, of whatever type or through whatever agency, as the embodiment of a principle of freedom. The aim of the cosmos itself will be the education of the race through

---

[1] *A Free Man's Worship.* (*Philosophical Essays*, p. 64.)
[2] Sir Oliver Lodge, *Making of Man*, p. 127.

liberty, and all deliberate forms of education will be co-workers towards the

> Far-off divine event
> To which the whole Creation moves.

And even if we view our destiny from the valley we shall probably find the despair of human existence softened by the undeniable presence of those lesser or greater hopes that keep alive the idea of progress in the human breast. The hopes themselves cannot be gainsaid, and so long as they live the consciousness of freedom and of progress lives with them.[1] The best evidence we have of progress is that of growth in our own lives and in the lives of others through education. On either view, the only good things in life are free activities which may be fostered through some type of educative process. We may deny or affirm that the cosmos is an educator but we affirm in either case that education proceeds through freedom.

To return to our analysis. We take the deliberate forms of education through the person of an educator as the *normal* type. The exact relationship of the educator to the individual and communal values which we have found in a concrete moment of educational activity, will be stated in the definition of freedom—the task of the succeeding chapters. In the meantime let us remind ourselves that his main task is to bring together the *disjecta membra* of our analysis, and that nearly all his mistakes seem to arise from over-emphasizing one or other of the two factors. The attaching of all importance to a self of absolutely personal values leads inevitably to the denouncement of education as despotism, imposition, hypocrisy, servility ; the exaggeration of the values offered by the educator to forms of teaching that stifle initiative, impede individual adjustment, and hamper self-expression. Both mistakes will be avoided by remembering that no self is a rigidly entrenched system of absolutely personal thoughts, feelings and volitions, completely sufficient, self-contained,

---

[1] Cf. Dean Inge's cautious view of progress (*Outspoken Essays*, Second Series, p. 176). ' The climbing instinct of humanity, and our discontent with things as they are, are facts which have to be accounted for, no less than the stable instincts of nearly all species. We all desire to make progress, and our ambitions are not limited to our own lives or our lifetimes. It is part of our nature to aspire and hope ; even on biological grounds this instinct must be assumed to serve some function.'

isolated, impervious, nor is it a completely expansive and passively benevolent receptacle for traditional customs, lifeless aphorisms and outworn creeds. Values, as we have seen, are never entirely imposed from without and are never completely unique and individual : their content inevitably bears the mark of an outside source even when their expression bears the mark of the highest creative activity. Life is the woof of self-expression crossing the warp of social values and education is the attempt to make life more complete and satisfying. There is neither a necessary despotism nor an inherent futility in trying to make a well-woven fabric rather than a haphazard union of strands.

It may be objected that in assuming an individual value that demands a fuller expression we are not fair to the hard facts of educational activity. Boys, we are told, must be helped up the slopes of Parnassus by the scruff of the neck : how can we expect childhood and youth to possess such desires as our analysis assumes ? To the question the obvious answer is that no education, worthy of the name, is possible in the absence of such desires, and that the stagnation assumed by the objector does not, in fact, exist in youth. The very subjectivity and immaturity of youth, its lack of knowledge, its perception of weakness, its instability, are positive advantages as well as limitations which lead it to make strong and continued effort to pass outside the circle of limitless self-contentment assumed by the objection. In truth the values of childhood and youth are of all values the most fluid : at no other stage of the educative process do we find the same active and persistent incorporation of external influences within the whirl of individual tendencies and purposes. The gradual weakening of the receptive tendencies, the development of the *laissez faire* attitude to life are characteristics of adult, not of immature, experience, and in the fact lie those very tragedies of so-called education that we wish to avoid. At the same time it must be admitted that some advocates of freedom unduly emphasize the ideas of creative activity and paint a picture of the school-boy's ceaseless efforts towards perfection that scarcely harmonizes with their delineation of the entrenched life of the adult. Here as elsewhere the truth seems to lie in the application to both young and old of the question : " Do men gather grapes of thorns or figs of thistles ? "

We shall, accordingly, decline to acknowledge any *radical* difference in the types of experience usually designated immature and mature. The distinctions are, no doubt, important for many purposes, but education has no other subject-matter or distinctive province than that of a *growing and developing experience*. It therefore views life from an angle of its own : its concern is with processes rather than with results, with the concept of growth rather than with momentary conceptions of maturity. It has some fixed points to which by times its partial aims are directed, but so far as it keeps true to itself and its own methods its goal ever recedes. Hence the philosophical discussions of freedom directed as they usually are to the *being* and not the *becoming* of freedom, and idealistic views of freedom tending, as they do, to emphasize the mental creation of the universe by the pupil rather than his active adjustment to the hard facts of reality, must be reviewed in the light of the needs of a developing, not of a fully developed, creature. Political conceptions of freedom, restricted as they usually are, to those mythical entities of Mill—' human beings in the maturity of their faculties '—have also little or no place in a science which does not arrogate to itself the relatively fixed concepts which most sciences choose as their distinctive subject-matter.

But if the meaning of freedom for education is specific it must not be narrow or partial. As we have seen, there is a tendency to limit the factors upon which it works to one instead of the two that are necessary to give meaning to the process as a whole. In actual practice there is also the further tendency to limit its operation to this or that aspect of these two partial factors. Thus we often find the emphasis of the social, or the intellectual, or the moral, or the aesthetic, or even the physical aspects of communal values and, on the individual side, the singling out of the creative, or the inventive, or the hedonistic, or the utilitarian tendencies, or even of the faculty of reasoning, or memory, or imagination, etc. But education based on a true conception of freedom is concerned with more than the merely social, or intellectual, or aesthetic, or moral, or creative, or pleasure-seeking, or useful aspects of life, and the person educated is more than a little man, a citizen, a miniature saint, a will to be strengthened, a memory to be cultivated, or an imagination to be chastened.   When animated by a spirit of freedom education is a message from, to, and through life. In our search for the meaning of freedom we must make a resolute effort to view the aspects and partial activities of life as elements in an inclusive whole.

It may be useful now to re-state the main points of our argument and to ask whether they throw light on the method to be adopted in our pursuit of the definition of freedom.   The term is implied in all types of education and its main function is that of a mediator between two very fluid factors—communal and individual values.   Its true force appears only when each of these is viewed as a complementary factor of a life process and is interpreted in the broadest and most comprehensive terms.   It is, nevertheless, a function exercised only within a specific kind of experience—one in which the limitations of an individual life are removed, so that the very act of removal fosters directly or indirectly the further removal of individual limitation.   The method of treatment must therefore (1) be broad in scope, (2) keep in mind the definite type of experience to which education restricts itself, and (3) avoid the tendency which, according to Tolstoy, is the *fons et origo* of the whole discussion.   In the definition of freedom the tendency to make another like oneself is apt to be present.

The only method, known to the writer, which is likely to fulfil these requirements is a survey of the views or partial aspects of freedom, propounded by writers on education.   This may profitably take the form of a historical survey, which need not be exhaustive but which must be suggestive of the typical methods of treating the subject.   The views of Socrates, Plato, and Aristotle and, in particular, Plato's conception of Justice, have a close bearing upon freedom.   Plato's scheme of studies in the *Republic* may be regarded as representative of theories which make communal values the predominating factor in education.   The further development of education, at least until the middle of the nineteenth century, may be envisaged as a continual re-adjusting of the traditional ' liberal arts ' which grew out of Plato's scheme to the changing demands of life and freedom.   Cicero, Seneca, Quintilian and

Plutarch show the modifications demanded by the practical mind, while the Christian Fathers, SS. Clement of Alexandria, Gregory Thaumaturgus, Tertullian and Augustine, reveal the difficulties of harmonizing the truth that made men free with the view of the universe presented in pagan literature. The Middle Ages give a picture of the adaptation of the liberal arts to the requirements of the Christian Church, and, as in the earlier period, give many indications of a belief in freedom as a means of efficient and economical learning. Alcuin and Rhabanus Maurus are worthy of special mention. With the Renaissance there comes a new vision of old values—a new vision of the studies that make men free. In Vergerius, da Feltre, Erasmus, and Vives (and especially in Erasmus) we can see the germs of Rousseau's interpretation of ' following nature.' The same period sees in the writings of Castiglione, Ascham, Elyot, and Mulcaster new outbursts of educational activity, and an appeal to tendencies in the pupil's life that had previously been ignored. Rabelais gives us a fantastic presentation of the aims and results of the old and the new views. With Montaigne a new glimpse of freedom appears in the history of education : in theory, at least, the pupil leads and the master follows. A notable anticipation of Pestalozzian ' concreteness ' appears in the Port Royalist schools, in Fénelon's ' play ' methods, in the pages of Milton, and in the little-known works of Hezekiah Woodward and John Dury. The general relation of this group of ' sense realists ' to freedom is seen in Dury's idea of ' no servile constraint in education.' Comenius attempts to combine this negative view of freedom with an elaborate pansophy. Locke comes boldly forth as the first direct advocate of freedom as a mean between restraint and licence. Watts, almost forgotten as a thinker in the educational field, makes ' a just liberty ' a cardinal feature of education and gives a concrete designation of freedom in the persons of Eugenio and Phronissa. Two almost unknown writers, de Crousaz and Fordyce, may be regarded as typical of many contemporary advocates of a reasonable freedom. Their presentations of the motives that underlay current conceptions of the pupil's ' freedom,' may enable us to understand more clearly the purpose of *Émile*. Rousseau, the usually accredited father of freedom, focuses the main ideas of his educational predecessors in his system of ' well-regulated liberty,' and for the first time places educational theory and practice on a firm foundation of freedom. Many critical evaluations of Rousseau's theory and practice follow—notably those of John Brown and Joseph Priestley, of William Godwin, David Williams, and the Edgeworths—writers who suggest experimental or critical methods of investigating the problem of liberty. Kant falls under Rousseau's spell, and lectures on Freedom through Obedience ; Pestalozzi struggles incessantly with the practical synthesis of the two ideas ; Fichte anticipates Dr. McDougall's presentation of the self-regarding sentiment (just as Sadoleto anticipated Fichte) and bases freedom on an instinct of ' self-respect ' ; Hegel finds the conditions of freedom in the fertilization of ideas gained from sources outside the self ; Froebel emphasizes a ' third ' (or mediating) term between the partially contradictory notions of Locke ; Herbart finds the essence of freedom in relevant ideas. The Hills initiate a system of self-government, and thus extend the ideas mooted by Trotzendorf three hundred years previously. A noteworthy contribution to the idea of freedom through good methods of teaching appears in Sir Thomas Wyse's little-known work on *Education Reform*. The same ideas of method, joined with a rather dogmatic prescription of science, run through Herbert Spencer's pleas for a non-coercive education and for the recognition of those rights of childhood which John Stuart Mill rules out of court in his famous *Essay on Liberty*. The views of individuality and freedom there sketched show the influence of the communistic schemes of education carried on for a time by Robert Owen and Josiah Warren. Their works may be regarded as enthusiastic forerunners of many sober efforts to bring the rudiments of a liberal culture to the lives of the masses caught in the maelstrom of the Industrial Revolution. Tolstoy in his early works fulminates against all compulsory culture and finally sees in freedom a legitimate result of suggestion. Madame Montessori brings the experimental studies of mentally defective children by Pereire, Itard and Séguin into relation with the work of the infant and primary school and formulates a biological theory of liberty. Professor Dewey finds the nerve of democratic freedom in co-operative activities. Other recent writers, notably Professors Gentile and

Nunn, emphasize the creative aspects of personality as the real basis of freedom. The works of Drs. Freud, Jung and Adler show the part played by the unconscious mind in the attainment of freedom. Many experiments made during the last two decades indicate the reaction of the pupil himself to such aspects of freedom as individual education and self-government.

These seem to the present writer the main milestones on the path of freedom, and they will be briefly described and interpreted in the following chapters. No claim for completeness of treatment is made ; many aspects of freedom are expressly omitted from the survey. The historical aspect of the subject is confined to western education ; its interpretations are confined to questions of practical rather than theoretical interest ; its treatment is limited to germinal ideas rather than to actual attempts to embody freedom in any fixed or final form.[1] Many problems directly connected with it or forming a substantive part of it are ignored. Thus, for example, the different degrees of freedom granted to the sexes at various stages in the history of the idea have been passed over in silence, and problems bearing upon the influence of the State on freedom are only slightly mentioned in passing.[2] On the other hand, the writer has ventured, even at the risk of a certain disproportion, to bring into the line of historical development a number of English writers whose contributions to liberty do not seem to have gained the recognition which they deserve.

[1] For the purpose of this essay a writer's views must be estimated by his distinctive contribution to freedom in education rather than by his success in bringing previous views of freedom into actual operation in the school. A complete history of the growth of freedom would include both aspects of the subject : an inquiry into fundamentals may perhaps be permitted to concentrate upon one, even though it passes over the work of schoolmasters like Arnold of Rugby whose influence upon the subsequent development of some aspects of freedom has undoubtedly been very great.

[2] Our problem is not to make freedom harmonize with this or that theory of the State but to define the fundamental conditions of the educative process so that any State, so long as it really desires to maintain its own existence, may accept them. Even if we hold that the State expresses the individual's aspirations and freedom more completely than he himself can ever express them, we have still to consider the best means of making the relatively immature individual grasp this supposed truth. In considering these means we come to grips with the problem of freedom in education. The ways in which State intervention may help or hinder education are important problems which follow naturally upon the discussions of the present volume.

CHAPTER II

PLATO'S FREEDOM THROUGH CONTROL

DR. LIVINGSTONE in his interesting study of the 'Greek Genius' names Freedom as one of the five or six outstanding attributes of the most brilliant period of Greek literature and thought. He shows that the Greek conception was wide and tolerant—an almost complete freedom for the intellect in aspects of life usually controlled by mere custom and tradition. Even in the sphere of religion the Greek mind was essentially creative. It fashioned its own gods and dressed them according to fancy, now in this garb, now in that garment. It had little, if any, place for the idea of an *eternal* verity, whether enshrined in a religious literature or voiced by a divine oracle. It tolerated few intrusions of the state even when it professed a general loyalty to its institutions : the slave was he who might not speak his thought. ' In theory and, on the whole, in practice the Greek state avoided interfering with its citizens. Here, too, the Greek was left free to see life steadily and see it whole. Neither priests nor politicians tyrannized over him.' [1]

One might therefore expect Plato's views on freedom to be those of an eleutheromaniac. In most respects he was reactionary. ' Though in a thousand ways Plato is a Greek of the Greeks, in all that is most distinctive in his thought he is so far a heretic, that if Hellenism had been a persecuting religion it would have been bound to send him to the stake.' [2] This it did not do, but to his teacher, Socrates, it offered the poison cup as a fitting reward for a life supposed to be devoted to the dissemination of religious and educational heresies. Liberty of thought had, even for the Greek mind, limits that could not be transgressed with impunity. The attempt to find these—

[1] R. W. Livingstone, *The Greek Genius and its Meaning to us*, p. 73.
[2] *Op. cit.* p. 183.

to answer the question why the master suffered and the pupil went free—may enable us to understand more clearly Plato's general conception of the function of freedom.

If we take a broad view of the work of the two great teachers it seems clear that both affirmed through different, yet really complementary, methods the Greek belief in freedom for the individual thinker, and both demonstrated to the full that active use of the intellect which for the Greek exhausted the means of exploring and unifying experience. But Socrates' method was not always encouraging to the superficially minded, nor was his impatience with the mental inertia of his fellows always moderated. His own thought, unremitting as it seemed to be, was not really sustained. He touched on everything and on nothing that he touched did he fail to leave a trace of scorn. He brought education down from the clouds and enveloped it in greater clouds when he had brought it to earth. Philosophers may perhaps be permitted to tie one another in knots so long as they speak of things that do not touch the everyday life of the people. But when the Athenians, who had both the leisure and the desire to discuss civic problems were continually befogged by a thinker who revelled in giving to philosophical abstractions unexpected, yet familiar and concrete, turns and settings, they could scarcely be expected to give to him the *only* mark of distinction which he himself claimed—that of pure scepticism. And this was the only mark which he claimed.[1] The crowd, no doubt, looked beyond the cloud of scepticism for the purpose that really animated Socrates' life and must have been impressed by his evident delight in teaching. They may have listened politely when he explained that he was a gadfly given by God to the State—that great and noble steed whose very size renders his motions so tardy—but in their heart of hearts they must have thought that the noblest of steeds might be excused for attempting to escape a gadfly that stings him out of a morass merely to bring him into a quagmire. To the crowd Socrates must have seemed to be perpetually destroying the thought that he was continually trying to bring

---

[1] *Apology*, 29 (Jowett's translation, vol. ii. p. 122). ' In this respect only I believe myself to differ from men in general, and may, perhaps, claim to be wiser than they are—that whereas I know but little of the world below I do not suppose that I know.'

to birth, and although the Greek could, and did, adjust himself to an occasional bankruptcy of reason, he could not restrain himself from hoping for its future liquidation by further intellectual exercise.   This was his solvent for life's contradictions, and in condemning intellectual scepticism he was true to his general conviction of intellectual freedom as the mainspring of a free man's existence.   Although he disparaged the merely utilitarian studies he sought a close connection between the highest theoretical flights of intellect and the service of the state.   He disclaimed a narrow utility because he emphasized the widest sphere of usefulness.   Socrates made useless the use of the intellect and for this sin against it he was put to death.

But Socrates in his life had given to the world something of great value for all time.   He had impressed not only a dull mind like Meno's but an acute mind like Plato's with the fundamental truth that the real starting point of education is a clear perception of the necessity for clearer ideas.   Education *began* with a personal sense of perplexity or limitation which brought with it the desire for more light.   The effect of his dialectical powers was well described by Meno : ' You seem to me both in your appearance and in your power over others to be very like the flat torpedo fish, who torpifies those who come near him and touch him as you have now torpified me, I think.   For my soul and my tongue are really torpid, and I do not know how to answer you; and though I have been delivered of an infinite variety of speeches about virtue before now, and to many persons—and very good ones they were, as I thought— at this moment I cannot even say what virtue is.' [1]   The intellectual result of the ' torpedo touch ' is still more adequately indicated by Socrates' question at the end of one of his lessons : ' Do you suppose that this boy would ever have enquired into or learned what he fancied he knew, though he was really ignorant of it, *until he had fallen into perplexity* under the idea that he did not know and had desired to know ' ? [2]   The general result of Socrates' excursions into the analogies that his nimble wit discerned in homely situations is well illustrated by Xenophon's story of Socrates and the shepherds.   At a time when Athens was being ruined by proscription and confiscation

---

[1] *Meno*, 80 (Jowett, vol. ii. p. 39).
[2] *Meno*, 84 (Jowett, vol. ii. p. 44).   (*Italics* mine.)

Socrates pointed out the inconsistency of thinking a man a bad shepherd whose sheep became poorer and fewer and not thinking a government bad which made its citizens fewer and poorer. Socrates was sent for by the government and told not to talk about the duties of shepherds! We do not know what his reply was, but we may imagine him, with his usual combination of reverence for authority, polite irony, and scepticism, remarking that it would indeed be an easy matter for him, as for them, to refrain from speaking about an art of which they were all ignorant. Whether Plato knew of the incident or not, he took care, in stating his educational views to refer to an ideal state, and thus in theory, at least, he could emphasize its divine right of domination over the individual. He was also careful to attempt to satisfy the perplexity of the aroused mind with a more certain and positive system of knowledge. He did not escape indignation but he died a natural death.

Plato was profoundly impressed by the scepticism of Socrates and by his skilful use of the ' torpedo touch.' Both spoke eloquently to him of the long and steep ascent from popular opinion, from the ' whim and pleasures of the many-headed multitude' to the mountain-top of scientific knowledge, from the shadows of the world of sense to the calm contemplation of the Good. Accordingly he roused the dull and sleepy souls by speaking to them through Socrates and tried to round off the scepticism of his master by translating it into a virtually positive and certain system of knowledge, revealed only to a small and select number of the community, who had been severely disciplined and prepared to recognize and receive it. Knowledge is not now impossible but it is the perquisite of a philosophical priesthood. It is acquired at great pains from those, and those only, who have seen the true light of reason. As the blind man has to trust another's hand to guide him in an unfamiliar path, so the pupil has to trust to teachers whose eyes have been turned towards the sun, and whose souls have been converted from the perception of things of time and sense to the contemplation of the immutable and eternal. And lest those of little faith might still have some reluctance in ascending Plato's staircase of the soul he clarifies the vision by constructing in thought an ideal state where the mistakes and superficialities of politicians cease to worry, and where, under the rule of the wisest of philosopher-kings and the guidance of the best teachers and the inspiration of the noblest artists, youth dwells in a land of health, amid fair sights and sounds, and receives the good in everything ; and beauty, the effluence of fair works, flows into the eye and ear, like a health-giving breeze from a purer region, and insensibly draws the soul from the earliest years into likeness and sympathy with the beauty of reason.[1]

Both Plato and Socrates were heretics in the sense of taking up an extreme position with regard to the possibility of knowledge ; the one, in theory at least, of the only man who knew, the other of the only man that knew he did not know.   Neither was heretical so far as the authority of the state was concerned : the one lived to inculcate obedience in life, the other died inculcating it even through death.   Personal liberty for both had to be found through it, and state control had to occupy in their schemes of education the position of a fundamental principle.   It will be necessary for us to state and examine the reasons assigned for this control, bearing in mind that many modern expositions of education give a similar precedence to authority whether of the family, the community, or the state. We shall consider, in the first place, the value of Plato's general theory and practice of control, and secondly, the value for a modern theory of education of a re-interpretation of his fundamental principles.   Thus we shall pass from the body to the spirit of his concept of freedom.

I

Plato's insistence upon state control of education follows naturally from his emphasis of the difficulty of attaining real knowledge, and from his keen desire to place reason on the seat of government.   An unquestioning submission to those who have expert knowledge runs through nearly every page of his philosophical discussions, and side by side with it there is the reminder that there are few really expert. ' Until a person is able to abstract and define rationally the idea of good, and unless he can run the gauntlet of all objections, and is ready to disprove them, not by appeals to opinion, but to absolute truth, never faltering at any step of the argument—unless he

---

[1] Cf. *Republic*, 401 (Jowett, vol. iii. pp. 87-8).

can do all this . . . he knows neither the idea of good nor any other good ; he apprehends only a shadow, if anything at all, which is given by opinion and not by science—dreaming and slumbering in this life before he is well awake here he arrives at the world below, and has his final quietus. . . . And surely you would not have the children of your ideal state whom you are nurturing and educating—if the ideal ever becomes a reality —you would not allow the future rulers to be like posts, having no reason in them, and yet to be set in authority over the highest matters.' [1]

In the family circle and on the lower level of understanding, similar conclusions are reached. The parents of Lysis really love their son, they desire his happiness, yet they do not permit him to do what he likes. His father will not allow him to mount a chariot and take the reins at a race ; his mother does not permit him to touch her spinning or weaving implements. All these things may be done by a hireling. His tutor is a slave. Strange that a slave should bear rule over a free man ! But Lysis is allowed to read and write and play the lyre. Why ? The youth answers : ' I suppose because I understand the one and not the other.' ' Yes, my dear youth, the reason is not any deficiency of years, but a deficiency of knowledge ; and whenever your father thinks that you are wiser than he is, he will instantly commit himself and his possessions to you.' [2]

Further, though with occasional waverings, Plato inclines to the view that Virtue is knowledge and that a knowledge may be implanted in the minds of young children which will serve them until reason, or a measure of reason, is attained. In his latest works he makes the imparting of knowledge almost synonymous with education. Thus he writes in the *Laws*: 'I mean by education that training which is given by suitable habits to the first instincts of virtue in children ;—when pleasure, and friendship, and pain, and hatred, are rightly implanted in souls not yet capable of understanding the nature of them, and who find them, after they have attained reason, to be in harmony with her. This harmony of the soul, taken as a whole, is virtue, but the particular training in respect of pleasure and

[1] *Republic*, 534 (Jowett, vol. iii. pp. 237-8).
[2] Cf. *Lysis*, 207-210 (Jowett, vol. i. pp. 54-7).

pain, which leads you always to hate what you ought to hate, and love what you ought to love from the beginning of life to the end, may be separated off ; and, in my view, will be rightly called education.'[1]   A little further on we are told where to look for guidance as to the habits which ought to be attached to the first instincts of virtue : ' Education is the constraining and directing of youth towards that right reason, which the law affirms, and which the experience of the eldest and best has agreed to be truly right.'[2]   In his belief that man himself should be ' under a rule like that of the best,' that he ought to be the servant of the best in whom the Divine rules, Plato finds his sanctions for the ' authority which we exercise over children and the refusal to let them be free until we have established in them a principle analogous to the constitution of a state, and by cultivation of the higher element have set up in their hearts a guardian and ruler like our own, and when this is done they may go their ways.'[3]

It would seem, however, that Plato never really contemplated the case of the *adult* ' going his way ' when it went contrary to the laws.   Socrates believed firmly in the rightness of his own actions, yet when the laws condemned him he pleaded their case against himself with an eloquence that surely has never been surpassed.   The arguments he brings forward for obedience, even to death, when Crito attempts to persuade him to flee, give a surer point of contact with the common values and aspirations of humanity than any appeal to mere reason (reasoned though the appeal undoubtedly is) could ever hope to secure.   They state so clearly and eloquently the natural ties of home, family, kindred and nation that we shall quote them at length.   Socrates puts the case for the laws and answers the questions which they address to him :

' What complaint have you to make against us which justifies you in attempting to destroy us and the state ?   In the first place, did we not bring you into existence ?   Your father married your mother by our aid and begat you.   Say whether you have any objection to urge against those of us who regulate marriage ?—None, I should reply.   Or against those of us who after birth regulate the nurture

---

[1] *Laws*, 653 (Jowett, vol. v. pp. 30-1).

[2] *Laws*, 659 (Jowett, vol. v. pp. 37-8).

[3] *Republic*, 590 (Jowett, vol. iii. p. 304).

and education of children, in which you also were trained ?   Were
not the laws, which have the charge of education, right in commanding your father to train you in music and gymnastic ?—Right, I
should reply.

' Well, then, since you were brought into the world and nurtured
and educated by us, can you deny in the first place that you are
our child and slave, as your fathers were before you ?   And if this
is true you are not on equal terms with us ; nor can we think that
you have a right to do to us what we are doing to you.   Would you
have any right to strike or revile or do any other evil to your father
or your master, if you had one, because you have been struck or
reviled by him, or received some other evil at his hands ?—You
would not say this ?   And because we think right to destroy you,
do you think that you have any right to destroy us in return, and
your country as far as in you lies ?   Will you, O professor of true
virtue, pretend that you are justified in this ?   Has a philosopher
like you failed to discover that your country is more to be valued
and higher and holier far than mother or father or any ancestor,
and more to be regarded in the eyes of the gods and of men of understanding, also to be soothed and gently and reverently entreated
when angry, even more than a father, and either to be persuaded,
or if not persuaded, to be obeyed ?   And when we are punished by
her, whether with imprisonment or stripes, the punishment is to be
endured in silence ; and if she leads us to wounds or death in battle,
thither we follow as is right ; neither may any one yield or retreat or
leave his rank, but whether in battle or in a court of law, or in any
other place, he must do what his city and his country order him ;
or he must change their view of what is just : and if he may do no
violence to his father or mother, much less may he do violence to
his country. . . .   Consider, Socrates, if we are speaking truly, that
in your present attempt you are going to do us an injury.   For,
having brought you into the world, and nurtured and educated you,
and given you and every other citizen a share in every good which
we had to give, we further proclaim to any Athenian by the liberty
which we allow him that if he does not like us when he has become
of age and has seen the ways of the city, and made our acquaintance,
he may go where he pleases and take his goods with him.   None of
us . . . will forbid him or interfere with him. . . .   But he who has
experience of the manner in which we order justice, and administer
the state, and still remains, has entered into an implied contract
that he will do as we command him.   And he who disobeys us is,
as we maintain, thrice wrong; first, because in disobeying us he is
disobeying his parents ; secondly, because we are the authors of his
education ; thirdly, because he has made an agreement with us that
he will duly obey our commands ; and he neither obeys them nor
convinces us that our commands are unjust ; and we do not rudely

impose them, but give him the alternative of obeying or convincing us—that is what we offer, and he does neither.' [1]

Before considering these arguments it may be profitable to seek for any evidence of sympathy with the individual's point of view, or any recognition of the rights of childhood and youth. Apparently the adult has the choice of one of four courses of action—obedience to the laws, amendment of them, exile, or death. Although Plato considers from time to time the force of (1) a perfect law above and beyond all rulers who are to be chosen for their wisdom and not for their wealth or strength or family claims,[2] and (2) law as the tyrant of mankind [3] who compels us to do many things which are against nature—the ' obstinate and ignorant tyrant who will not allow anything to be done contrary to his appointment ' [4]—and although he sees clearly that the ' endless irregular movements of human beings do not admit of any universal and simple rule,' and that ' no art whatsoever can lay down a rule which will last for all time,' [5] he does not really waver in his admiration for law as the mainspring of authority and as a perfect expression of human virtue and aspiration. On the one hand all is perfect wisdom and fixity; on the other hand, there is the individual with his mere opinion and fickleness of purpose. Obedience to the law is the Hobson's choice of Plato's theory.

The subordination of freedom appears in many ways. Its meaning was never deemed worthy of serious discussion in the *Dialogues* : it is mentioned incidentally in several of them and nearly always in a derogatory sense. Thus, it is coupled with anarchy ; [6] it is held to be the chief good and glory of democracy ; [7] it makes fathers descend to the level of their sons and puts sons on an equality with fathers ; it banishes respect and reverence, leads the schoolmaster to flatter his pupils and the pupils to despise their master ; it levels everybody—the citizen and the metic, young and old, male and female, bond and free.

---

[1] *Crito*, 51-2 (Jowett, vol. ii. pp. 152-3).

[2] *Laws*, 715 (Jowett, vol. v. p. 98).

[3] Hippias' remark in *Protagoras*, 337 (Jowett, vol. i. p. 160).

[4] The remark of the Stranger in the *Statesman*, 294 (Jowett, vol. iv. p. 497).

[5] *Statesman* 294 (Jowett, vol. iv. p. 497).

[6] *Republic*, 562 (Jowett, vol. iii. p. 270).

[7] *Republic*, 562 (Jowett, vol. iii. p. 270).

Even the dogs and asses bred in its atmosphere acquire a dignified gait and a bellicose assertiveness. All things are 'just ready to burst with liberty.' By reaction it passes into excessive slavery.[1]

And if Plato has little room for freedom, as he understands it, he has less room for individual happiness. He thinks that this may, and probably will, result from the attempt to make the state as a whole happy, but the legislator cannot be a respecter of persons. Citizens are to be held together by persuasion and necessity : being benefactors of their country they are to be benefactors of one another. ' To this end he created them, not to please themselves, but to be his instruments in binding up the state.'[2] Here the individual is lost in the community life : he finds his highest life, even his religion, in its service. So clearly does Plato subordinate the self to communal demands that, as some one remarks, his republic is not a state but a church. But, for all save the guardians, the general spirit of the state, and indeed the spirit of the guardians' education, was a religious conformity to, rather than a religious co-operation with, established precedent.

The earlier stages of education show the same spirit in a more marked degree. An oft-quoted passage in *Protagoras* describes the practice in vogue in Plato's day, and we have no reason to believe that in any of his more mature writings he seriously dissents from it. Education and admonition begin in the first years of childhood and last to the very end of life. As soon as the child is able to understand what is said to him, mother and father, nurse and tutor, vie with one another in setting forth what is just and what is unjust, what is honourable and what is dishonourable, what is holy and what is unholy. ' And if he obeys, well and good : if not, he is straightened by threats and blows, like a piece of bent or warped wood.'[3] The same dutiful submission runs through the whole of the elementary instruction. The boy is sent to teachers who see to his manners as well as to his reading and music ; he learns by

---

[1] Cf. also *Laws*, 701 (Jowett, vol. v. p. 82).

[2] *Republic*, 520 (Jowett, vol. iii. p. 220). Cf. also *Republic*, 420 (Jowett, vol. iii. pp. 108-9).

[3] *Protagoras*, 325 (Jowett, vol. i. pp. 146-7).

heart the tales of the poets, so that he may imitate or emulate what he reads ; the teachers of the lyre introduce him to the lyric poets for the double purpose of keeping him out of mischief and of making him more gentle and harmonious.   The master of gymnastic fits his body for ministering to his mind.   Here, for most children, education ends.

In the *Republic*, however, there is some recognition of an intermediate stage of education resulting from the submission of the first period and preparing for the conformity of a third.   Children, beginning with right diversions, receive loyalty into their minds by the instrumentality of music, and this loyalty accompanies them into everything and promotes their progress.[1]   Or as another translation has it : ' When they have made a good beginning in play, and by the help of music have gained the habit of good order, then this habit of order . . . will accompany them in all their actions and be a principle of growth to them.'[2] But behind Plato's ' principle of growth ' there is always a plea for adherence to the old order of things which ill consorts with youthful visions and dreams.   All through the process here, as in the former and the latter stages, the spirit seems continuous and unmistakable.   The state compels the youth to learn the laws and to live after their pattern and not after his own fancies.   Just as the writing master draws lines with a style for the beginner and makes him follow the lines, so the city draws laws for the conduct of the young man— whether he is commanding or obeying—and calls him to account if he transgresses them.[3]   In the intermediate stage the animating principle of education seems not to be intelligent loyalty but habitual allegiance.

From the pupil's point of view dutiful submission, habitual allegiance, religious conformity ; from the teacher's side the exercise of authority, the implantation of values in souls not yet capable of understanding them, the establishment of a principle of reason—these are the main points of Plato's doctrine.   But along with the law there are signs of the gospel of grace—signs only, for Plato's general view of man's original

---

[1] *Republic* (translation by Davies and Vaughan), 425 (G. Treasury Edn. p. 123).

[2] *Republic* (trans. Jowett, vol. iii. p. 113).

[3] Cf. *Protagoras*, 326 (Jowett, vol. i. p. 147).

nature is too pessimistic to lead him to repose any real trust in spontaneity. Education is essentially a process of conversion, yet, by times, Plato disclaims any intention of ' forcing ' his system of education.[1] ' A freeman ought not to be a slave in the acquisition of knowledge of any kind. Bodily exercise, when compulsory, does no harm to the body ; but knowledge which is acquired under compulsion obtains no hold upon the mind.' [2] Education, therefore, should be a sort of amusement, for by this means we shall more readily discover the ' natural bent ' of the pupil. In the *Laws* the Athenian stranger advocates play as the best training for the work of after-life : educators should provide children with mimic tools. ' They should learn beforehand the knowledge which they will afterwards require for their art. For example, the future carpenter should learn to measure or apply the line in play ; and the future warrior should learn riding, or some other exercise, for amusement, and the teacher should endeavour to direct the children's inclinations and pleasures by the help of amusements, to their final aim in life. . . . The soul of the child in his play should be guided by the love of that sort of excellence in which, when he grows up to manhood, he will have to be perfected.' [3]

A theory of play is likely to test severely an educator's attachment both to the conservative and the progressive aspects of his art, and Plato's statement of the anticipatory nature of play clearly shows his link with both old and new. It does not betray any belief in the value of play as a really *free* activity. It defines an *attitude* towards an activity, rather than an activity itself, and Plato apparently thinks that the play spirit may be present where the activity itself is externally conditioned. But the recognition of the playful spirit is not without a certain reserve. Play is due to the incapability of children to endure serious training. It is because of their lack

[1] *Republic*, 536 (Jowett, vol. iii. p. 240).

[2] Cf. the translation of Davies and Vaughan (p. 264). ' You must train your children to their studies in a playful manner and without any air of constraint with the further object of discerning more readily the natural bent of their respective characters.' It would be difficult to compress more adequately into a single sentence the spirit of most modern views of freedom in early education.

[3] *Laws*, 643 (Jowett, vol. v. p. 21).

of endurance that harmony is implanted in their minds through plays and songs, " just as when men are sick and ailing in their bodies their attendants give them wholesome diet in pleasant meats and drinks, unwholesome diet in disagreeable things, in order that they may learn, as they ought, to like the one and to dislike the other.' [1]   Plato's main concern is clearly the permanence and peace of the state, not the health of the individual.   He will allow mathematics to be made into a game, for it has objective and external controls that restrain individual fancy.   ' Music,' however, being a concrete form of presenting virtue must be rigidly scrutinized by the state.   Hence the view (described by Plato himself as singular and unusual) that ' the plays of childhood have a great deal to do with the permanence or want of permanence in legislation.' [2]   Fixity of play allows the solemn institutions of the state to remain undisturbed. When the young never speak of having the same likes or dislikes the state is in extreme peril.   ' Children who make innovations in their games, when they grow up to be men will be different from the last generation of children, and, being different, will desire a different sort of life, and under the influence of this desire will want other institutions and laws.' Little by little, the spirit of licence will penetrate into manners and customs, invade contracts between man and man, and finally will overthrow all rights, private as well as public.   In short, any innovation in play, in music, or in gymnastic, will foster a spirit of disloyalty which, sooner or later, will spread to all activities of life, whereas uniformity of play will establish a habit of order and an ideal of loyalty, which will serve as a ' principle of growth.'

We may now re-state the main points of Socrates' argument. The laws are supreme because they are prior to the individual and, in a real sense, the source of his being ; they are the ultimate agents of his nurture and training ; they supply a ' principle of growth ' necessary for his preservation ; they are flexible, not fixed, standards ; though amenable to persuasion, they exercise a control which must be accepted by every individual as a basic condition of life.   In our discussion we shall regard the laws as representative of the customs

[1] Cf. *Laws*, 659, 660 (Jowett, vol. v. p. 38).
[2] Cf. *Laws*, 798 (Jowett, vol. v. pp. 178-9).

and traditions of the social group to which the pupil belongs and ignore their flexibility, for, as we have seen, *limits* of compulsion seem to be ruled out of Plato's scheme of education.

The only indisputable fact of Socrates' statement is the *priority* of the laws. On reflection, however, it does not seem possible to base on it the right of *exacting* obedience from the younger generation. If mere priority established such a right no departure from usually accepted ways of thinking could be permitted—even to adults. The more ancient the law the greater would be its claims upon our obedience. We ought all according to this reasoning to begin to eat acorns and to go back to the wearing of old Adam's pelts—as Mulcaster advised those to do who *must* cleave to the oldest and not to the best. Conservatives would, no doubt, point out that there are many good reasons for venerating the old values of the race. They may be the race's vital values : acorns and pelts may not be fashionable but they may tend to preserve society. Two points may be urged in reply. Mankind, as a whole, is not conservative and youth shows a noteworthy sympathy with the old racial life. Being born into a society is thus, as Samuel Butler pointed out long ago, not an event but a process whereby a relatively old organism is given an opportunity to become as young as the social group which it finds around it. Even if the modern doctrine of ' recapitulation ' [1] has as slender a basis as Plato's conception of ' reminiscence ' the similarity between the child's tendencies and the racial life is undeniable. If the argument for obedience to what is prior has any real force it is the adult that ought to venerate the child ! And if we deny that the child is the heir of all the ages and narrow his obedience to the demands of his immediate ancestors we are driven to admit that parents and friends and country exercise the most potent influence, not because they are *prior* and *exact* obedience but because they are *co-existent* and *attract* it. They evoke obedience partly (at least) because they satisfy the needs of young life.

It was in this sense that Aristotle urged the priority of the state. The individual, as he pointed out, is not self-sufficing when isolated from his fellows and therefore he is like a part in

[1] Further considered in Chapter XXIX.

relation to the whole.[1] In the long run the argument from priority resolves itself into some superior quality or power, whether of the strong right arm, of knowledge, of virtue, or of natural right possessed by society. It is useless to deny that the absence of these qualities, and the perception of the individual's lack of them, largely determine his adjustment to his social group. Education finds its very being in the fact. But it does not follow that the best means of making the individual realize his limitations is obedience *quâ* obedience. Xenophon knew another method : ' This, my son, is the road to compulsory obedience, indeed, but there is another road, a short cut, to what is much better—namely to willing obedience. For people are only too glad to obey the man who they believe takes wiser thought for their interests than they themselves do.' [2] In a perfectly rounded system of social relationships, like those of Plato's state, or those of an educational establishment permeated with a clock-work routine of nicely adjusted activities, there is little opportunity for the individual to perceive either his limitations or the greater efficiency and wisdom of the social group. It is he who has liberty to dare who realizes his weakness, and it is the teacher of wise thought for his pupils' interests who best changes weakness and fickleness into willing obedience to the laws.

The nurture and training of youth are often conjoined in education. The child is given shelter, support, protection, and these gifts are sometimes made the pretext of a compulsory training. Society, it is said, gives safety and exacts obedience.[3] Safety is indeed a prime consideration of early training—so important that we prefer to attach to it the note of adult compulsion and to reserve to obedience the quality of a youthful gift. Society exacts safety and receives obedience. In favour of this re-interpretation we would urge that safety can never really be *given* but that, in some sense of the term, it must be the result of a really educative process.

---

[1] *Politics*, i. 2.

[2] *Cyropaedia* (I. vi. 21, trans. by W. Miller in Loeb Classical Library). In I. ii. 6-8 there is an interesting anticipation of modern school courts. The education of Cyrus has many points of interest for freedom.

[3] See the forceful and eloquent presentation of this view in Professor Campagnac's *Education in its Relation to the Common Purposes of Humanity*, especially Chapter II.

Doubtless safety in a relative sense may be received or enjoyed, but its function is to aid us in attaining some definite aim in life. Biologically, it affords opportunity for testing our impulses and rightly evaluating them. Its function seems to harmonize with nature's general design for man's equipment. Having prolonged the period of human immaturity, and therefore having increased the child's dependence on his parents, and having made the guidance of instinct less definite and certain, nature further demands safety so that he may more readily and truly escape from his limitations. To give him safety through the easy path of compulsory obedience would merely thwart the purposes for which immaturity and dependence and plasticity stand: to enable him to learn where safety lies would utilize the general indeterminateness and indefiniteness with which nature has endowed him. The ' safe ' plan of sacrificing youthful plasticity to compulsory regulations seems to have no vestige of utility and no real guarantee of safety. Anything gained by it is *faute de mieux*. Real safety comes only through a willing obedience. This is the gift of the pupil's whole being. It is not a requirement or an exaction but a response to educational conditions that are in harmony with the natural laws of his life.

In some respects these conditions are relatively fixed and unalterable. The child must acquire the speech and manners, and understand the mind of the society into which he is born. It is absolutely necessary that he should be made to feel the value of a clear, correct, and precise expression of thought ; very desirable that he should accept the social conventions which we call politeness ; most desirable that he should grow up to respect and venerate his elders. But once again it must be insisted that these values do not become influential forces in the pupil's life by mere obedience ; the speech and manners and thought of the child's social group do not give any *educational* control other than that which comes to it in virtue of its predominating position in the child's environment. Every extension of the child's course of studies—foreign languages, history, geography, science, art, music—is a recognition of the necessity of introducing to him other standards of life than those which, by their nearness, must naturally exercise the *greatest* influence over his early training. And with the recognition of an extended social group as a controlling influence of early education the plea for the absolute supremacy of the social environment of a particular time and place loses much of its force.   The values of all mankind—humanity in the broadest sense—are the only ultimate controlling forces of even the early stages of education.   On the other hand the necessity for understanding the social group and for adjusting himself to its demands is so great that to emphasize the idea of *exacting* obedience to it is to confess inability to show a natural connection and reasonableness in the outward manifestations of the adult's innermost life forces.   If compulsion must be exercised here, then all education is, and must be, a tyranny.   Here, if anywhere in education, there should be room for the qualities which we usually call intelligence, loyalty and co-operation : here it is most unwise to rely on an obedience that is nothing more than submission to external demands.

The disintegration of society in the absence of obedience is a fact that will not be denied even although the powers of any generation to predict the amount of change which would really imperil the continued existence of society be doubted. We have only to look at the type of innovation which Plato dreaded to see how baseless were his fears.   He would, no doubt, have ruled out the learning of any language save the vernacular, just as he ruled out this or that type of literary composition, expunged this or that passage of Homer, rejected this rhythm, and accepted that, included this physical exercise and forbade that type of play.   To prescribe, in the interest of the state, fixed and uniform courses of study in literature, in music, in gymnastic, and to forbid any innovation in play now seems fantastical even to those who are not disposed to question the unlimited ' spread ' of loyalty or licence assumed by Plato's argument.   Our own prescriptions of culture, manners, and behaviour may seem no less absurd at the end of another two thousand years.

The whole force of the preceding arguments lies in the tacit admission of spontaneity—of individual aims that are not to be entirely deflected by external forces.   The strength of the spontaneous impulses is admitted by Plato.   The boy is the most unmanageable of animals, the most insidious, sharp-

witted and insubordinate.[1] But instead of attempting to
utilize his qualities Plato attempts to curb him with many
bridles, to put him under the management of tutors, to control
him by studies and teachers—' no matter what they teach.' [2]
These repressions limit the operation of education to the second
and third-rate values of the personality ; they deaden childhood in the hope of vitalizing the days of maturity. In spite
of them, however, the creature who ' has the fountain of reason
in him not yet regulated ' escapes his bridles and his teachers
and so regulates his reason that he becomes intelligently loyal.
He *receives* ' loyalty ' into his mind through the instrumentality of music. Here, as elsewhere, forces which the educator
ignores or despises become the mainstays of the pupil's mental
structure. At some point an element of spontaneity enters his
process of ' induction ' and changes dutiful submission into
willing obedience, habitual allegiance into intelligent loyalty,
and religious conformity into zealous co-operation. But these
transitions may be much more effectively accomplished by
activities that suggest co-operation, arouse loyalty, and sustain
obedience.

The educative basis of obedience is spontaneity. When this
truth is reflected in education the value of obedience can
scarcely be exaggerated. The individual (and even the young
child) has tendencies that urge him to identify himself with the
behaviour of his fellows : he is a gregarious, an imitative, a
suggestible, a submissive, a sympathetic, a curious being. All
these tendencies prompt him to yield a real obedience which is
not incompatible with any, save extreme, views of freedom. So
important is the attitude of *willing* obedience that education
must strain every effort to attach it to the values which the
pupil himself wishes to develop further in his life, and to prevent
its limitation to the values which others wish to introduce into
that life. The latter may be *received* by the personality but
they have never the same directive influence over life as the
former. The one type owns us, we own the other type.
Education may have to work upon both, but if it attempts to

[1] Cf. *Laws*, 808-9.

[2] On reading this passage one cannot help wishing that Socrates had discussed the problem of freedom with Polemarchus. It would have been of
great interest to follow a discussion of the question : *Can a free-born boy by the
denial of freedom be made free ?*

remove limitations so that the act of removal fosters growth, it must make sure that its *main* point of contact is with the values which the pupil already partially owns and which he himself wishes to develop.   These values are given a secondary position in Plato's theory and in many practical schemes of education.   The relative weakness, helplessness, and ignorance of childhood tend to make us exaggerate its receptivity and thus lead us to make out of the very qualities which give a positive contact with the outer world a reason for imposing in all directions an obedience that before long destroys the finest possibilities of educative influence, and often arouses an emotional attitude towards authority that makes education sterile or impossible.   It must be remembered that we can only touch the fringe of a child's life by compulsion, that even where we touch it we cannot enforce real obedience, and where we succeed in enforcing a momentary submission we are likely to exert an influence in the direction opposite to that which we wish the child to take.

For the present, then, we note failure to find in Socrates' arguments for the laws any real support for the idea of compulsory obedience.   We reject it as an educative agency because (1) it touches only the relatively unimportant aspects of the pupil's life, (2) it arouses emotional dispositions unfavourable to growth, (3) it neglects the mental forces upon which educational influence is most effective, and (4) it arrogates to itself the right of a general principle that in the end is indistinguishable from despotism.   And our mediating concept must view life as a whole, make growth possible, appeal to individual values, and preserve a balance between licence and subjection. The attempt to find a particular type of balance is the central point in Plato's *notion* of justice.

II

Our task now is not to discuss the meanings Plato assigns to this term but to estimate the bearing of his general discussion on freedom in education.   We shall therefore ignore the details of his educational system, his general conservatism, his limitation of education to particular sections of the community, his over-emphasis of obedience.   All these follow from his idolatry of the state, and in rejecting it we have rejected them. Our problem is Plato's shorn of Plato's political prejudices and may thus be stated : Given a class of people in the community who are to be educated in the spirit of justice, to what fundamental features of their nature shall we appeal ?

It may be helpful to state the essential data and functions of Plato's educational scheme in the *Republic*.

(1) In the early pages the *raison d'être* of the state is found in certain negative characteristics of the individual. He is not independent : he has wants that he cannot satisfy and needs that he himself cannot supply. Satisfaction requires some form of association with his fellows and this brings in its train the need of protection. Guardians and soldiers and citizens form the state. With great pedagogical insight, and with much greater respect for the individual than our discussion of obedience would lead us to expect, Socrates considers carefully the natural endowments of those whom he singles out for education *before* he attempts to draw up a practical scheme for their training. And though he limits his inquiry to the natural endowments which qualify for the guardianship of a state, [1] his view is broad and universal enough to be readily generalized and applied to all types of education.

(2) Two qualities (or tendencies) in the individual are regarded as fundamental—gentleness and high spirit. They are recognized to be conflicting, or, at least, partially opposing qualities. The first is further described as ' philosophical,' as a ' disposition or turn for learning,' as ' love of wisdom ' ; the second as ' invincible,' ' unconquerable,' ' indomitable,' ' savage,' ' angry,' ' fearless.' Physical qualities like swiftness and strength are also mentioned. The ideal pupil unites in himself philosophy, spirit and strength. But how are the first two to be reconciled ? ' How shall we find a gentle nature which has also a great spirit, for the one is the contradiction of the other ' ? Thus Plato traces the ' inherent contradiction ' of the educative process, mentioned in the previous chapter, to its source—the presence of contradictory tendencies in human nature. This incompatibility of natural qualities in the pupil's endowment leads him, on one hand, to strive for the satisfaction of his needs and maintain his own values, and on the other

[1] Cf. *Republic*, 374-5.

hand to be receptive to the values of others, to be fond of learning from them and to be gentle in disposition.

(3) The whole range of studies is designed to nurture these fundamental qualities.

(4) The aim of education is to harmonize the individual's conflicting tendencies by nurturing them.   This is accomplished when justice pervades the soul, or, in other words, *when each principle or part of the soul does its own and only its own work.*[1]

It is by no means easy to state either Plato's meaning of this principle or its relation to its twin-sister freedom.[2]   The chief feature of the early educational scheme of the *Republic* is the attunement of the gentle and spirited elements through music and gymnastic, but the exact relationship of these elements to the regulative principle of reason and the part played in its development by the two educational agencies are not clearly defined in Plato's pages.   Several stages of education are described which we may profitably review in turn.

(*a*) We see in the early exposition a picture of the receptive (or gentle) element attaching itself to objects to which it feels itself naturally attracted.   In the words of one of Plato's most sympathetic interpreters : ' It is an instinctive feeling, which often does not rise to the height of affection, but remains a sense of quiet pleasure or comfort ; it attaches to things, to places, to persons ; much of the love of home and of country, and even of humanity, is traceable to its presence ; much of the antipathy to foreigners, or to novelties, to its absence.   In a rudimentary feeling of attachment for what belongs to us Plato saw the first germ of that which seemed to him highest in human nature.'[3]   It must be remembered, however, that although the terms which are used to describe the qualities of gentleness are those which characterize the true philosopher, and are therefore those which are in some sense applicable to the highest flights of reason, the continuity is possibly only one of terms.   Plato would probably have refused to apply the term ' reason ' to the homely relationships and impulses which he finds in the first operations of gentleness but, as we shall

[1] Cf. *Republic*, 443.

[2] The phrase of one of His Majesty's Judges in *The Riddle of Justice*, by James Mulligan, K.C.

[3] Nettleship : *Hellenica*, p. 78.

see, it is just these elements which Pestalozzi and Froebel emphasized as the basis of the higher moral life, and it is in similar elements that Dr. Dewey and Dr. Montessori and other modern educators trace some of the earliest and surest operations of a budding reason and a dawning intelligence. Even if in Plato's mind there was no such anticipation of modern theories there was certainly the recognition of two important educational facts, (1) that the early forms of education proceeded through the pupil's predisposition to attach himself to certain objects in his environment and to adjust himself to the demands which these objects made upon him, (2) that in some sense of the term the objects were those which the *pupil* recognized as having import and value for the development of his own life.

(*b*) At a later stage of Plato's discussion the receptivity of the gentle element is still further emphasized.[1] Through it the pupil becomes increasingly susceptible to the various modes of social expression as they are presented to him, for example, in music and in literature. He is responsive to the appeal of beauty ; he appreciates such qualities as orderliness and quietness ; he tends to be more obedient and more amenable to persuasion. The adjustment to merely familiar objects which characterized the first stage has been gradually extended so as to include the ' taste ' of learning, of inquiry, thought, culture, propriety, grace, persuasion and beauty. There is no longer any direct emphasis of the quality of instinctive attachment to other objects which we found in the earlier passage, but Plato's general treatment again draws attention to two important facts. In the first place, a due balance must be preserved between the activities of the ' gentle ' and the ' spirited ' elements. It is he who mingles music with gymnastic in the fairest proportions and best attempers them *to the soul* who is the true educator, a view which may be taken to imply the recognition of limits to the natural receptivity of the pupil. In the second place, Plato is at considerable pains to show that the softening and soothing effect of music may be carried to excess, wasting away the spirit and cutting out the sinews of the soul, and that a too ardent devotion to gymnastic enfeebles, dulls, blinds, and starves the mental powers. It is clear that the ' principle of growth ' that Plato wished to establish in the young mind is not a

[1] *Republic*, 410-412.

principle which worked in opposition to the powers of the soul. On the contrary it is, in theory at least, the expression of those powers.

(c) The fourth book of the *Republic* brings several interesting points of difference into Plato's exposition. As Nettleship points out, the highest form of the soul no longer has the designation 'philosophic.' There is no direct reference to gentleness; there appears instead the forbidding and guiding voice of reason. The discussion has, however, the closest possible reference to 'spirit' which no longer appears as a co-ordinate element of the soul but as the servant of the rational principle. A third element or principle creeps into the discussion—desire, appetite, or concupiscence. A new type of harmony, that of the naturally better and the naturally worse elements, appears with it. Reason, or reason in alliance with spirit, controls the appetites and results in that harmony of the higher over the lower nature which Plato calls temperance.

Are we justified in assuming (as Nettleship, for instance, assumes) that the early instinctive impulse towards the familiar, and the later receptivity to the appeal of the good, the true and the beautiful are stages in the development of the regulative and directing functions of reason? Does gentleness merge into reason, or is reason a new and supervenient power of the soul? The question is of first importance for freedom. If 'reason' is really and totally absent from the young life, if youth lacks any vital principle of self-mastery, there is no other method of early education than that of a wise control which will seek, as Plato sought, first to establish in the heart a principle analogous to the constitution of a state, and then to give it greater powers of self-direction. On the whole, this seems to be Plato's view in the *Republic*, and it harmonizes with the burden of his desire for adult obedience to the laws of the city-state.

But the pains with which Plato traces the beginnings of education to experiences which are familiar and valuable to the young seem to indicate that such a view does not express the whole truth of his theory of education. It is very usually admitted that his exposition in the *Republic* does not attempt to give a presentation of continuous mental development. He takes up the problem of education, now from one angle now from another, and deals now with psychological powers in the individual and at the next moment with ethical qualities in the distinctive classes which form his ideal state. The continuity or discontinuity of gentleness and reason must, therefore, be largely a matter of inference.

Against continuity may be quoted views like those ascribed to Aristotle in *De Virtutibus et Vitiis* (1249*b*) which suggest that in Plato ' gentleness ' and ' bravery ' are virtues of the passionate, not of the rational, part of the soul. The whole of the early educational training in the *Republic* would then operate upon the passions and the attunement might aim simply at the choice of the mean, the avoiding of extremes which Plato declares to be the way of happiness both in this life and the life to come (*Republic*, x. 619). In the *Laws* (vii. 792) this middle state—gentle and benign—is directly connected with the ' beginning,' ' the most critical part ' of education, but this product of Plato's old age and, indeed, the passage in the closing pages of the *Republic*, are by no means representative of either Plato's advocacy of the disinterested pursuit of truth, or of the importance of the early training as a means of its attainment.

(*d*) Everything in that great work seems to converge towards the one supreme object, a free and just life—a life that will embrace all that is human and divine. But the later books of the *Republic* emphasize the pursuit, not merely the love, of truth : the effort to see things as they really are, the fullest possible comprehension of all time and all existence. For the attainment of this end Plato has further and severe courses of study, courses which are really reflections of man's dissatisfaction with the mutable, evanescent, manifold world of experience. They sketch the partial satisfactions of the integrative impulses which lead him inexorably to dialectic. From ' images,' ' shadows,' ' reflections,' ' presentations,' to the noting of ' resemblances ' and the making of ' conjectures,' from these to the more certain steps of ' belief ' and ' conviction,' and from the manifold, specific, and relative embodiments of all these to the immutable ' principles,' or ' forms ' which make them what they are in reality, and from these ' hypotheses ' ultimately to the form of the Good—to a coherent and systematized body of truth—these are the steps of Plato's staircase of the soul.

A survey of these four stages may give the impression of two main periods—one in which the mind is receptive and passive, and one in which it is directive and active. But such an interpretation, as we have already insisted, is not really fair to Plato's whole theory. It views each of the stages in a partial light. There is certainly implied in the first two stages above, a direct activity and controlling power of the mind which differs from that of the last two in degree rather than in kind, and there is in the final phases of the guardians' education an acceptance of control which is much more striking than the receptivity emphasized in the earlier training. Both of these points must be briefly developed.

(1) The early discussion in the *Republic* implies the unity of function and the co-ordinate powers of the gentle and the spirited elements. They are two distinct principles and are nurtured by two specific arts which serve to mitigate or chasten their modes of expression. Just as the strings of a musical instrument may be relaxed or tightened until they are attuned to an external standard, so music and gymnastic may be attempered to the needs of a soul which is itself in harmony with the demands of goodness, truth, and beauty. In respect of the receptivity of the soul, however, the gentle element plays the less dominant part, even if the education of it through music figures most prominently in Plato's discussion. The rôle of gentleness as compared with spirit may be seen in the results assigned to an undue devotion to either music or gymnastic. Music, in excess, weakens the gentle element unduly, and it has also an ultra-softening and soothing effect upon spirit. But a too rigid course of gymnastic does not really control or harden the gentle element. The intellectual qualities are merely starved and enfeebled. The mind, says Plato, never wakes up, or receives nourishment and, in consequence, becomes a hater of philosophy. Thus while the spirited element is receptive to music, the gentle element is *not* receptive to gymnastic. We are therefore driven to the conclusion that the attunement or adjustment of the two elements of which Plato speaks is, in effect, an influence, or perhaps even a control, of gentleness over ' spirit,' to which ' spirit ' responds but which it cannot exercise

in return. The only clear evidence of ' spirit ' acting as a controlling agent is to be found in its control of the appetites.[1]

(2) When we examine the many stages by which the soul passes from ' images ' to the contemplation of the Good, the submission of the ruling reason to the control of reality is apparent. The aim of the whole process is the contact of true being with true being—the adjustment of the stabilized and disciplined mind to things as they really are, or rather to that inner reality which sustains everything and makes out of it all a universe. The mind is really active because it is continually being adjusted to and harmonized with the active principle of the universe. It is active *because* it is receptive ; it is free and untrammelled because it is rightly controlled. Again and again Plato insists that the stagnant life is that which portions out to itself a limited and arbitrary field of reality within which it is content to slumber. Expansion, activity, receptivity, acceptance of control are all conjoined, as the following passage shows :

' It is in the nature of the real lover of learning to be ever struggling up to being, and not to abide amongst the manifold and limited objects of opinion ; he will go his way, and the edge of his love will not grow dull, nor its force abate, until he has got hold of the nature of being with that part of his soul to which it belongs so to do, and that is the part which is akin to being ; with this he will draw near, and mingle being with being, and beget intelligence and truth, and find knowledge and true life and nourishment, and then, and not till then, he will cease from his travail.' [2]

Our survey gives evidence of Plato's *real concern in all these stages* (1) for the *activity of the soul itself,* whether in its instinctive, imitative, suggestible, or habitual aspects, in its response to the influences of beauty, order, rhythm, harmony, or in its highest flights of understanding and reason, (2) for its

[1] Even here Plato's contention that spirit is always on the side of reason when a conflict between reason and appetite takes place gives some support to the idea of similarity in the functions of gentleness and reason. For the education of youth in ' simple music ' is declared to inspire temperance (*Rep.* 410), a virtue which implies self-control (*Rep.* 389) as well as obedience to authority. The context shows that the control is exercised over the appetites and it must therefore be that of gentleness alone, or that of gentleness in its adjustment to spirit.

[2] *Republic,* 490 (trans. by Nettleship, *Hellenica,* p. 85).

receptivity and its *adjustment* to forces and values *akin to itself*, yet greater than it, and beyond the circle of its positive attainments at any given moment.

This concern is the real continuity of the Platonic theory of education, and perhaps it explains the points of resemblance between the later and more liberal education of the guardians and the earlier and more prescriptive period of training through music and gymnastic. The resemblances are striking. Thus, even when reason ' which is wise and has the care of the whole soul ' rules over spirit—its *subject and ally* (a combination of functions which, it will be noted, harmonizes with the notions of control and adjustment suggested above) it is the *united* influence of music and gymnastic that brings reason and passion into accord ' nerving and sustaining the reason with noble words and lessons, and moderating and soothing and civilizing the wildness of passion by harmony and rhythm.' [1] And although education through mathematical and astronomical subjects was intended to be an intermediate course leading the pupil gradually to higher powers of abstraction and reflection, Plato urges that mathematics should be presented to the mind in childhood. By this means ' the natural bent of the pupil might be discovered '—a remark which suggests a continuity of the earlier and later aims and processes of education rather than the mere advocacy of play ways or the concrete presentations of mathematical concepts. In the final stages, too, where the aim is to produce the ' philosopher and the warrior ' it is the ' gentle ' aid of dialectic that lifts upwards the eye of the soul, and it is ' philosophy tempered with music ' that is the soul's best guardian. Whether gentleness is the matrix from which reason springs, or merely the precursor of reason, it seems to be *at least* co-ordinate with spirit and not a mere quality of the passionate element as, for example, bravery or courage undoubtedly is. The many points of agreement in the terms used to describe gentleness and reason, in the functions of these elements, and in the aims and methods of education which nurture them, give further support to the suggestion of a genetic relationship between the two elements.

In the *Republic* we see, then, a picture of the receptive (or gentle) element uniting with, or merging into, reason as a result

[1] *Republic*, 442.

of musical and gymnastic training.   Later the pupil receives
the good into his soul and salutes the friend with whom his
education has made him familiar.[1]   Simultaneously, and as a
result of the same training the spirited element is tempered like
steel and made useful instead of brittle and useless.[2]   Education (1) nurtures the gentle element, (2) moderates the
spirited principle, (3) develops both of these so that they are
mutually attuned and obedient to the things usually accounted
good and true and beautiful, (4) develops reason so that it
controls the whole inner life and increasingly recognizes its
affinity to the whole universe.

From our discussion it follows that Plato's educational scheme
in the *Republic* embodies four principles : gentleness, spirit,
desire, reason.   The linking of gentleness with reason, as some
suggest, would result in a trinity of elements amongst which
two types of adjustment take place.   The earlier of these is the
attunement of gentleness and spirit, the later, the harmony of
the higher and lower nature, is itself the outcome of the earlier
attunement, and results from the control of attuned gentleness
and spirit over the appetites.   This, briefly, is the system which
underlies Plato's designation of justice—each element doing its
own.   What is its relation to freedom ?

Let us first consider briefly its relation to the control and
supremacy of the laws discussed in the earlier section of this
chapter.   Is Plato's basal idea of elements each fulfilling its
own function not synonymous with a wide view of liberty?   Do
not the early stages of education, as we have shown above, suggest
an almost complete harmonization of the means and methods
of culture with the demands of the pupil's nature ?   How are
we to reconcile the liberalism of Plato's conception of justice
with the fixity and rigour of his ideas of the laws, with his prescription of play activities in youth, and with his apparent
distrust of even adult human nature ?

The two points of view are reconcilable only on an assumption which seems to be so thoroughly embedded in Plato's
whole thought that the necessity for any discussion, or the
probability of any questioning of its validity, never crossed his
mind. *That assumption is the conjunction if not the identification of mental activity with mental receptivity*.   The light, as

---

[1] *Republic*, 402 (Jowett, iii. p. 88).   [2] *Republic*, 411.

he urged against the professors of education, was in the eye of the soul, but the eye had to be turned to the sun before any vision of the Good could enter.   The good was received into the soul only when it was saluted and recognized as a friend. It became a fully living and directive force of the life only when the mind was in perpetual travail to bring forth truth.   Plato disliked the term freedom because its popular implications divorced the natural expression of the elements—each doing its own—from the natural control which expressed the very condition of their activity.

This control, as we have seen, was of two kinds.   The first has been sufficiently illustrated in Plato's emphasis of the control of the laws, of the values of the social environment, of the idea of things as they *are*.   The other type of control was relatively internal but presupposed always the external aspect of control.   Gentleness and spirit were attuned through the influence of music and gymnastic, and music, in particular, was the representative of the laws.   The internal adjustments give evidence of a type of behaviour complementary to that which the external control presupposes.   Thus it is that the ' gentle ' element, rigidly controlled by the conditions of the early training, really controls the spirited element which, in its relation to the outer world, is the relatively domineering and assertive element.   Thus, too, reason, the directive agency of the inner life, is made the subject of a whole series of disciplines which adjust its activities to the universal principle of all being—the form of the Good.

But both types of control sustain mental activity—their aim is *to mingle true being with true being*.   The phrase itself is very suggestive of the full Platonic theory, and of the identification of mental activity with the acceptance of control.   It emphasizes Plato's positive characterization of justice—that of each element pulling its own weight.   The functions of each are more or less clearly stated.   There is a very clear picture of a disinterested reason endeavouring to penetrate the arcanum of the Good—a notable presentation of the pursuit of knowledge for its own sake, a view of the goal of education too often hidden from those who rightly trace the beginnings of the educative process to utilitarian studies.   Spirit, too, has a markedly definite part to play in early education : it may be regarded as the executive officer of the ruling reason. The appetites do not really enter into the sphere of education : they are controlled but not educated. It is only in Plato's striking pictures of their rebellious manifestations that we see that they, too, have their own part in the activities of the soul.

In the relationship of the appetites to reason (and to spirit), and in that of spirit to reason there is a negative characterization of justice—one which expresses the inner harmony of the whole being. Plato states it in the form of ' not permitting the several elements to interfere with one another, or any of them to do the work of others.' [1] This principle of non-interference expresses a function of each of the elements which is only implicit in the idea of ' each doing its own.' It emphasizes the fact that *each element owes to, and receives from, the others a type of expressive behaviour which is determined by the purpose of the whole life*, or in Plato's words, by the activity of the man who has ' set in order his own inner life, and is his own master, and his own law, and at peace with himself.' [1] This is a principle of freedom rather than of justice— a term which has too close a connection with man's social environment to express adequately the animating principle of the citadel of selfhood.

Plato's general theory may best be evaluated in the light of his own principle. Does he give the conditions that permit each element to perform only its own work ? His discussion, it may be replied, at least shows the difficulty of setting free all the activities that go to make a man—whether guardian, or artisan or philosopher. In two respects, perhaps, he does not meet the requirements of his theory. He undoubtedly exaggerates the plasticity and receptivity of childhood and envelops a code of unnecessary prescriptions and regulations with the insignia of spontaneity. He assigns to reason a governing function which is foreign to its mode of expression in the lives of even highly intellectual men. For, as one of his discerning critics insists : " If a man must be governed by understanding, it will be by the understanding of the lower things of life, for the highest things pass understanding ; of peace (true peace), of righteousness, of wisdom a man has a suspicion, a vision, a gleam, a divination (as Plato says, *Rep*. vi. 505*e*), but not yet compre-

[1] *Republic*, 443.

hension : ' through a glass darkly ' he sees, if at all. And therefore the demand that life be based upon logic, reason and comprehension inevitably sinks into a basing of life on that common sense merely ' which is intolerable without metaphysics ' ; on that horse sense which is only one degree, I apprehend, removed from jackass-sense ; and on materialism ; hence Greek intellectualism tends to end in a commonplace and rather sordid Positivism and Utilitarianism." . . .[1] It is, in short, only in theory that an idealization of a part of life (even of reason) ever rules : when it really controls it ceases to be an ideal.

Our exposition up to this point has been confined to views that are common to Plato's early and later works, but it is interesting to note that the disillusionment of old age led Plato to admit that the rule of justice—the supremacy of certain individuals or tendencies—is not incompatible with the reign of freedom.[2] And however unfair these later views may be to the vision of the *Republic* we must note those of the Athenian stranger when, forgetting the control of an external law, the supremacy of a governing class, the lordship of a cold reason, he takes man as a creature of flesh and blood, of high purposes and lower tendencies, of instinct and passion as well as reason and boldly declares that ' when the opinion of the best, in whatever part of human nature, states or individuals may suppose that to dwell, has dominion in the soul and orders the life of every man, even if it is sometimes mistaken, yet what is done in accordance therewith and the principle in individuals which obeys this rule and is best for the whole life of man is to be called just.' [3]   We prefer to call the principle freedom and forgetting the *body* of Plato's state with its attempt to implant virtues through external coercion, to recognize in his designation of justice a statement of some of the essential marks of liberty, and in the pronouncement of the Athenian stranger a notable anticipation of the most enlightened elements of educational theory during the twenty centuries that have followed him.

We may, then, re-interpret the concept of justice as a statement of four characteristics of freedom in education.

(1) It harmonizes two partially conflicting yet fundamental tendencies—the receptive and the active.

---

[1] Maurice Hutton, *The Greek Point of View*, p. 57.
[2] Cf. *Laws*, 962.   [3] *Laws*, 864 (Jowett, vol. v. p. 247).

(2) It adjusts each of these to the requirements of the social environment.

(3) It emphasizes the idea of the full life through adequate and carefully regulated nurture.

(4) It relates all the tendencies and values to an inner law which is so delicately adjusted to the requirements of society that it is at once the embodiment of an *individual* and a *social* ideal of life.

CHAPTER III

ARISTOTLE'S FREEDOM THROUGH THE MEAN

' A " COMPLETE " good is one the presence of which leaves us
in need of nothing ; an " incomplete " good is one which may
be present while yet we need something further ; for instance,
we may have justice and yet need many things besides, but
when we have happiness we need nothing more.' [1] This quotation from the *Magna Moralia*, whether it comes directly from
Aristotle or from a later writer, gives in a single sentence the
relation of the Aristotelian to the Platonic concept of the Good
(in the *Republic*) and at once brings Aristotle's fundamental
views on education into connection with the Platonic concept
of justice discussed in the preceding chapter. There, under the
name of freedom, we included the dual notion of reconciliation
of opposing tendencies and fullness of life. Aristotle, as we
shall see, gives us a general formula for the reconciliation and
a concrete setting for completeness. Like Plato, he has little
direct place for liberty in his conception of the complete good,
but some elements of his view of happiness are suggestive for
freedom. A blend of justice and freedom may be said to
express his conception of happiness.

Before developing this conception we must note the difficulty
for education of the notion of a ' complete good.' It is not the
difficulty of individual completeness, for Aristotle, like Plato,
urges that association with other human beings[2] is a condition
of the complete life. It is rather the difficulty which any
notion of completeness brings for an incomplete process, or for
a process which exists only so long as it is incomplete.[3] The
notion, as it exists in Aristotle, leads to the exclusion of the

---

[1] *Magna Moralia*, 1184a (edited by W. D. Ross, *Works of Aristotle*, Oxford,
Clarendon Press). The authorship of the *Magna Moralia* is not of importance
for our purposes. Mr. Ross points out (Introduction, p. xiii.) that its main
doctrine is Aristotle's.

[2] Cf. *Politics*, i. 1, 2.   [3] Cf. *Nicomachean Ethics*, 1, 6.

child. No child, urges Aristotle, can be happy. His age makes it impossible for him to ' display this activity at present, and if a child is ever said to be happy, the ground of his felicitation is his promise, *rather than his actual performance*. For happiness demands, as we said, a complete virtue and a complete life.' [1]

Our view of education seeking, as it does, to bring within its scope the immature as well as the comparatively mature phases of development, must emphasize both in child and adult the promise rather than the attainment of happiness, and, however unfair the interpretation may be to Aristotle's conception of early education, must regard happiness as a continual effort towards a ' complete ' good shared by all persons who are really being educated. We thus regard happiness and completeness as relative terms applicable in some degree to all human beings and not fully enjoyed even by a person desirous of further education. Both terms are relative to the past attainment of the individual, and Aristotle's general delineation of adult happiness is to be taken as conditioned at all stages of development by the ' nature ' of the individual.

We have ventured to characterize Aristotle's concept of happiness as a blend of freedom and justice, and we have now to consider his view of freedom and to attempt to state its relation to that completeness and efficacy of the several tendencies of life which we found in the Platonic concept of justice. Aristotle's main point is that freedom is not equality.

In the *Politics* he reviews several types of human relationship and finds no justification for the belief that human beings are *equals*. ' There must be a union of natural ruler and subject that both may be preserved.' [2] ' That some should rule and others be ruled is a thing not only necessary but also expedient —from the hour of their birth some are marked out for subjection, others for rule.' [3] ' In all things which form a composite whole and which are made up of parts, whether continuous or discrete, a distinction between the ruling and the subject element comes to light.' [3] Some men, he urges, are by nature free, others are slaves, the slave being a part of the composite whole which includes the master's life and interests.

[1] Cf. *Nicomachean Ethics*, i. 10 (trans. Welldon).
[2] *Politics*, i. 2 (Jowett's translation).   [3] *Politics*, i. 5.

The husband and father rules over the wife and the children, for the male is by nature fitter to command than the female, and the elder and full-grown is superior to the younger and the immature.[1]   Hence the democratic idea of freedom is contradictory to the interests of the state : ' Men think that what is just is equal : and that equality is the supremacy of the popular will ; and that freedom and equality mean the doing what a man likes.   In such democracies everyone lives as he pleases, or in the words of Euripides, ' according to his fancy,' but this is all wrong ; men should not think it slavery to live according to the constitution ; for it is their salvation.' [2] True equality consists in the *same* treatment of *similar* persons, and Nature herself has made a difference between old and young ' of whom she fitted the one to govern and the others to be governed.   No one takes offence at being governed when he is young, nor does he think himself better than his governors, especially if he will enjoy the same principle when he reaches the required age.' [3]

In referring the concept of liberty to the nature of the individual and to the natural relationships of individual to individual Aristotle emphasizes truths, which, however partial they may be for some aspects of life, are of fundamental importance for education.   There is no education within a circle of equals [4] :   if men are equal in attainments, in skill, in knowledge, in virtue, there is no possibility of educating or instructing them.   It is the consciousness of one's inequality, of a something that transcends self, of something greater than self which makes education a reality.   This consciousness when clearly understood gives to the teacher no right of domination and to the pupil no sense of real inferiority.   To the teacher it brings home the need for intimate contact with some aspect or element of the pupil's life in which real equality of teacher and pupil exist, but it, none the less, makes him sensitive to the claims of a greater value which he presents.   He does not dominate his pupil because the starting point and the maintenance of growth lie within the pupil's life.   The greater value is in the hands of the teacher, the potentiality of growth

---

[1] Cf. *Politics*, i. 12.   [2] *Politics*, v. 9.   [3] *Politics*, vii. 14.

[4] The special case of self-government is discussed in Chapters XXII and XXXI.

with the scholar. The relationship is not unlike Aristotle's idea of a natural inequality which becomes less and less marked as education proceeds and which therefore tends to make less and less appropriate the ideas of domination and slavery.

The demand for the equality of teacher and pupil comes from those who confuse two very different values that enter into education, (1) the values, representative of the outer world, that the teacher presents, (2) the pupil's values which must be studied in order that they may be nurtured. In the study of the pupil there must be a certain attitude of teacher to disciple, an attitude which Dr. Montessori characterizes as a blend of reverence and science. It is very easy to transfer to the pupil's education the mental attitude that enables us to study him, and particularly easy since the studying and educating of him proceed *pari passu*. But the transference often leads to a foolish worship of the pupil, to an exaggerated idea of the sacredness of his inner life, to the demand for conditions of education that no pupil *quâ* pupil really desires, to conditions which too frequently enervate, paralyse, and even destroy the relationships which education demands. That the pupil should live according to his fancy, that his acts and thoughts and feelings should be the expression of his *own* inner forces and motives, and of these *alone*, is a possible view of freedom and equality, but it is incompatible even with the beginnings of education. As Plato and Aristotle both urge, the individual is not self-sufficing : he must find his freedom, his justice, his equality, his happiness in those adjustments to external (as well as internal) forces in which the educative process consists. A child is not, educationally, the equal of another child or of an adult, nor is one adult the equal of another, although socially and politically, equality *may* or *should* exist in such cases. The rights that appertain to the educative process are not those enjoyed by equals, but those that permit *individual growth*.

In agreement with Aristotle's clearly cut distinction between the ruling and the subject element is his disapproval of the second principle of liberty as it appears in the democratic state— that all should rule and be ruled in turn.[1] The real force of this idea may best be presented through a statement of the

[1] *Politics*, vi. 2.

psychological and ethical implications of his conception of rule within the soul.   This will bring us to his practical formula for the adjustment of the inner tendencies which we have already touched upon in an earlier chapter.

In many respects Aristotle's conception is suggestive for education.   Like Plato he divides the soul into two parts, the rational and irrational.   The irrational has two principles or parts, one vegetative or nutritive which ' has no activity and having no activity, in no way co-operates towards happiness ; ' [1] the other part, the appetitive, is 'irrational, yet in a sense partakes of reason,' listens to and obeys reason.   Appetite or desire or concupiscence is thus obedient in the sense in which we speak of ' paying attention to a father,' or to friends, but not in the sense of ' paying attention to mathematics.' [2]   It is rational in the sense of being receptive to reason, although it is not capable of directing and initiating a reasonable course of action :   it is responsive but not responsible.   Its passivity and receptivity lead Aristotle to emphasize the importance of habituating it to reasonable actions, the harshness of Plato's idea of implanting virtues being mitigated by the affinity (or ' nearness ' in the Pestalozzian sense) of the reasonable action to the appetitive or concupiscent element of the soul.   Aristotle recognizes that reason presented in concrete form is transparent to the pupil.   In thus finding a *positive* point of contact in the child's soul with rudimentary forms and functions of reasoning he repairs a serious omission in the Platonic doctrine.   As one translator puts it :   ' Aristotle's point is that the ἄλογον (the faculty of desire) can be said to have λόγος only in the sense that it can obey a λόγος presented to it by reason, not in the sense that it can originate a λόγος—just as many people can " take account of " a father's advice who could not " account for " a mathematical property.' [3]   It must be granted that this receptivity—the being ruled in gentle fashion by reason—is one of the *fundamental* qualities of youth and one of the *fundamental* conditions of education.   Its value may be seen in the fact that ' all correction, rebuke and exhortation is a witness that the irrational part of the soul is in a sense subject to the

---

[1] *Magna Moralia*, 1185a.   [2] *Nic. Ethics*, xiii.

[3] W. D. Ross, Note to *Eth. Nic.* 1102b (Works of Aristotle, Oxford, Clarendon Press).

influence of reason.' In recognizing the semblance of reason·
in the irrational part of the soul Aristotle may fairly be said
to be the father of the modern doctrine of instincts as the
handmaidens of intelligence, and in finding in liberty the
characteristic mark of ' being ruled ' as well as ' ruling ' he
stands almost alone among educators.

The prior place is given to the *rule* of reason over passion,
yet many passages point to co-ordination of the two rather than
to the subordination of passion. Thus in *Ethica Eudemia* he
speaks of the ways in which the parts of the soul express reason
as the ' natural tendency to command,' and ' the natural tendency to obey,' obedience being thus as fundamental as rule.
While the intellectual virtues are reserved for the rational
part ' which governs the soul by its possession of reason,' the
moral virtues are relegated to the irrational part ' which is by
its nature obedient to the part possessing reason.' [1] The moral
life takes its origin in the appetites, desires and instincts, their
adjustment to reason being as truly natural as their direct
expression apart from reason can ever be. Character is thus
a function of the irrational element and grows by habit.
' Neither by nature or contrary to nature do the Virtues arise
in us ; we are adapted by nature to receive them and are
made perfect by habit.'

There are many passages, however, which emphasize the
positive rule of the emotions and passions. Thus in the
Nicomachean Ethics Aristotle asserts that the ' irrational
emotions seem to be as truly human as the reason itself, and
therefore we are as truly responsible for our emotions as for
our reasoning.' [2] And the co-ordination of the two is forcibly
presented in a remarkable passage in the *Magna Moralia* : [3]

' For we assert that then, and only then, is there virtue, when
reason being in a good condition is commensurate with the passions,
these possessing their proper virtue, and the passions with the
reason ; for in such a condition they will accord with one another,
so that reason should always ordain what is best, and the passions
being well disposed find it easy to carry out what reason ordains.
If, then, the reason be in a bad condition, and the passions not, there

---

[1] *Ethica Eudemia* (trans. Solomon), 1219*b* and 1220*a*.

[2] *Nic. Ethics*, iii. 4.

[3] *Magna Moralia*, 1206*b* (trans. St. George Stock).

will not be virtue owing to the failure of reason (for virtue consists in both). . . .

Speaking generally, it is not the case, as the rest of the world think, that reason is the principle and guide to virtue, but rather the feelings. For there must first be produced in us (as indeed is the case) an irrational impulse to the right and then later on reason must put the question to the vote and decide it. One may see this from the case of children and those who live without reason. For in these, apart from reason, there spring up, first, impulses of the feelings towards right, and reason supervening later and giving its vote the same way as the cause of right action. But if they have received from reason the principle that leads to right, the feelings do not necessarily follow and consent thereto, but often oppose it. Wherefore a right disposition of the feelings seems to be the principle that leads to virtue rather than the reason.'

This has been called the crowning word of Peripatetic Ethics : it is, in a very real sense, the crowning word in the charter of freedom. Fully acted upon, it would lead to the abandonment of the Platonic idea of implanting habits in natures not yet capable of receiving them, and with the disappearance of this idea there would also disappear the specious doctrine, some-times deduced from Aristotle, that since one becomes good only by doing good acts, children must be *made* to do good acts before they appreciate the quality in virtue of which the acts themselves are good. The satisfaction of impulses that arouse pleasurable feelings, or, in other words, of impulses that *seem* good to the individual is rightly emphasized as the *terminus a quo* and the *terminus ad quem* of the virtuous life. It is in the working out of such impulses that the child ' pays attention ' to the voice of reason whether it speaks from within or from without himself. And, although Aristotle is true to his funda-mental principle of the rule of the best, rather than to that of ' ruling and being ruled in turn,' the reason that here rules over passion is not a reason *external* to the individual life but one that comes warm with the glow of personal emotions and tendencies. It is the rule of the best, but of a best which carries a two-fold sceptre.[1]

[1] Cf. Professor Burnet's Note (*Aristotle on Education*, p. 43, note 2), ' So long as we recognize the existence of appetition, Aristotle is quite indifferent as to whether we assign it to the rational or the irrational part. All he insists upon is that it cannot be simply identified with either. If it is irrational, it never-theless partakes of reason ; if it is rational, it is not so in the full sense, but only in a secondary and subordinate way.'

In the Aristotelian scheme of education, while reason is kept in view, the training of the irrational element has first place, and the doctrine of *catharsis* bears witness to the importance of rightly treating the emotions. In effect, Aristotle's method of reaching the mind is to stir up the feelings by means of music, and by systematically discharging them to bring the mind back to a normal condition. A direct expression of the emotions is thus regarded as an essential condition of normal life. People ' liable to become possessed of pity or fear,' for example, are brought back by appropriate melodies ' to a normal condition as if they had been medically treated and had taken a purge.' [1] Thus from the educational, as well as from the ethical and psychological points of view, ' ruling and being ruled ' means exercising and obeying a reason commensurate with the passions, and if reason is given the chief place the passions are by no means ignored.

The practical means of adjusting the commanding and the obeying elements and the delineation of the full life are both to be found in Aristotle's doctrine of happiness through the mean. Happiness is described in psychological terms, although it is recognized that a certain sufficiency of external goods is one of its desirable conditions. It is an activity of the soul in accordance with virtue and in a complete life.[2] Aristotle discusses the meaning of virtue at length. The moral virtues are mean states which in each case lie between two vices, the vice of excess on one hand and of deficiency on the other. Virtue is a deliberate moral purpose consisting in a mean that is relative to the individual and determined by reason. Happiness is thus an activity (1) deliberately adjusted to a mean determined by one's own reason, and (2) operative in a complete life. This is but a more elaborate statement of the concept of freedom in education considered in the previous chapter. If we agree that the first part of the definition is an amplification of freedom as there interpreted, and that the second, the complete life, expresses the Platonic idea of justice with a fullness of which Plato never dreamed, then we may regard the Aristotelian supreme good as a conjunction of freedom and justice. For our purposes, however, both notions

---

[1] Cf. *Politics*, viii. 7.
[2] Cf. *Nic. Ethics*, i. 6.

are again essential, and we shall, therefore, retain the term freedom for the union of both concepts.

The discussion of the adjustments that lead to the mean emphasizes several points of importance for freedom. Psychologically, the mean state is very extensive, and varied: it embraces tendencies and qualities arising from instincts or emotions such as fear, anger, and acquisitiveness, from states of consciousness like pleasure and pain, from quasi-ideals like truthfulness and liberality, and from sentiments such as friendship. In practice it is itself an activity, although it unifies in an empirical formula two sets of opposing tendencies—on the one hand those which over-step the bounds of reason, and on the other those which fail to meet reason's demands. And the activity is not only exceedingly complex but infinitely varied in its manifestations. In respect of one virtue there may be excess in one individual and defect in another, while in respect of another virtue the first may be deficient and the other may err through excess. Ethically, it is a rather colourless idea, for although Aristotle recognizes some tendencies to be intrinsically bad, his general teaching is that virtue and vice are made of the same stuff and are the products of the same capacity.[1] The mean is therefore *individually* conditioned, and if we accept the teaching of the *Magna Moralia*, and the actual operation of education as sketched in the *Politics*, rather than the general spirit of the *Ethics*, it is conditioned by a *best* in which reason and passion are commensurate. Even if reason finally issues orders and ordains what is best, its orders are issued to an equal rather than to a slave. The first principle of liberty, that of equality among similars, is therefore *implicit* in the theoretical conception of the mean as a state of consciousness actually attained. Equality as a kind of mean is explicitly admitted by Aristotle.[2] In the process of attaining it,

---

[1] In the *Nicomachean Ethics*, ii. 5, Aristotle's general position seems to be that the capacities for goodness and badness of character are one and the same. Natural capacities (such as the capacity of the stone for falling) give rise to only one type of activity : training and habituation determine the way in which the activity functions. And he proceeds to argue that the material which makes and unmakes goodness is the same : playing the lyre makes good and bad lyre-players, business transactions make both just and unjust men. But, given good conditions of training and habit, the mean is individually conditioned, and, in practice, the feelings as well as reason enter into the conditioning process.

[2] Cf. *Eth. Nic.* ii. 5.

however, reason rules and passion obeys : Aristotle, emphasizing the 'right rule' of Plato,[1] cannot here accept the idea of 'ruling and being ruled in turn.' The second principle of liberty is implicit in the general idea of a sympathetic reason dominating an influential as well as a submissive irrational element.

It should be noticed that the discussion of these points in Aristotle has little, if any, direct reference to education : here, as in Plato, politics, ethics, and education intermingle. But Aristotle would certainly have had little room for the *equality* of the pupil with the teacher. Even the cathartic influence of music is designed to bring the pupil back to an emotional mean. The general note of his education, so far as we know it, is corrective rather than inspired by any faith in spontaneity ; the general note of his teaching is an appeal to a nature which is receptive rather than assertive. The reasoning of others would no doubt have obtained its first entry to the mind through the feelings and instinctive tendencies. At what stage of development he supposed the pupil's reason to exercise control, or to respond directly to the reason of another we have no means of judging, but we know that he believed the *intellectual* virtues to be both originated and fostered by teaching.[2]

If we apply Aristotle's views to education we may find in them a recognition of the fact that equality of teacher and pupil does not really characterize freedom in education. We may also find an interpretation of ' ruling and being ruled ' which adds vividness and concreteness to Plato's ideas. All the activities of the soul according to the teaching of the *Magna Moralia* are capable of rule and obedience. In making reason commensurate with the passions Aristotle gives a much more complete view of the sphere and function of education than Plato's general theory affords. He also gives a much surer point of contact with the young pupil's life, and therefore a greater measure of equality. His theory of the *mean* emphasizes the rule of an *individual* reason which Plato's idolatry of the state is inclined to ignore. Its attainment assumes the idea of a continuous effort which serves as a valuable corrective to the static conceptions of completeness and happiness. It gives a much clearer glimpse of freedom at work than Plato's principle

[1] Cf. *Eth. Nic.* ii. 2.   [2] Cf. *Eth. Nic.* ii. 1.

of non-interference. It illuminates those moments in which we try to adapt the self to the vision of what the self ought to be, moments which we associate with the struggle for freedom rather than with the possession of happiness. In the actual process of education freedom seems to be the best watchword even if happiness be its desired reward.

CHAPTER IV

FREEDOM AND THE ἐγκύκλιος παιδεία

ONLY a passing reference has been made in the preceding chapters to the course of studies proposed by Plato and Aristotle. Time and bitter experience led Plato to soften the rigour of his philosophical training. In the *Laws* [1] we see him regretfully parting company with divine dialectic, robing mathematics in a sombre garment, and, followed by music and gymnastic, making a last attempt to descend into the cave as a Director of Education. Aristotle, too, had bowed to the whim of the many-headed multitude by arranging a simple course of rhetoric, dialectic, and political theory for men of ordinary education. These concessions were probably due to the success of the sophists, and, in particular, to the success of Isocrates. It has been very unfortunate both for the development of education and for the prestige of educational science that the contempt of a great thinker like Plato has been associated with that study of the pupil's requirements which has made the sophists famous—or infamous.

Their teaching gifts must undoubtedly have been considerable. They had a certain charm of manner, a versatility, a flair for the problems that aroused youthful curiosity, a knack of linking up their lectures with adolescent ambitions and interests, and a facility for presenting abstract ideas in forms and activities that invited youthful co-operation. And qualities like these usually appeal to youthful minds more impatient, as they generally are, of abstract discussion than of superficiality, and tolerant of frankly utilitarian and sceptical tendencies. Isocrates was a sophist of outstanding gifts. Even Socrates admitted that he had ' a certain philosophy inborn in him.' [2] His aim of education was not dialectical attainment

---

[1] 810-827 Jowett, vol. v. pp. 192-208.

[2] *Phaedrus*, 279 (Jowett, i. 489).

61

but political wisdom and eloquence. He sought to press literary and linguistic disciplines into the making of a man who could not only think clearly and speak well but make active use of these gifts in civic life. Gradually, and with varying content in successive writers, this conception of a ' practical ' culture was specialized into schemes for the education of the orator, and generalized into the idea of an ' ἐγκύκλιος παιδεία,' a ' general ' education, or an education through the liberal disciplines or arts.[1] Through the teaching of grammar, (or literature), dialectic, rhetoric, arithmetic, geometry, astronomy, and music Greece became, in effect, the schoolmistress of the world. Out of the relatively final conception of studies suggested by Plato there emerged a curriculum sufficiently comprehensive and enlightened to focus the educational activity of Europe for a period of nearly two thousand years. Its modifications are, in a very real sense, the history of freedom for they present the successive adjustments of cultural values to the special requirements of a long succession of peoples and nations and therefore show on a large scale that adaptation of values which lies at the heart of freedom in education. The history of these changes is Freedom writ large. In the present chapter we shall illustrate the earlier adjustments by reference to the views of Cicero, Seneca, Quintilian and Plutarch.

Two main points in their writings seem relevant to our purpose. The first is the presentation of certain disciplines as the necessary equipment of the free man ; the second the distinct recognition of freedom as an aid in the early stages of discipline.

I

The extension of the Platonic scheme of studies is well illustrated in Cicero's delineation of the ' doctus orator.' The orator's studies are almost as wide as those of the philosopher who surveys all time and all existence. Ethics, psychology,

---

[1] Quintilian (De Inst. oratoria, i. 10, 1), and Plutarch (De Mus. 1135d) use the Greek designation. Cicero prefers artes liberales (De Or. i. 72), doctrina liberaliter institutus (De Or. ii. 162), liberales doctrinae et ingenuae (De Or. iii. 127), bonae artes (De Or. i. 158), while Seneca (Epist. 88) uses both the Latin and Greek terms.

history, jurisprudence, military and naval science, medicine, and geography are necessary in addition to the other ' liberal ' studies. But more striking than the content of his studies is their close connection with everyday activities, and with all forms of human life. He must appear in the camp, the forum, and the field. He must practise everything and test the strength of his understanding continually. The writers and teachers of the liberal arts must be read, considered, praised, interpreted, corrected, censured, refuted. Both sides of every question must be disputed. Laws must be understood ; the facts of antiquity known ; the nature of government, the rights of allies, the conditions of treaties, and all that concerns the interests of the state must be studied. A certain intellectual grace must be extracted from every study and with it, as with salt, every oration must be seasoned.[1] In this higher education there must be abundance of matter rather than of words—the knowledge of the keen and sympathetic man of the world responsive to the needs and aspirations of his fellows. The ' abundance of words ' is not to be that of the mere rhetorician but the embodiment of an eloquence that is firmly based upon the facts and conditions of life. Cicero's conception of the studies that make a man free is as broad as that of Plato or Aristotle ; it is educationally deeper in so far as it works itself out in life activities that give purpose, direction, continuity and natural conditions of growth. In it there is a glimpse of a truly liberal training—one that is definitely purposive yet not merely utilitarian, broad and inspiring yet not vague or nebulous, concrete and personal yet not egocentric.

Cicero's pansophic leanings find a corrective in Seneca. A stoic by conviction, and proud that even in old age he preferred a hard couch and a simple life, Seneca brings to education two ideas of great importance. First, he urges that our desires and wants must be diminished if we would increase our possessions.[2] Wisdom is the only liberty. It is to serve nothing, neither necessity, nor fortune. Fortune may wage war but she may be shaken off and kept at arm's length : ' that day I myself understand that I can more than she may, she can do nothing.' [3] In the second place, he shows the uselessness of the childish

---

[1] Cf. *De Orat.* i. 15, 64 ; i. 34 (154-159) ; ii. 17, 72.

[2] *Epistles,* 2.   [3] *Epistles,* 61 (trans. by T. Lodge, 1641).

(*pueriles*) arts ' which the Greeks call " ἐγκύκλιοι " and the Romans " *liberales*." ' There is only one really liberal study—that which gives a man his liberty.   It is the study of wisdom and that is lofty, brave and great-souled.' [1]   Rousseau's *Émile* is based upon these two principles.

Seneca's idea of the active invincible mind colours all his views of education.   Every study is to be related to the self and to give it positive nutriment.   So long as a man is ignorant he ought to continue to attend school : however old he may be he ought always to learn.   But all studies should nourish the wit.   In learning he ought to imitate the bees which wander up and down, pick fit flowers, and dispose what they have gathered in their combs.   The liberal arts do not teach virtue.   One by one, with the exception of rhetoric and philosophy, Seneca passes them in review.   He shows that they make no pretence to the teaching of virtue.   They give neither sustenance, nor vision, nor direction to the soul.   Studies in language and history, the uttering of syllables and the scansion of poetry do not banish fear, repress covetousness, or restrain lust.   It is important to learn the things that made Homer wise, but to know whether Homer or Hesiod were the older, or where Ulysses was tossed, or why Hecuba bore her years badly is of little value to human beings exposed to the storms of daily passion, assaulted by terrible monsters of lust and enticed by sirens.   The attunement of treble and bass does not bring harmony into the purposes of the mind ; the practice of mournful tunes does not teach how to bear oneself in adversity.[2]   The mathematician's measurements do not teach me to measure myself as a man.   Arithmetic may increase my avarice but not my happiness.   What is the use of knowing how to divide a field into two equal parts if I know not how to divide with my brother ?   Why learn the times when Saturn and Mars are in opposition if I am not convinced that all the stars are propitious and that they are not subject to change ?   What good is there in overcoming many men in the palaestra if I am myself overcome by anger ?

To these views of wisdom as delivering deeds not words, as a great and spacious thing that had ' need of an empty place,'

[1] *Epistles*, 88, trans. by R. M. Gummere (Loeb Classical Library).

[2] Compare Plato's claims for music, and Aristotle's theory of Catharsis.

and for whose entrance ' many things should be expelled, nay even the whole breast emptied,' Seneca adds the further view that a superfluity of learning is a kind of intemperance and therefore blameworthy. It makes men troublesome, unreasonable, full of words and ignorant of necessary knowledge. Didymus wrote four thousand books, but life is short, and great are the labour and trouble of all this writing and counting of syllables. The philosophers, who should know better, are infected with the same disease. They know rather how to talk than to live. Protagoras will have everything disputed on both sides ; Parmenides and Zeno teach a new knowledge—that of knowing nothing. The liberal studies are profitless but the philosopher takes away the hope of knowledge.

Notwithstanding his scepticism Seneca is not really the father of negative education. Even if he believes learning to be vanity, he thinks it is better to know too much than to know nothing. He cannot say whether he is more angry with those who would have us know nothing or with those who have left us nothing to know. On the whole, he inclines to the more positive view sketched in the *Consolation of Helvia*.[1] There he advises his mother to return to her early study of the liberal arts for they will give comfort and delight, and banish sorrow, loneliness, and affliction. He is really desirous of returning to the central things of life, and wishes education to embody not so much the Ciceronian ideal of ' humanitas ' as the warm human values which form the basis of every human activity. Teach me, he says, my duty to my country, to my father, to my wife, teach me honesty, purity and contentment, fortitude, fidelity and temperance, simplicity, modesty, economy and self-restraint.

And although he thinks that the liberal arts are childish he does not reject them as entirely useless. They are the rudiments of wisdom and are to be learned when the mind is capable of nothing greater. As men, our duty is not to study them but to have studied them. They prepare the understanding for wisdom. They cannot give virtue but they prepare the mind to receive it. It is probable that Seneca is influenced here by Plato's general theory. He points out that just as the primary course in grammar, as the ancients called it, taught

[1] Seneca, *Ad Helviam Matrem*, c. 16.

not the liberal arts but prepared a place for them, so liberal arts lead not the mind to virtue but make it fit for virtue. Of the way in which this preparation is brought about Seneca is silent. Perhaps we are nearer the heart of his meaning if we see in his criticisms of school studies not an exposition of their inherent futility but the conviction that they are wrongly presented to young minds. His epistle on liberal studies lends support to this view. ' Let us see,' he says, ' whether geometry and music teach virtue or not. If they do not teach they do not indeed deliver virtue, if *they do teach they are Philosophers.*' His pleas for real activity of mind, rejection of useless studies, closeness of teaching to the demands of life, emphasis of human values, contact of learning with personal conduct, simplicity, restraint, and reasonableness show him to be one of the most notable pioneers of freedom in education.

The enthusiasm for philosophical studies has almost disappeared in Quintilian's view of philosophy, although his *vir bonus dicendi peritus* is reminiscent of Cicero and his education of the orator may be regarded as an appeal to Cicero from Seneca. He speaks scathingly of those who sit for a while in the schools of the philosophers and affect an intellectual and moral superiority. ' Philosophy may be counterfeited but eloquence never.' [1] The Ciceronian conception of the cultural values of philosophy, law and history, is replaced by a detailed statement of the grammatical, literary and technical studies which are necessary for the production of the perfect orator. The orthodox liberal studies are accepted although music, geometry (and literature) are studied *pari passu* and more or less subordinated to rhetoric. There is an emphasis of utility that is absent in Cicero. The one is broad, philosophic, humane, the other is specific, utilitarian and thorough. Quintilian writes like a schoolmaster who has his eye on examination and scholarship results. In his pages the conception of liberal studies has just that note of ' practical ' utility that suggests illiberalism. His views are considerably broadened by his assumption that the orator is a ' good ' man. Seneca, had he wished to reply to Quintilian's strictures on philosophy, would doubtless have pointed out that a combination of goodness and

[1] Cf. *Inst. Oratoria*, xii. 3. 12 (trans. H. E. Butler, Loeb Classical Library, vol. iv., p. 407).

eloquence is as rarely found as a union of virtue and philosophy.

In Cicero, Seneca, and Quintilian we see the gradual but sure transition from philosophical to oratorical and from oratorical to rhetorical studies. Plutarch embodies both the Greek and the Roman view so skilfully that it is easy to understand why the ' ἐγκύκλιος παιδεία ' remained the almost universal basis of education down to the fall of the Roman Empire and powerfully influenced the early and later forms of Christian education. In his writings we breathe once more the Greek conviction of positive value in education and in philosophical studies. But moral excellence is no longer to be found in a *vision* of the good ; theory, or training in reasoning, natural powers of ability, and practice in working at one's craft or occupation are all conjoined. Three types of life are distinguished, the advantages of which are to be combined in suitable schemes of education. The life of mere enjoyment is paltry and animal, the practical life without philosophy is unlovely and harsh, the contemplative life without the practical is useless. Plutarch's statement of the values of philosophy, is a blend of Plato and Seneca, and has the vision of the Greek, as well as the personal attachment of the Roman, mind. With philosophy as guide we know what is honourable and what is dishonourable, what is just, what unjust ; what is to be sought after and what is to be avoided ; how we ought to behave to the gods, to parents, to elders, to the laws, to foreigners, to rulers, to friends, to women, to slaves—how we ought to worship the gods, honour parents, reverence elders, obey the laws, submit ourselves to rulers, love our friends, be chaste in our relations with women, kind to our children, considerate to our slaves . . . to be neither over-elated in prosperity nor over-depressed in adversity, nor to be dissolute in pleasures, nor fierce and brutish in anger.[1] This blend of ' music and gymnastic,' had it given a more prominent place to the pleasures that are ' not dissolute '—a feature of the full life at which Plutarch hints—would have been a noteworthy perception of the blend of conation, cognition and feeling implicit in his statement of the values of philosophy. But Plutarch just

---

[1] Cf. *Essay on Education* (the authenticity of which has been questioned) in Bohn's trans. of Plutarch's *Morals* (ch. x. p. 11).

misses the significance of those aspects of life that are neither contemplative nor practical, aspects which are, for some lives at least, so important that in their absence life could never be fully free.

II

The hour had not yet come for the full recognition of the rôle of feeling in the educative process ; nevertheless the movement towards liberal studies brought in its train a greatly enhanced idea of the pupil's freedom. Cicero indicates the force and the limitation of this idea in a single sentence : ' The authority of those who teach often injures those who wish to learn.' [1] Seneca points out the bad effects of dulling and damping the spirit of pupils, and insists that the mind's power is increased by liberty and depressed by servitude. In several passages [2] anticipatory of Locke and Rousseau he states the disadvantages of undue praise, excessive exultation, and excessive self-esteem, and pleads for reasonable and consistent treatment of the young. The curb at one time, the spur at another is his formula for discipline, an empirical type of adjustment that finds favour with many subsequent writers and notably with Plutarch.

If Quintilian adds little to the Roman conception of a liberal training he makes a valuable contribution to the idea of freedom as an aid to effective learning. Convinced of man's reasoning power—as natural a faculty for human beings as flying to birds, speed to horses and ferocity to birds of prey—he counsels us not to waste the early years. ' Small children are better adapted for taking in small things and just as the body can only be trained to certain flexions of the limbs while it is young and supple so the acquisition of strength makes the mind offer greater resistance to the acquaintance of most subjects of knowledge.' [3] No previous writer had so clear a perception of this resistance and none set himself so persistently to avoid it. He is thus the first serious student of the pupil's reaction to teaching.

Three analogies used by Quintilian are not only educative in themselves but illustrative of his general point of view. The first shows his guarded use of freedom : ' We may draw a

[1] Cicero, *De Nat. Deorum*, i, 5. 10.   [2] E.g. *De Ira*, ii. 18, 21.
[3] Quintilian, *Inst. Orat.* i. 1. 22 (trans. by Butler, i. p. 31).

lesson from the birds of the air, whom we see distributing the
food which they have collected in their bills among their weak
and helpless nestlings ; but as soon as they are fledged, we see
them teaching their young to leave the nest and fly round
about it, themselves leading the way ; finally when they have
proved their strength, they are given the freedom of the open
sky and left to trust in themselves.' [1] The textual reference is
to the declamation of themes and Quintilian emphasizes the
need for careful correction of faults and a liberal supply of
models, but insists that pupils should sometimes be left
entirely to their own devices so that they may not be spoilt by
always relying on another's efforts and so prove incapable of
originality.

A second figure shows how he would utilize the pupil's own
impulses in the process of education. Early in his exposition
he insists that he is not so blind to differences of age as to think
that the very young should be forced too prematurely. ' Above
all things we must take care that the child, who is not yet old
enough to love his studies, does not come to hate them and dread
the bitterness which he has once tasted, even when the years of
infancy are left behind. His studies must be made an amusement, he must be questioned and praised and taught to rejoice
when he has done well ; sometimes, too, when he refuses
instruction it should be given to some other to excite envy,
at times also he must be engaged in competition and should be
allowed to believe himself successful more often than not, while
he should be encouraged to do his best by such rewards as may
appeal to his tender years.' [2] As if in apology for this appeal
to ambition he tells us that though it may be a fault in itself
it is often the mother of virtue, and confirms his statement by
a reference to his own school experience. To be leader of the
class was a coveted honour, but the position was not made
permanent. Once a month there was a competition. If the
honour was to be retained there could be no slackening of
effort, while if it were lost the defeat served as an incentive to
wipe out the disgrace. ' I will venture to assert,' he writes,
' that to the best of my memory this practice did more to
kindle our oratorical ambitions than all the exhortations of our

[1] Quintilian, *Inst. Orat.* ii. 6. 7 (Butler, i. p. 261).
[2] Quintilian, *Inst. Orat.* i. 1. 20 (Butler, i. p. 31).

instructors, the watchfulness of our *paedagogi* and the prayers of our parents.' [1] He notes that beginners derive greater pleasure from imitating their comrades than their masters, because it is easier, or, as he goes on to suggest more truly, because children ' can scarce dare hope to reach that complete eloquence which they understand to be their goal.' Had Quintilian had any experience of youthful eloquence when really free and unfettered, he might have been still more appreciative of children's standards of oratory,[2] but no analogy could give a better general idea of the imitative, receptive, and clinging tendencies of youth than his idea of children ' imitating the vine which has to grasp the lower branches of the tree on which it is trained before it can reach the topmost boughs.' [2]

The third comparison is one that has been quoted again and again by educational reformers. After insisting that the teacher who prefers practical utility to ambitious programmes will not burden his pupils with tasks to which their strength is unequal, but will come down to the level of their abilities, he writes : ' Vessels with narrow mouths will not receive liquids if too much be poured into them at a time, but are easily filled if the liquid is admitted in a gentle stream or, it may be, drop by drop ; similarly you must consider how much a child's mind is capable of receiving : the things which are beyond their grasp will not enter their minds, which have not opened out sufficiently to take them in.   It is a good thing, therefore, that a boy should have companions whom he will desire first to imitate and then to surpass : thus he will be led to aspire to higher achievement.' [3]

The above exposition gives some idea of Quintilian as a student of the child's tendencies and an advocate of wisely utilizing them.   But he is not to be taken as a blind worshipper of childhood : he is really concerned with the content and results of instruction, and at times speaks of originality as impossible in the early years, and of memory as the only faculty that can be developed.[4] He is convinced that the skilful teacher's first care is to ascertain the ability and character of

[1] Quintilian, *Inst. Orat.* i. 2. 25 (Butler, i. p. 51).
[2] Quintilian, *Inst. Orat.* i. 2. 26 (Butler, vol. i. p. 51).
[3] Quintilian, *Inst. Orat.* i. 2. 28, 29 (Butler, vol. i. p. 53).
[4] Quintilian, *Inst. Orat.* i. 1. 36 (Butler, vol. i. p. 39).

his pupil, but he is of the opinion that the surest indications of these qualities are to be found in the child's memory and his powers of imitation.[1] His ideal pupil will absorb instruction with ease and he will even ask some questions, but he will follow rather than anticipate his teacher![2] He warns us that precocious intellects rarely produce sound fruit; the context shows that his real fear is of superficiality, not of early originality. He draws attention to the advantages of using different methods with different types of pupil, and of variety in studies.[3] 'Study depends on the good will of the student, a quality that cannot be secured by compulsion.'[4] But some boys are slack unless pressed on; others are impatient of control; some are amenable to fear while others are paralysed by it; some require continued application, others rapid concentration.[5]

In the greater things of school life it is fair to class Quintilian among those who 'follow nature.' He considers the value of the view that each pupil should be pushed forward in the sphere for which his talents seem specially to design him—the view that 'nature when cultivated goes from strength to strength, while he who runs counter to her bent is ineffective in those branches of the art for which he is less suited and weakens the talents which he seemed born to employ.'[6] He thinks that this is only partially true. 'It is undoubtedly necessary to note the gifts of each boy, and no one would ever convince me that it is not desirable to differentiate courses of study with this in view. One boy will be better adapted for the study of history, another for poetry, another for law, while some perhaps had better be packed off to the country.'[7] But he points out that if natural talent is sufficient there is no need for education, and asks whether the pupil of depraved tastes shall be allowed to go his own sweet way. If it be right to remove certain qualities may we not be permitted to add what is lacking, to feed up, for example, the naturally dry and jejune disposition

---

[1] Quintilian, *Inst. Orat.* i. 2. 31 (Butler, vol. i. p. 55).

[2] Quintilian, *Inst. Orat.* i. 2. 31 (Butler, vol. i. p. 55).

[3] Cf. Quintilian, *Inst. Orat.* i. 3 2-4; i. 12. 4-9; ii. 8. 1.

[4] Quintilian, *Inst. Orat.* i. 3. 9 (Butler, vol. i. p. 57).

[5] Quintilian, *Inst. Orat.* i. 3. 6 (Butler, vol. i. p. 57).

[6] Quintilian, *Inst. Orat.* ii. 8. 5 (Butler, vol. i. p. 265).

[7] Quintilian, *Inst. Orat.* ii. 8. 7 and 10 (Butler, vol. i. p. 267).

of this or that pupil ?   ' Not that I would set myself against the will of nature.   No innate good quality should be neglected but defects must be made good and weaknesses made strong.'[1] When Isocrates ruled that Ephorus needed the spur and Theopompus the curb, he did not mean that the sluggish temperament of the one and the headlong impetuosity of the other alike required modification by instruction, but rather that each would gain from an admixture of the qualities possessed by the other.   Here there is a clear recognition of the two fundamental tendencies which we have found in Plato and a clear perception of the positive function of education for *each* of them, and, moreover, a glimpse of the truth that freedom is to be found in their adjustment.   Education is required because of individual limitation ;   there are defects of nature which necessitate the intervention of the teacher, but the wise teacher works *with* the forces of nature already strong and functional in the pupil's life.   A view like this seems to underlie Quintilian's methods and aims, and, as we shall see, it is by no means an impracticable or an illiberal theory.

Quintilian's appeal to the naturally strong and functional values has already been illustrated, but a great many of his teaching devices as, for example, his method of teaching a child to read, and his endeavour to make early education an amusement, are not so much novelties and play ways as means of utilizing native tendencies for a directly utilitarian and at the same time a decidedly educative purpose.   He wishes to secure the good-will of the student because it brings with it a greater fixity of purpose, a greater energy and a greater power of assertion.   ' I approve,' he says, ' of play in the young ; it is a sign of a lively disposition, nor will you ever lead me to believe that a boy who is gloomy and in a continual state of depression is ever likely to show alertness of mind in his work, lacking, as he does, the impulse most natural to boys of his age.' [2]   He emphasizes the educational value of games, particularly those in which pupils ask each other questions—turn and turn about—a suggestion which in one shape or another vitalized the school-room of the middle ages and still lives in the twentieth century.   His insight into the educative pos-

[1] Quintilian, *Inst. Orat.* ii. 8. 7 and 10 (Butler, vol. i. p. 267).

[2] Quintilian, *Inst. Orat.* i. 3. 10 (Butler, vol. i. p. 59).   Cf. also i. 3. 11 and 12.

sibilities of play is remarkable. He sees in it a means of moulding character : through it the youngest child may learn to distinguish between right and wrong. Thus the early or preparatory stage of education may not only, as Seneca urged, prepare for virtue but can be used so as to give a practical acquaintance with it.

Quintilian's remarks on punishment are worthy of quotation not only because of the light they throw upon the practice of the schools but also because of his clear perception of the limitation of punishment as a force in the pupil's later life, and because of his noteworthy anticipation of the results attributed to it by psycho-analysts in our own day.

' I disapprove of flogging, although it is the regular custom and meets with the acquiescence of Chrysippus, because in the first place it is a disgraceful form of punishment and fit only for slaves, and is in any case an insult, as you will realize if you imagine its infliction at a later age.   Secondly, if a boy is so insensible to instruction that reproof is useless, he will, like the worst type of slave, merely become hardened to blows. Finally, there will be absolutely no need of such punishment if the master is a thorough disciplinarian.   As it is, we try to make amends for the negligence of the boy's *paedagogus*, not by forcing him to do what is right, but by punishing him for not doing what is right.   And though you may compel a child with blows, what are you to do with him when he is a young man no longer amenable to such threats and confronted with tasks of far greater difficulty ?   Moreover, when children are beaten, pain or fear frequently has results of which it is not pleasant to speak, and which are likely subsequently to be a source of shame, a shame which unnerves and depresses the mind and leads the child to shun and loathe the light. . . .   I will content myself with saying that children are helpless and easily victimized, and that therefore no one should be given unlimited power over them.' [1]

The same mildness of treatment and encouragement of personal effort mark Quintilian's observations on the methods of dealing with adolescence.[2] The teacher is to be self-controlled and fatherly, strict, but not austere, genial but not too

[1] *Inst. Orat.* i. 3. 14-16 & 18 (Butler, vol. i. pp. 59, 61).
[2] *Inst. Orat.* ii. 2 (Butler, vol. i. pp. 211 ff.).

familiar ; his instruction is to be free from affectation, his industry great, his demands on his class continuous, but not extravagant. He must be ready to answer questions and to put them unasked to those who sit silent. He must be neither grudging nor over-generous in giving praise ; he must avoid sarcasm and abuse. He must regulate the order of his class in answering, not allowing boys to leap from their seats in their expressions of applause, and he must preserve an orderly audience. He must be lucid and intelligible in his teaching, for clearness is the first virtue of eloquence. Above all he must not demand or expect a perfect style from boys.

Quintilian, true to his encouragement of the stronger traits of the personality, sees signs of promise in a certain luxuriance of mind and ambitious effort even though it may be exuberant to the point of extravagance. He wishes his pupils to be daring and inventive and will rejoice in their inventions, even though correctness and restraint must yet be acquired. Exuberance is easily remedied ; barrenness of thought is incurable. He likes to see the first fruit of the mind copious to excess and almost extravagant in profusion. ' The years as they pass will skim off much of the froth and reason will file away excrescences.' [1] Undue severity in correcting faults must be avoided ; it tends to weaken the boy's own efforts, makes him lose hope and give way to vexation, and finally brings hate of work and fear of action. The instructor must be kindly. ' Remedies which are harsh by nature, must be applied with a gentle hand ; some portions of the work must be praised, others tolerated, others altered ; the reasons for the alteration should be given. . . . If a boy's composition is so careless as not to admit of correction, I have found it useful to give a fresh exposition of the theme and to tell him to write it again, pointing out that he was capable of doing better ; for there is nothing like hope for making study a pleasure. . . . When boys ventured on something that was too daring or exuberant, I used to say to them that I approved of this for the moment, but that the time would come when I should no longer tolerate such a style. The result was that the consciousness of ability filled them with pleasure without blinding their judgment.' [2]

---

[1] Cf. Butler, vol. i. p. 227 (Book ii, 4. 4-8).

[2] Quintilian, *Inst. Orat.* ii. 4. 12-14 (Butler, vol. i. pp. 229 and 231).

This portrait of the kindly schoolmaster is an embodiment of the essential qualities of freedom. Quintilian uses the natural forces, and tries to provide an atmosphere which will free them from their inherent limitations. Even when he deals with defects he gives the pupil the impression of ability and encourages him to persevere. Effort without compulsion, directed activity without severity, ingenuity and invention without conceit, are some of Quintilian's aims, and they are among the most worthy aims of education through the centuries. But as we have hinted there is here and there the idea of final satisfaction that is the precursor of decay if not the herald of death. He is willing to allow the ' weaker understandings to follow the call of their own nature.'[1] Thus they will do more effectively what lies within their power. But the youth who is to be trained as an orator does not enjoy so full a freedom. In his presence Quintilian is a schoolmaster rather than a follower of nature. He leaves no oratorical virtue untended. The justification of supervision is found in the supposed fact that the really bright pupil will not be repelled by his weaker subjects, but by working hard at them will develop his powers until he reaches the same level of proficiency in all studies. Even if we grant the possibility of this ' levelling up ' we can scarcely agree that Quintilian makes a good case for compulsion, for the argument in favour of allowing freedom in the choice of subjects to weaker pupils will surely apply with equal force to pupils of decided ability, and will apply with greater force in a course of professional training than in one of general education. Quintilian finds his justification in the education of the skilled gymnast who must become expert in the use of both fists and heels, and in that of the singing master who must excel in all registers. ' Eloquence is like a harp and will never reach perfection unless all its strings be taut and in tune.'[2] His concern for a *specific* training in *all* the departments of oratory, and his desire to keep it close to the conditions of life are, no doubt, justified by many recent experiments which throw doubt on the ' transfer ' of training from one type of activity to another, and which suggest the necessity for a close connection between the training and the life activity

---

[1] Quintilian, *Inst. Orat.* ii. 8. 12 (Butler, vol. i. p. 269).
[2] Quintilian, *Inst. Orat.* ii. 8. 15 (Butler, vol. i. p. 271).

in which it is to be tested. But he really begs the point at issue in assuming that the orator's abilities in all the subjects of his training are positively and highly correlated. In his sense of the term the ' good ' orator must be a *rara avis*. Even the *vir bonus dicendi peritus* would have chafed at Quintilian's long list of prescriptions.

Before attempting to estimate the bearing of these early modifications of the liberal arts upon freedom in education it may be well to remind ourselves that they were not typical of the educational practice of their day, and that their direct influence was comparatively short-lived. Even if the Greek view of education was vitalized for the moment by the sober Roman conception of virtue, and in its new garb revealed an ideal of life fertilized by broad notions of social duties and responsibilities, it failed to contribute in any marked way to the solution of the real problems of freedom. The failure of the early idea of ' liberal arts ' to give freedom is apparent from its later history. The arts became more and more frankly utilitarian, and before long degenerated into an artificial and mainly traditional body of studies. As a recent writer points out,[1] the schools of literature and rhetoric which sprang from them tended more and more to give a merely literary education ; to narrow it to a training in rhetorical composition ; to make the training itself, not a means of educative influence, but a superficial round of amusements and pleasant exercises ; to neglect the physical aspects of education ; in Seneca's phrase to educate for the class-room and not for life. The result may perhaps be explained by the fact that the ἐγκύκλιος παιδεία merely extended the two types of value central in all education. On the one hand, it brought education down from the clouds of dialectic and the fictions of the philosopher-king, and by its appeal to the practical and emotional, as well as to the intellectual life, made a distinct contribution to the Platonic and Aristotelian theories. On the other hand, it took a much broader view of the forces and potentialities of the pupil's life and paid a noteworthy and even devoted attention to his attitude towards learning. But it lacked any really mediating principle between these two

[1] *Roman Education from Cicero to Quintilian*, by Aubrey Gwynn, S.J., chap. x.

values. It gave a fuller, yet a definitely prescribed, type of curriculum, and a measure of freedom, yet a freedom that was but a means to the better learning of prescribed tasks. Its additions lacked a principle vital enough to resist misinterpretation. The worst of all impositions in education are those that are made under the guise of a partial interpretation of 'liberal' studies.

These faults were due to misinterpretations of Cicero, Seneca, Plutarch, and Quintilian. Again and again in the course of history these writers made the dry bones of education live.

CHAPTER V

CHRISTIANITY AND FREEDOM

PROFESSOR G. BURTON ADAMS remarks that a new increment of ethical force seems to have been added with Christianity to the sum total of energies in action in human history.[1] This in its turn has brought a new conception of human freedom which has left its mark upon education. Its influence in the first three or four centuries of the Christian era is the subject of the present chapter.

First, let us consider the nature of the ethical force to which Professor Adams refers. In order to understand its influence we may remind ourselves of the Roman love of ancestral custom and tradition. The acceptance of Greek studies came on the whole easily and naturally yet not without protest. In 161 B.C. the praetor was empowered to expel all teachers of philosophy and rhetoric from Rome. The censors of 92 B.C. reminded the people that their ancestors had ordained the lessons which Roman children should learn, and that the new studies were contrary to Roman customs and ideals. But the conflict with Hellenic culture raised no deep *religious* issues, such as those which Christianity by its very *raison d'être* provoked. It was the conflict not of one form of polytheism with another but of a monotheism with a polytheism that had been nurtured at least as effectively by the newer Greek studies as by the old Roman customs and traditions. Christianity was thus in its early days the conflict of a new way of life with ways of thinking that had been preserved through centuries by a carefully designed system of early instruction and training. The roots and influence of paganism even three or four centuries after the advent of Christ and after the official adoption of Christianity may be seen from the vivid pictures of Prudentius. In his *Contra Symmachum* he shows infancy drinking in error

[1] Cf. *Civilization during the Middle Ages*, pp. 50, 59.

78

with its mother's milk, the child 'raised high on his nurse's shoulders, pressing his lips to the sacred stone that stood by the house,' and later honouring with blood of lambs the gods of his family. Pagan cult and ritual, custom and phantasy, Lares and Penates, demons and spirits of nature, charms and superstitions—were the central forces in the instruction of childhood, and neither Greek culture nor Oriental cult could for a time vitally weaken their influence. As Mr. Glover reminds us, 'no polytheistic religion can exclude gods from its pantheon ; all divinities that man can devise have a right there.' [1]

This complex system of ritual and ceremony, of religion and superstition, of sacrifice and prayer, the Christians met with an almost uncompromising hostility. They opposed to its easy and superficial morality a way of life that probed every action of the individual. They characterized the worship of all other gods as a vanity, pronounced the teachings of other religions false and even refused to countenance the simplest preventive rite of pagan worship. Never did religious or educative system make so great havoc with the idols of a conservative people. Never did any revolution more speedily accomplish its purpose. For, despised as the early Christians were—' a mere handful of ignorant workmen '—conservative as were the Romans with their dreams of world empire and conquest—intolerant as the Christian religion was of the aims and aspirations of those whom it wished to win to its side, the fact remains that within a single generation Christianity ' had been taught in all the central provinces of the Roman Empire and far beyond its boundaries. . . . In less than three hundred years from the crucifixion it had become the recognized religion of the imperial court, and had been placed on a footing of legal equality with paganism throughout the Empire, and before the century closed it was the only legal religion.' [2] In the course of time the Emperor himself ' bent to become the worshipper of a crucified provincial of his Empire.' [3]

It is usually held that all this was accomplished without any revolution of the existing schools, or of the usual methods of

[1] T. R. Glover, *The Conflict of Religions in the Early Roman Empire*, p. 24, and *Life and Letters in the Fourth Century*, pp. 271 ff.

[2] Adams, *Civilization during the Middle Ages*, p. 41.

[3] Freeman, *Periods of European History*, p. 67.

instruction. The Christians evolved specific types of school, but in the main, though with reservations, they tolerated the 'liberal' course of studies discussed in the preceding chapter. At some points in the course of their history they even dared to *teach* the literature that sounded the praise of Jupiter. Their influence as teachers in the pagan schools is shown by Julian's edict of 362. In it he virtually asks them whether the interpreters of Homer and Hesiod should not honour the gods honoured in the writings that they professed to interpret, and whether, if they, as Christians, believed the poets to be in error, they should not themselves go to the churches of the Galileans and interpret Matthew and Luke.[1] This they apparently did not wish to do.[2]

[1] Cf. Walden, *Universities of Ancient Greece*, p. 110.

[2] See Dr. Parry's *Education in the Middle Ages*, Chapter II, for an interesting discussion of the relation of the 'episcopal' and 'monastic' schools to the schools of the Graeco-Roman type. The Bishops' schools have been traced to an institution at Caesarea opened by Origen after his departure in 231 from the Catechetical School of Alexandria, one of the specific types of Christian school referred to above. St. Augustine, who had been a student and teacher of rhetoric opened a seminary founded on community principles soon after his consecration as Bishop of Hippo in 391. This served as a model for the foundation of other institutions, particularly in Gaul, and Dr. Parry gives reasons for supposing that these, rather than the pagan schools, were the real prototypes of the schools of England. In their early days, at least, the Bishops' schools seem to have concentrated their energies on the training of candidates for ordination or for some other office in the Church, although there is evidence of a wide range of studies in the curricula of Pantaenus (who founded the Catechetical School at Alexandria), and Clement and Origen who in turn succeeded him. Gregory Thaumaturgus tells us that Origen taught physics, geometry, astronomy, ethics, logic and philology. The Christian schools at Jerusalem, Rome, Athens, and other cities followed, and while their growth is wrapped in obscurity there is probably sufficient evidence to justify the supposition that the Christian schools in some measure leavened the whole lump of pagan learning.

The *primum mobile* of the 'monastic' school is probably to be found in Oriental ideas of isolation but there is some evidence of a cœnobitic system being favoured by early Christians (cf. Miss Hodgson's *Primitive Christian Education*, p. 226), and also of a community living under definite rules drawn up by Pachomius about 320. In this some provision was made for instruction of an elementary kind. St. Basil of Caesarea (*c*. 330-379) developed several industrial monastic communities and did not, in spirit at least, limit instruction to children marked out for a monastic life. The elements of grammar, rhetoric, scripture, history and trades, like weaving and tailoring, were taught.

It would seem, therefore, that there is some basis for Dr. Parry's objection to Mr. Leach's view that the Graeco-Roman schools were the true models and source of English schools. His reasons for this view bring us back to the beginnings of Christianity and they may be briefly stated and examined. He argues, in the first place, that the pagan schools could not have been models for in them there 'was no thought of the moral aspect of instruction' (*op. cit.*

Looked at from an educational point of view, the success of Christianity requires explanation. It seems at first sight to run counter to the principles which we have found underlying previous views of sound education. It sweeps away not only the customs and traditions, but also the divinities, of adult life instead of beginning with them and working from them ; it remains aloof from the work of the schools and allows the inculcation of heathenism to proceed almost unchecked. How are we to explain its success and where are we to find evidence of its sympathy with human freedom ?

The answer to the first question brings us directly to the new ethical force of which Professor Adams speaks. Christianity swept away adult values which should have been vital

p. 21). This fact, in our opinion, states one of the main reasons why the Christians did not seriously attempt to re-model the Roman schools. He quotes, as his second reason, Professor Woodward's view that ' it is an invariable law that the accepted ideals of the adult generation shape its educational aims ' and points out that scepticism in religious matters was characteristic of the thought of Varro, Lucretius and Cicero, that religion had lost its control over the moral life, and that therefore the pagan schools could not furnish a model for the Christian institutions. The difficulty here is in applying Woodward's law of ideals to its limiting case, or in other words, in stating exactly what is meant by ' accepted ideals of an adult generation ' when they take the form of scepticism, and in showing how such scepticism could shape an educational aim. The basic fact, however, is as Dr. Parry urges : ' The ideals of Christianity and the ideals of the Graeco-Roman schools were fundamentally opposed.' This may be true and at the same time it may be equally true that the positive ideals of Christianity were consistent with an aim of laissez faire so far as Graeco-Roman culture was concerned. This we believe to be the true view of its position—at least in the first three centuries. In the third place, Dr. Parry refers to the antagonism of the early Christians to classical literature and says that it ' serves to illustrate still further the attitude of the Christians towards the pagan schools.' But classical literature was by no means obnoxious to all Christians and to most of them its beauty and charm of expression by no means made ' little or no appeal.' Julian's edict of 362 was not issued without a reason. It had the effect of inducing some Christians to make a revision of the classical literature, but it was soon repealed. When the time came for a re-organization of the Imperial schools it was a Christian that restored the former methods and text books. And as Professor Ayer points out (Monroe, Cyclopaedia of Education, vol. i. p. 651), when Christianity had become the religion of the State nothing stood in the way of Christian schools, yet young Christians still patronized heathen culture. Eminent Christians brought up by pious Christian parents, sent their children to the Imperial schools : Gregory Nazianzus, son of Bishop Gregory, Basil of Caesarea, Chrysostom, Jerome, and many others of less distinction were among their pupils. After the fourth century the Church became still more tolerant, as Julian's edict indicates. Even if it is true that the English schools were modelled on those of Gaul, and these in turn on that of St. Augustine, it is well to remember that Augustine himself had agreed that ' all branches of heathen learning, while containing much superstition, contain

but were not really so, and appealed to deeper forces and values that lay dormant in human nature.   In tolerating the heathen schools its success was not imperilled, for, as we have seen, even a pagan philosopher like Seneca recognized that their studies did not touch the deeper values of life.   Christianity in its early stages chose the adult as its pupil, the world for its school, and the instruction that directly affected the issues of everyday life for its curriculum.   It was a definitely specific form of moral discipline directed towards basal human tendencies.   It succeeded because of its definiteness and its directness.   It put first things first.

First in order of importance Christ placed the Kingdom of God.   His followers were to know the truth and the truth was to make them free.   The truth immediately to be grasped was the truth as to His own life and mission.   The distinctive note of that life was entire surrender to the will of God.   He taught that only in the service of something transcending the individual life was perfect freedom to be found.   Freedom in His teaching was real *self*-submission.   In appealing to it He was appealing to one of the most fundamental of all human tendencies as the facts of primitive religious beliefs show.

Submission to one's innermost realities was not unknown to the Romans.   Seneca refused, as a true Stoic, to be mastered even by fortune.   Marcus Aurelius asked himself which of the things that swirl past in the river of change a man should

---

also liberal instruction adapted to the use of the truth,' and perhaps, as Mr. Leach points out (Article on Middle Ages in Monroe's *Cyclopaedia*, iv. p. 220) ' the reasoned defence of learning not only of grammar, but rhetoric and even logic, contained in this work of Augustine (*Christian Teaching* written in 427) was one of the main influences which prevented the monastic furore, which attacked schools as it attacked marriage and other institutions, from converting the Dark Ages into absolute blackness.'   Whatever may have been the model of the first Christian missionaries to England, it is beyond doubt that before many years some of the English schools had acquired a reputation for erudition in ' liberal as well as ecclesiastical learning.'   It seems probable, therefore, that the courses and methods of the episcopal schools, limited as their outlook was to the service of the Church, were not uninfluenced by the ' liberal ' studies of the pagan schools, and that apart from the foundation of the Catechumenal and Catechetical institutions the activity of the early Church did not include any very definite and active policy of general education. Mr. Leach's statements (*Cyclopaedia*, iv. p. 218) that ' the early Christians took the schools as they found them ' and that they ' used the public grammar schools and rhetoric schools as they had come down from the unendowed schools of Athens and Alexandria ' is probably true only of the Christians of the first and part of the second century.

prize. It is not mere existence, not the things of time and sense, not our appetites and passions, not fame. What is left ? ' To limit our action or inaction to the needs of our constitution.' [1] This expressed his aim of education and his conception of liberty. Our needs were indicated by reason. ' The ruling reason wants for nothing unless it create its own needs and nothing can disturb it, nothing impede it, unless the disturbance or impediment come from itself.' [2]

This inspiring conception of the rational nature not, as with Plato, merely contemplative but ' content with itself when it speeds well on its way ' in the activities of life—the ' only impregnable fortress of liberty for the noblest Romans ' [3] under the tyranny of the early Caesars—is virtually a form of submission ' to a higher Power and all that he sends us.' It has many points of connection with Christ's teaching. It is, nevertheless, an unsatisfying, a cheerless, and a partial view of liberty. The ordinary man may admit that everything *may* be only as he thinks it, but he likes to think of life as not entirely made by his own thinking. He feels too insecure of his own nature, too distrustful of its tendencies to submit himself unreservedly to it. And if, in the last resort, he believes that he is himself the final arbiter of his conduct he asks for some assurance that, as judge, he shall act with all the powers of his highest self. He longs for something more fluid than the fiats of a rigid destiny, and something more secure than the verdicts of a ruling reason, for some view of life which will transcend fate and give a hope of continued existence, for some means of re-organizing and integrating the conflicting tendencies of his life, for something that will give sacredness and value to the Universe, something that will sustain him in the task of mastering his passions, and that will enable him to live in accordance with the laws of his nature. He seeks for a real self-submission—submission to something that transcends his highest self.

The search for a transcendental good may be thought to be a delusion but mankind universally acknowledges it and Jesus

[1] Marcus Aurelius, *Communings*, vi. 15, 16.

[2] Marcus Aurelius, *Communings*, vii. 16 (trans. C. R. Haines in Loeb Classical Library).

[2] C. R. Haines, Introduction (Loeb Classical Library, p. xxi).

Christ gave promise of success in the quest.   He presented in His own life the example of a complete submission to a God whom He pictured as a father in sympathy with the infirmities of men and moved by the desire of drawing them to Himself, and of providing through His son the means of escape from the sense of sin that weighed upon the individual soul.   In Christ's own life and in the life of most of His followers there was a perpetual appeal to something infinitely more heroic than the mastering of the passions : there was the appeal to the idea of life gladly and willingly devoted to the service of the King-dom.   Nothing higher can human or divine life show ; nothing lower can satisfy the aspirations of man.   Christianity suc-ceeded as an educational force because it gave actual hope of union with a God responsive to human aspirations, because it gave promise of a unified life in the present and reasonable hope of life in the future, because it offered an outlet for the heroic tendencies latent even in a Roman mob obsessed with feelings of hate and cruelty.

We shall discuss very briefly the bearing upon freedom of the actual teaching of the early Christians.   Although Jesus had a great deal to say about the qualities and outlook of childhood he had nothing to say about education.   His own teaching was mainly unsystematic.   He taught but one lesson—the fatherhood of God—and that lesson was ever presented in a new form and ever suited to the needs and capacities of His hearers.   Absolute clearness and definiteness of thought and language ; simplicity and concreteness both in developing His subject and in indicating its relation to the duties of life ; appositeness of symbol and image, of figure and analogy, all were notably present in His teaching.   His work as a teacher was a challenge for all time to the idea of a systematic and fixed method of presentation ; there was no art behind His work save the supreme art of utilizing the common experiences of life, those of the fisherman, the shepherd, the husbandman, as a starting point for the discernment of inner relationships and spiritual values.   But a teacher who has insight into the needs of life and who is sincere in directing the aspirations of his pupil to a single and simple, yet all-embracing principle of daily life, can ignore pedagogical rules and precepts.   The life of such an one is the embodiment of the truth that makes men free.

In sketching the educational views of the Christian Fathers we must limit the discussion to topics of immediate interest. Clement of Alexandria gives us a fairly vivid picture of the model training of the Catechetical school, and Gregory Thaumaturgus an extraordinarily clear account of the educational aims of Clement's successor, Origen. Tertullian's view of the difficulties of Christian teachers in heathen schools has a close bearing on freedom. Passages in the writings of Jerome, Chrysostom, and Augustine give glimpses of a sympathy with the pupil's point of view that are not only interesting in themselves but of importance for our subject.

In Clement's treatise, the *Pedagogue*, the usual conditions of education seem to be reversed. It is not a picture of children aiming at the culture of the adult, but of adults striving, with the aid of the Instructor (Christ), to attain the virtues of childhood. The aim is not to teach, but to improve the soul, to train it to a virtuous, not to an intellectual life.[1] The youthful qualities which Clement wishes to inculcate are simplicity, innocence, purity, gentleness. To become as a little child does not mean that adults should be unlearned or childish, but that, loosed from the world, they should touch the earth on tiptoe. That is the secret of the life-long springtime of youth.[2]

There is also a sterner note. Reproof and punishment are necessary helps in the training of children.[3] Many passions are cured by reproof : it is the surgery of the soul. Plato rightly urged that the spirit of those who are justly punished is improved. Christ taught that the unpruned vine grows to wood. Admonition, complaint, reproof, invective, censure, denunciation, and indignation have a positive educational function, for they show us to ourselves as we really are. ' As the mirror is not evil to an ugly man because it shows him what he is like, and as the physician is not evil to the sick man because he tells him of his fever, so neither is he that reproves ill-disposed towards him who is diseased in soul.'[4] The ascetic note pervades almost every page.[5]

---

[1] *Pedagogue*, i. 1 (trans. Ante-Nicene Library, vol. iv. p. 114).

[2] *Pedagogue*, i. 5.   [3] *Pedagogue*, i. 8.   [4] *Pedagogue*, i. 9.

[5] Dainties and delicacies, from lampreys to oysters and from mussels to dried figs, are prohibited. Table manners are prescribed and the limits of

Yet there is a distinctly liberal attitude towards learning. In the *Stromata* Clement insists that each soul has its own proper nutriment—some growing by science, others feeding on the Hellenic philosophy ' the whole of which, like nuts, is not eatable.' [1] His real love for learning, despite his meticulous prescriptions in other things, appears in the remarkable admissions : ' As we say that a man can be a believer without learning so also we assert that it is impossible for a man without learning to comprehend the things which are declared in the faith. . . . And we avow that at once with more ease and more speed will one attain to virtue through previous training.' [2] Truth, he urges, is one. In geometry there is the truth of geometry, in music that of music, and in right philosophy there will be Hellenic truth.

In Tertullian there is a more grudging recognition of moral value in heathen studies. He distinguishes between the learning and the teaching of literature. If the believer teach literature he cannot refrain from commending the praises of idols,[3] but the learner neither receives nor allows the truth of the things he learns. One may accept poison yet not drink it. In both Clement's and Tertullian's point of view the Platonic idea of receptivity is clearly discernible ; Tertullian's figure of the poison-cup may be regarded as a re-inforcement of Seneca's views concerning the uselessness of school studies. But both of the Fathers add to Plato's notion of receptivity a positive belief in the value of some at least of the liberal arts for life. Tertullian asks how, without literature, one could be trained unto ordinary intelligence or unto any sense or action whatever, since it is the means of training for all life. This is a

seemly laughter defined. Even smiling is the subject of discipline. Men who try to trick time by anointing their grey locks, and women who ' chill the skin and furrow the flesh ' with cosmetics are admonished. The hairs of the head are numbered, also those on the chin. There must therefore be no ' plucking out contrary to God's appointment.' The bath is to be taken by women for cleanliness and health, by men for health alone. Scarcely any detail of life is omitted. The times, no doubt, called for some regulation of the acts mentioned in *Pedagogue* 2 and 3, but Clement's pages show the futility of a too rigorous prescription of custom either for child or adult.

[1] Clement, *Stromata*, i. 1.

[2] Clement, *Stromata*, i. 1. 6 (cf. Gregory's statement of Origen's views : ' It was not possible for any one to be truly pious who did not philosophize.' *Panegyric*, vi.)

[3] Tertullian, *On Idolatry*, 10 (Ante-Nicene Lib. vol. xi. p. 154.)

notable admission of the value of pagan studies in one who eschewed a ' mottled Christianity of Stoic, Platonic, and dialectic composition.' [1]

Clement and Tertullian may be regarded as typical of the Christian Fathers' attitude towards liberal studies. With a certain hesitancy they accept them as valuable not only in preparing the mind for the reception of religious truth but also as sustaining the everyday activities of life. They do not enter into a lengthy discussion of literary values, but they seem to have had some idea of the liberalizing influence suggested by Keats in *Sleep and Poetry* and in *Endymion* :

> ' What though I am not wealthy in the dower
> Of spanning wisdom ; though I do not know
> The shiftings of the mighty winds that blow
> Hither and thither all the changing thoughts
> Of man : though no great minist'ring reason sorts
> Out the dark mysteries of human souls
> To clear conceiving : yet there ever rolls
> A vast idea before me, and I glean
> Therefrom my liberty ; thence too I've seen
> The end and aim of Poesy.'

. . . .

> ' What care, though owl did fly
> About the great Athenian admiral's mast ?
> What care, though striding Alexander pass'd
> The Indus with his Macedonian numbers ? . . . . . Juliet leaning
> Amid her window-flowers, sighing, weaning
> Tenderly her fancy from its maiden snow
> Doth more avail than these ; the silver flow
> Of Hero's tears, the swoon of Imogen,
> Fair Pastorella in the bandit's den
> Are things to brood on with more ardency
> Than the death-day of empires.'

Aristotle rightly urged that poetry was truer than music ; all great literature is the embodiment of those feelings and aspirations that are really universal. It is only in so far as any study revives these universal passions in the individual breast that it may fitly be prescribed as liberal. Clement, Tertullian, Jerome, and Augustine felt something of the liberalizing power

---

[1] Tertullian, *De Praes. Haeret* 7 (Ante-Nicene Library, vol. xv.).

of such studies and ignored the garb in which their moral issues were dressed.

One of the clearest presentations of the right relationship of teacher to pupil and of the conditions of freedom that sustain it is indicated in the *Panegyric* of Gregory Thaumaturgus on his teacher, Origen. Gregory describes the beginning of his law studies at the time when the human and the divine reason began to act at once and together—the one giving help with a power inexplicable, though proper to itself, and the other receiving help.[1] He shows how Origen's rare combination of persuasiveness and constraint captured the youthful imagination of his pupils who were drawn to him by the power of his reasonings as by the force of some superior necessity. He is reminded of the friendship of David and Jonathan in whom ' those things were knit together which are the ruling powers in man—their souls—those objects which, even though all the things which are apparent and ostensible in man are severed, cannot by any skill be forced to a severance when they themselves are unwilling. *For the soul is free, and cannot be coerced by any means, not even though one should confine it and keep guard over it in some secret prison-house. For wherever the intelligence is, there it is also of its own nature and by the first reason.* And if it seems to you to be in a kind of prison-house it is represented as there to you by a sort of second reason. But for all that, it is by no means precluded from subsisting anywhere according to its own determination ; nay, rather it is both able to be, and is reasonably believed to be, there alone and altogether, wheresoever and in connection with what things soever those actions which are proper only to it are in operation.' [2]

The appeal to intelligence seems to have had results which may not appear consistent with liberty. The pupil is taken captive. He is knit to his superior so that he has no power of loosing himself from his bonds. But Gregory is at pains to show that good use is made of intelligence. In an arresting series of figures he shows the advantages and disadvantages of one's own powers of reasoning. The work of the husbandman shows the union of internal and

[1] *Panegyric*, v. (trans. Ante-Nicene Library, vol. xx. p. 49).

[2] *Panegyric*, vi. (trans. Ante-Nicene Library, vol. xx. p. 54). *Italics* mine.

external forces. Even at this early date the process of en-graftment is seen to be suggestive for education. After describing the making of a fissure and the binding of a culti-vated shoot to the stem ' until the sap in each flows in one stream and they both grow with the same nurture,' [1] Gregory gives a detailed statement of Origen's method : ' In suchwise, then . . . did he receive us at first ; and surveying us, as it were, with a husbandman's skill, and gauging us thoroughly and not confining his notice to those things only which are patent to the eye of all . . . but penetrating into us more deeply, and probing what is most inward in us, he put us to the question, and made propositions to us, and listened to our replies ; and whenever he thereby detected anything in us not wholly fruitless and profitless and waste, he set about clearing the soil, and turning it up and irrigating it and putting all things in movement, and brought his whole skill and care to bear on us, and wrought upon our mind. And thorns and thistles and every kind of wild herb or plant which our mind (so unregulated and precipitate in its own action) yielded and produced in its uncultured luxuriance and native wildness, he cut out and thoroughly removed by the process of refutation and prohibition ; sometimes assailing us in the genuine Socratic fashion, and again upsetting us by his argumentation whenever he saw us getting restive under him . . . until with a strange kind of persuasiveness and constraint he reduced us to a state of quietude under him by his discourse, which acted like a bridle in our mouth. . . . Not simply by dealing with things patent and prominent, which are sometimes delusive and sophistical, but also by teaching us to search into things within us, and to put them all individually to the test, lest any of them should give back a hollow sound, and by instructing us to make sure of these inward things first of all, he trained us to give our assent to outward things only then and thus, and to express our opinion on all these severally. In this way that capacity of our mind which deals critically with words and reasonings was educated in a rational manner ; not according to the judgments of illustrious rhetoricians . . . for theirs is a discipline of little value and no necessity : but in accordance with that which is most needful for all, whether Greek or bar-

[1] *Panegyric*, vii.

barian, whether wise or illiterate, and, in fine . . . in accordance with that which is most indispensable for all men, whatever manner of life they have chosen, if it is indeed the care and interest of all who have to converse on any subject whatever with each other, to be protected against deception.' [1]

In many passages Gregory refers to the care taken by the master to encourage his pupils to think for themselves, to discriminate, to shake themselves free from prejudices and fixed ideas. The pupil's account shows how successful the teaching had been. ' Being bound by our ideas ' is a pregnant phrase which he elaborates by a series of analogies, into a vivid picture of the enslaved mind. Men caught in a swamp and neither able to go on or to go back, struggling till they meet their end, men lost in a forest and wandering among by-paths until they despair of any other place of abode, men trapped in a labyrinth of unending passages—all are like the man whose mind is filled with prejudices. ' But,' says Gregory, ' there is neither any labyrinth so inextricable and intricate, nor any forest so dense and devious, nor any plain or swamp so difficult for those to get out of, who have once got within it as is discussion ($\lambda\acute{o}\gamma\text{os}$) . . . wherefore to secure us against falling into the unhappy experience of most he (Origen) did not introduce us to any exclusive school of philosophy ; nor did he judge it proper for us to go away with any single class of philosophical opinions, but he introduced us to all, and determined that we should be ignorant of no kind of Grecian doctrine. And he himself went on with us, preparing the way before us, and leading us by the hand, as on a journey, whenever anything tortuous and unsound and delusive came in our way. And he helped us like a skilled expert who has had long familiarity with such subjects, and is not strange or inexperienced in anything of the kind, and who therefore may remain safe in his own altitude, while he stretches forth his hand to others, and effects their security too, as one drawing up the submerged. Thus did he deal with us, selecting and setting before us all that was useful and true in all the various philosophers, and putting aside all that was false. And this he did for us, both in other branches of man's knowledge, and most especially in all that concerns piety.' [2]

[1] *Panegyric*, vii. (*op. cit.* pp. 56-59).
[2] *Panegyric*, xiv. (*op. cit.* p. 73).

We have quoted at length from St. Gregory's pages because we see in them one of the clearest delineations of freedom to be found in the history of education. For the times in which they were written they show a marked sympathy with the idea of a *full* life. Religion may be the ultimate aim but Origen's methods do not subordinate the intellectual to the moral powers. In Gregory's words, he creates in his pupils ' a love for the beauty of righteousness by his own virtue.' There is a heroic attempt to direct the ' ruling ' powers of teacher and pupil, to one object ' dear and worth desire.' The emphasis of an inferior and a superior element in the educative process, though involving the submission of the pupil's reason to the conditions imposed by the teacher, brings no form of coercion, for Gregory and Origen saw, as Tertullian and others of the Christian Fathers saw, that stone walls do not make a prison.[1] Liberty is, in the last resort, independent of coercion, but it is always consonant with submission. The reference of everything in life to an intelligence, ' present of its own nature,' and passing judgment in accordance with its own proper nature, however it may emphasize the intellectual aspects of life, is surely the condition of a liberty that has become in any real sense a conscious liberty. And, finally, Origen seems to have escaped the dangerous view of liberty that is best characterized in his own words : ' being bound by the chain of one's own ideas.'

In the life of St. Jerome there appears to have been an almost perpetual conflict between religious tendencies and love of pagan learning. Even in the seclusion of the monastic life he mingles Cicero and Plautus with his fastings and penitence,[2] and is repelled by the careless style of the Prophets. His *Letter to Laeta* on the education of her daughter is at once ascetic and liberal in its general point of view. Everything that does not lead her to the fear of God is to be removed from her path ; everything that makes learning pleasant and that

---

[1] Tertullian makes the same plea in *Ad Martyres*, 2 : ' The leg does not feel the chain when the mind is in the heavens. The mind compasses the whole man about, and whither it wills it carries him.' (Vol. xi. Ante-Nicene Library, p. 3.)

[2] The famous dream in which he heard his life work condemned by the great Judge as Ciceronian and not Christian might be interpreted as the working of a repressed fear of condemnation because of his devotion to pagan learning.

promotes effort is commended.   The teaching of the elements,
as in Quintilian, is to be done through play ; prizes and gifts
are to be offered.   She is not to be scolded if she is slow to
learn ; praise must be the main inducement to real effort.
She must have companions to excite emulation so that she may
be glad when she excels others and sorry when she is excelled
by them.   Above all, care is to be taken that her lessons are
not made distasteful, lest she may conceive a dislike for them
in childhood which will continue in maturer years.   Detailed
instructions bearing upon conduct, food, and dress, as well
as studies, are added, and Jerome concludes a paragraph on
the difficulty of her education by advising that she should be
brought up in a monastery, one amid companies of virgins
where, ignorant of the world, she may live the angelic life.
The alliance of emulation with asceticism and seclusion is
noteworthy.   Later writers condemned emulation unless it took
the form of comparing one's present with one's past attainments.   But Jerome, hermit though he is by inclination,
realizes the force of Origen's insistence upon the value of a
superior element in education.   He sees that we tend to
evaluate attainments (if not conduct) by comparing them with
those of our fellows, and that comparison brings with it the
desire to excel.   He perhaps realizes (what the critics of
emulation tend to forget) that it is impossible to pass a well-
founded judgment upon our own attainments if we close ourselves within the circle of our own accomplishments.   He is
aware, too, of the value of rivalry as a motive to further progress.

These motives, as they exist in child life, are described with
wonderful psychological insight in the writings of St. Augustine.
Few writers so successfully appeal to the memories of their
own tender years, and no one of his day gives so many valuable
hints for the reform of teaching.   Even his advocacy of the
doctrine of original sin does not entice him into a repressive
theory of education.   His memory of the ' miseries and
mockeries ' [1] of childhood is too vivid to allow him to fall
into such an error.   Although in mature years he thinks that
constraint was for his good and that without it he would never
have taken to learning, he adds : ' Nor did they that forced
me to my book do very well. . . .   *For no man does well against*

---

[1] Augustine, *Confessions*, i. 9, 10, 12.

his will though that which he does be good.' [1] Hating Greek, and
loving Latin which he learnt without fear or torment from
his nurse and his companions, he chafed at the discipline of his
school days. ' One and one make two, and two and two make
four was a harsh song to me, but the Wooden Horse full of
armed men and the burning of Troy and the Ghost of Creusa
was a most delightful spectacle of vanity.' Why then, he asks
himself, was Greek distasteful ? Homer was full of such fictions.
His dislike was due to compulsion : ' I believe that Virgil is no
less harsh to Grecian children when they be compelled to learn
him, as I was to learn Homer : for to say truth, the difficulty
of learning a strange language, did sprinkle as it were with gall
all the pleasures of those fabulous narrations. For I understood
not a word of it, yet they vehemently pressed me and with
most cruel threatenings and punishments to make me understand it.' [2] In his learning of Latin there was no painful
burden for, as he writes, ' mine own heart put me to it to bring
out mine own conceptions. . . . Hereby it clearly appears that
a free curiosity hath more force in children's learning of languages than a frightful enforcement (*quam meticulosam neces-
sitatem*) can have.' [3] This is a direct recognition of the pupil's
values as the right starting point of education.

The futility of presenting elements that fail to arouse
interest is clearly stated in a discussion on the proper method
of learning rhetoric. Augustine has little sympathy with rules
such as Quintilian propounded, although he admits that boys
may profitably give some attention to them. He prefers to
learn from the speeches of eloquent men, rather than to learn
rules about eloquence : ' In the speeches of eloquent men we
find rules of eloquence carried out which the speakers did not
think of as aids to eloquence at the time when they were
speaking, whether they had ever learnt them, or whether they
had never even met with them. For it is because they are
eloquent that they exemplify these rules ; it is not that they
use them in order to be eloquent.' Then, no doubt, thinking
of his own early dislike of grammar, he pens the following

---

[1] Augustine, *Confessions*, i. 12 (trans. by W. Watts, 1631. The Loeb
Classical Library, i. p. 37).

[2] *Confessions* (i. 13). (Loeb Classical Library, p. 43.)

[3] *Confessions* (i. 14). (Loeb Classical Library, p. 45.)

singularly clear appreciation of the uselessness of presenting the elements of a subject rather than the subject itself as it functions in actual life. Had this paragraph been really understood the history of freedom in education from 400 A.D. would have been very different from that which we shall find it to be. Were it really understood to-day a reformation of the schools would be effected within one generation.

' And, therefore, as infants cannot learn to speak, except by learning words and phrases from those who speak, why should not men become eloquent without being taught any art of speech, simply by reading and learning the speeches of eloquent men, and by imitating them as far as they can ? And what do we find from the examples themselves to be the case in this respect ? We know numbers who, without acquaintance with rhetorical rules, are more eloquent than many who have learnt these ; but we know no one who is eloquent without having read and listened to the speeches and debates of eloquent men. For even the art of grammar, which teaches correctness of speech, need not be learnt by boys, if they have the advantage of growing up and living among men who speak correctly. For without knowing the names of any of the faults, they will, from being accustomed to correct speech, lay hold upon whatever is faulty in the speech of any one they listen to and avoid it ; just as city-bred men, even when illiterate, seize upon the faults of rustics.' [1]

Augustine had previously pointed out that there is sometimes less difficulty in naturally attaining eloquence and correct reasoning than in going through the ' very intricate and thorny discipline ' of rules. ' It is,' he adds, ' just as if a man wishing to give rules for walking should warn you not to lift the hinder foot before you set down the front one, and then should describe minutely the way you ought to move the hinges of the joints and knees. For what he says is true and one cannot walk in any other way : but men find it easier to walk by executing these movements than to attend to them while they are going through them, or to understand when they are told about them. Those, on the other hand, who cannot walk, care still less about such directions, as they cannot prove them by making trial of them.' [2] And as if in face of such a *reductio*

---

[1] *On Christian Doctrine*, 4. 3. 5 (trans. Dods : *Works*, vol. ix. p. 123).

[2] *On Christian Doctrine*, 2. 37. 55 (trans. Dods : *Works* vol. ix. p. 73).

ad absurdum he feels some apology for existing practice to be necessary, he suggests that in drawing up rules for speech, eloquence, and reasoning, ' we derive more pleasure from them as exhibitions of truths than assistance in arguing or forming opinions, except perhaps that they put the intellect in better training.' [1]

St. Augustine's treatise on the *Catechising of the Uninstructed* illustrates two principles of method embodied in the work of the Christian Fathers and explicitly formulated by Chrysostom —the regulation of teaching by the capacity of the pupil and the giving of help only when it is necessary. The real theme is ' How to catechise without weariness.' Augustine advises the teacher to be brief, direct, and simple in his treatment, to give a prominent place to the most important facts, to omit details, and, when they must be included, to weave them into the narrative ; to get from some source an idea of the cate-chumen's state of mind and his previous instruction. Even if our pupil is not strictly truthful or frank in his profession we should commend and praise the purpose which he puts forward so that we may make him feel it a pleasure to be the kind of man that he wishes to seem to be. Digressions into knotty

[1] Is St. Augustine the father of formal training ? (We have not discussed formal training in Chapter II. for we accept Mr. E. C. Moore's suggestion (*What is Education*, c. 3), that Plato's assertion that he hardly ever knew a mathematician capable of reasoning acquits him of the charge of fathering this educational fallacy. The arguments against Professor Moore's view in Dr. Rusk's *Doctrines of the Great Educators* do not seem to be conclusive. Plato's observation that those who have a talent for calculation are generally quick at every other kind of knowledge (*Rep.* 326) may be but a simple way of stating that ability in arithmetic is highly correlated with ability in other school subjects. And even the increased retentivity, quickness and shrewdness noted in *Laws* 747, is not conclusive, for Plato at the time of writing may have held the Pythagorean doctrine that number is the rational essence of all things. On this hypothesis a training in number might have the effect of ' an art divine.' More conclusive passages in support of Dr. Rusk's views are to be found in Plato's ideas of the child's ' receiving loyalty ' and certain other virtues into the soul through specific courses of training. Here, however, Plato seems to assume a general receptive tendency (? submission) and the training of a general congenital tendency may possibly result in a large ' transfer '.)

St. Augustine's cautious advocacy of rules ' or concepts ' seems to be an anticipation of the pleasurable process of induction emphasized by Herbert Spencer. His whole argument insists that only those who are cognisant of the complex whole in which an activity functions can draw up rules for the synthesis of the elements into which it is analysed. His *Confessions* show that the pleasure which the teacher may enjoy through such analysis and synthesis does *not* always transfer to the pupil.

and intricate questions are to be avoided. ' The simple truth of our explanation . . . ought to be like the gold which binds together a row of gems and yet does not interfere with the choice symmetry of the ornament by any undue intrusion of itself.' [1]

The irksomeness of teaching mainly arises from the need of repeating frequently what seems simple to the well matured mind, and of little interest to the pupil who may remain ' unmoved, either because he is not actually stirred by any feeling, or does not indicate by any motion of the body that he understands or that he is pleased with what is said.' For this ennui there is one suggestion—to remember Him who emptied Himself taking the form of a servant—who made Himself ' weak to the weak in order that He might gain the weak.' After many illustrations of the reasonableness of this service Augustine concludes : ' For if intelligence brings delight in its purest recesses, it should also be a delight to us to have an intelligent understanding of the manner in which charity, the more complaisantly it descends to the lowest objects, finds its way back, with all the greater vigour to those that are most secret, along the course of a good conscience which witnesses that it has sought nothing from those to whom it has descended except their universal salvation.' [2] This statement admits that everything of supreme importance in education is to be found in the pupil, and that only by recognizing this fact we can escape the drudgery of teaching him. Augustine thinks of the process of teaching as ' a dwelling in each other,' the result of a sympathetic disposition that affects the pupil while the teacher speaks, and affects the teacher while the pupil learns ; a unity of hearts which renews its enjoyment in the pupil's mental growth, just as the pointing out to others of spacious and beautiful scenes to which we ourselves have become accustomed, renews the pleasure and delight with which we first viewed them.

Finally, Augustine emphasizes the importance of the pupil's mental activity. Questions, in order that we may find out whether he understands us ; encouragement to give free expression to objections or to voice difficulties ; appeal to his

[1] On Catechising, ch. vi. (Dods, vol. ix. p. 279).
[2] On Catechising, ch. xi. (p. 289).

former acquaintance with the subject ; the continual shaping of our discourse in accordance with his answers ; simplicity, illustration, explanation, conciseness, attractiveness, kindliness, and conciliation—all are commended in a passage [1] which might serve as a model for the practice of to-day. If these fail, at any time in the task of education, if the pupil is ' of a sluggish disposition ' and ' senseless,' we can do nothing more than carry out Augustine's suggestion : ' We ought rather to address ourselves to God for him than address much to him concerning God ' . . . or anything else !

The writings of the Christian Fathers, when viewed in relation to the circumstances in which they appeared, show a remarkable sympathy with the idea of freedom in education. They had a healthy conception of serving the cause of truth through the activities of life and were enthusiastic over all studies that equipped them for such a service. Though the more timid souls doubted the wisdom of that free appeal to truth which characterized Christ's teaching, the early Christian teachers and disciples went out bravely to test a wide view of freedom in the dangerous field of actual experience. In so doing they placed the seal of their approval on all education which aims at setting free the activities of the mind and giving to the soul that strength which the search for truth demands. In meeting the challenge of pagan literature they showed a remarkable insight into the value of studies that aim at truth even though they only partially embody it. In the highest values of life, and even at the peril of their own existence, they respected the ordinary human activities and recognized in them the true forces upon which education should work. And with singular wisdom they avoided any formal or elaborate technique in their teaching, preferring to make the appeal to the pupil's own

---

[1] *On Catechising*, ch. xiii. pp. 293 ff. Many of the Christian Fathers show extreme anxiety to catechise ' without weariness.' See *e.g.* St. Cyril's *Catechetical Lectures* (in *Pusey Library of the Fathers*), 10, 11. The importance of thoroughly receiving the truth is shown through several analogies— planting in deep, well-tilled soil, building on strong foundations, stone on stone and course by course. The pupils are reminded that if they do not connect into one whole and remember what is first and what is second, the builder buildeth indeed but the building is unstable. As Miss Hodgson remarks (*Primitive Christian Education*, p. 164) : ' There is nothing dull, hard, tedious, in St. Cyril's invitation; it savours of hope, light, and warmth.' Simple, orderly, clear, vivid, and concrete, the lectures are models of exposition.

values the main guiding principle of their art, and trying to bring into play his own mental activity, his own judgment and intelligence, his powers of emulation and his love of praise. Influenced perhaps by the necessity of making a personal appeal to the unlearned, they favoured a simplicity of language and an orderliness of expression which kept their teaching in close grips with the central facts of life.

It may be well to remember, however, that the appearance of liberal views of education need not imply any necessary point of contact with educational practice. So far as we can gather, the vitalizing influence of Graeco-Roman culture, focused, directed, and transformed as it was by Christianity, left the schools almost untouched. ' Their practice seems to have been mechanical, lifeless, artificial. They were unable to stimulate the reasoning or reflective powers, depended mainly on rote-memory, and gave themselves up to a round of literary and rhetorical futilities. Augustine's experiences seem to have been typical : the veil which hung over the entrance of the grammar school was, as he said, ' a covering of error rather than the honour due to a mystery.' Many years were to elapse before the liberal ideas of Greece, living through Rome, and both living through Christianity, vitally influenced the every-day work of education.

CHAPTER VI

FREEDOM IN THE MIDDLE AGES

AT first glance the mediaeval conception of education may seem to have little direct connection with freedom : it may even seem to be a direct challenge to the general argument that, implicitly or explicitly, a concept of freedom regulates all forms of educational activity. It is often held that during the thousand years from 450-1450 comparatively little progress was made in educational curricula, methods or institutions. A brief survey of this period, even if it contributes little of positive value for our study, may serve, just as the Middle Ages themselves served, to consolidate the views already discussed. We shall regard aspects of it as offering the same help towards our analysis of freedom as the slow motion camera affords in studying the elements of a complex movement.

It will be appropriate to view its distinctive qualities from the angles suggested in the introductory chapter, namely the values emphasized as the aim of education, the existent values by which educational activity was sustained and the nature of the mediating concept of freedom. In all these aspects the Middle Ages offered a direct and definite point of view.

In the formulation of aim we penetrate what is usually held to be the secret of the mediaeval mind. As the late Mr. Leach writes : ' Till the middle of the fifth century the object of education was to fit a man to be a good citizen and a successful man of the world. From the middle of the fifteenth century the same object began again to be put forward, and from the middle of the sixteenth century became the accepted object of education. But in the thousand years between education had a different object. The main object of education was no longer to prepare a man for this world but for the next ; no longer to make him a good citizen or to be successful in this life, but to be a good Christian and to attain successfully the world to come. For patriotism was substituted religion ; for the promotion of society the saving of a man's own soul. The whole of education was dominated by the Day of Judgment and the dread of the world to come, and the necessity of the appeasement of the Judge by self-abasement and self-torture, by constant prayer and by assiduous asceticism. The Stoic philosopher and the Essene met together and, re-incarnated as monk, conquered the world.' [1]

The influence of this re-incarnation on education cannot be studied in detail. The public schools of grammar and rhetoric disappeared throughout the Roman Empire, the futility of much of their instruction, and their almost exclusive attention to the ' *ornamenta* of pagan culture,' [2] being in marked contrast with the strictly utilitarian aims of the Christian institutions which succeeded them. The relative parts played by the monastic schools, the schools of cathedrals, the collegiate, parish, and song schools, the gilds and chantries need not, for our purposes, be differentiated. They all served in different ways the same purposes—the study of the sacred Scriptures and the maintenance of ecclesiastical ordinances. For the Church, as Professor Adamson points out,[3] was from the very nature of its everyday routine an educator—' educating its members not only by the public recital of its offices and by the symbolism of its pictures, sculpture, and architecture, but even more by its contact with daily life. The parish church was the centre of all forms of communal activity, "secular" as well as "sacred"; the trade gilds were at least as much religious as industrial associations. Social life found its highest expression in a common worship which employed a liturgy whose sources were the Hebrew scriptures or Greek derivations from them ; the language of this common worship was Latin, an alien tongue in most places, even within the limits of the Roman Empire. All ecclesiastical persons, therefore, had some knowledge of Latin ; lay people shared this knowledge, more or less, according to individual circumstances.' The Church, too, was a centre of learning as well as of teaching—the serious study of

---

[1] Article on *Middle Ages* in Monroe : *Cyclopaedia*, vol. iv. p. 218.

[2] Cf. J. B. Mullinger, *The Schools of Charles the Great*, pp. 13 ff.

[3] *A Short History of Education*, pp. 4-5.

the Scriptures making necessary an appeal to the grammatical and sometimes to the philosophical and other learning of the pagan schools, and its daily services necessitating the provision of elementary instruction. As a rule, the early schools limited their courses to such exercises as were absolutely necessary for the maintenance of church services, and even the monks were taught the rudiments of learning in close association with the sacred books and the church festivals.

Although the first-hand knowledge of classical authors soon declined, writers such as Martianus Capella, Boethius, Cassiodorus and Isidore of Seville, preserved the content of pagan learning by their treatises on the ' liberal ' arts. One of these productions, ' sapless as the rods of mediaeval schoolmasters,' [1] gives an allegorical interpretation of the arts as the seven bridesmaids attendant upon Philology on the occasion of her marriage with the god Mercury. Subsequent writers like Cassiodorus and Isidore connect the number of the liberal arts with the seven pillars of wisdom mentioned in *Proverbs*, and thus satisfy the demand of the mediaeval mind for definiteness in the course of studies, for allegorical interpretation, and for agreement with ancient authorities. And although at the end of the sixth century Pope Gregory thought it his duty to reprove the Bishop of Vienne for teaching grammar, the general consensus of opinion was expressed in Isidore's dictum that it was better to have grammar than heresy. Thus ere long the pagan learning ceased to be a source of offence and a subject of dispute. Yet we find that before the end of another couple of hundred years learning had almost fled from the Continent of Europe.

The main reason for this decline was undoubtedly the new adjustment of educational effort which the German invasions of the fifth century rendered necessary. The fall of Rome, as Professor Adams urges, was not the destruction of the ancient civilization, but a necessary reorganization and rearrangement preparatory to a new and higher civilization.[2] In this readjustment we may see Roman civilization playing the part of schoolmistress to a number of barbarian tribes, or perhaps with

[1] The criticism of H. O. Taylor in the *Classical Heritage of the Middle Ages* on part of Capella's *De Nuptiis Philologiae et Mercurii* (*op. cit.* p. 51).
[2] *Civilization during the Middle Ages*, pp. 86-7.

greater truth, we may see the Germans educating themselves through the assimilation of such features of Roman-Christian civilization as appealed to their own view of life. The picture is one, not of stagnation, but of educational activity ; the period one in which the employment of the pupil's own powers temporarily slows the process of education, but in the long run contributes to educational progress. And rude and crude as the barbarians were they had qualities other than those of mere physical prowess. ' Their love of freedom was unconquerable.' [1] They were simple in habits, devoted to family life, independent and venturous in spirit. Complete absorption of Roman civilization was therefore impossible. ' The crowded thoroughfares, the theatres, the games, the enervating dissipation amid which the inhabitants of the Gallic and Italian cities frittered away the strength and dignity of manhood, had for the German no charm. He built no cities, but fixed his little homestead near some perennial stream, amid fruitful pastures, shut in by woodland, and there ruled supreme over his family and dependants. Living thus very near to Nature and rendering a rude instinctive obedience to her laws, he received from her as his reward a robust and powerful frame and exulted in an invigorating sense of freedom which, unlettered and unrefined though he was, enabled him to look down with not all-unmerited scorn on the degenerate races whom he subdued.' [2]

To such a race the rhetorical, dialectical, and grammatical studies of the pagan schools would have been useless ; the utilitarian and concrete instruction of the Church schools made a real appeal. From a pedagogical point of view, many features of the Church's educational scheme were of considerable value. She had a fixed and definite aim theoretically co-extensive with life, and she was in possession of methods that were clearly related and subservient to that aim. She had a natural and concrete system of daily activities round which her instruction centred. A huge concentration scheme, with a practical, if at times a highly symbolic contact with life, permeated with the ideal of utility—such was the system of ecclesiastical education in the early Middle Ages and, so pre-

---

[1] Mullinger, *Schools of Charles the Great*, p. 21.

[2] Mullinger, *Schools of Charles the Great*, pp. 21-2.

sented, it has qualities manifestly superior, in some respects, to the education of our own times.   What is the reason for its failure in the early Middle Ages ?

Before admitting failure it may be well to remind ourselves that the statement of its general results is likely to refer more clearly and directly to the teacher than to the pupil.   A system may have passable results so far as the pupil is concerned, yet have a deplorable effect upon the teacher.   This seems to have been the state of affairs in the sixth and seventh centuries. Isidore of Seville was regarded as the most widely informed man of the early seventh century, yet a competent critic regards his huge book (*Etymologiae*) as ' utterly without original value and so full of absurdities and puerilities that it may be considered as an index of the retrogression in learning.' [1]   We find, too, that in Charlemagne's famous capitulary of 787 the main reference is to the illiteracy of the monks, and that abbots are exhorted to choose ' men who will not neglect the study of letters,' men ' *who are both able and willing to learn, and also desirous of instructing others.*' [2]   The one really enlightened teacher of the eighth century, Alcuin, expressly took as his motto *disce ut doceas*,[3] but in at least one of his epistles assigns the one function to boyhood and the other to old age.   The ecclesiastical view of education, although it referred everything in this life to the requirements of the other world, tended in practice to confine the preparation for that world to well defined exercises and studies that failed to keep alive the teacher's intellectual powers.   It failed to recognize fully the legitimate exercise of the reasoning powers so forcibly presented in Plato's *Republic* ; it enslaved the intellect not so much by its bringing the most trivial matters to the judgment seat of the faith, as by denying the free, unimpeded exercise of reason in aspects of life that are, or should be, free from meticulous moral precepts ; it crippled the aesthetic and literary powers by subjecting them needlessly to moral regulations.   Pedagogically it was on sound lines in presenting its first instruction in concrete and practical form ; it was wrong in allowing the instruction of both teacher and pupil to end there.

[1] A. F. West, *Alcuin*, p. 26.
[2] *Op. cit.* p. 51.   *Italics* mine.
[3] Cf. Alcuini Epist. 88, ' Qui non discit, non docet.'

While restrictions of this kind were bound to have a narrow-
ing influence, it does not appear that in the vital aspects of
education the Middle Ages were so limited as they are often
supposed to be. If we judge the results of an educational
system by its general contribution to civilization we must
admit that those of the early Middle Ages were considerable.
Professor Adams urges that the idea of the independence and
the supreme worth of the individual was strongly felt and
expressed in the early mediaeval centuries ; that a closely
related idea found expression in feudalism ; that the primitive
German institutions developed into those modern political
contrivances by which the individual secures the greatest possible freedom under an efficient government.[1]

The adjustment of Christianity to pagan culture had increased its efficiency as a teacher, and the Church with its
power, its gorgeous ceremonial, its complex organization, and
its authoritative teaching made a profound impression on the
barbarians.[2] It was well organized and strongly entrenched
before the Germanic invasions, and its successful adjustment
to pagan culture had revealed the secret of successful teaching
—that of working upon the life tendencies of the pupil.   And
although the mediaeval period may have been meagre in
scholarship it was essentially a creative age ; its products are
witness to many developments of the human spirit often untouched by more elaborate and more scholarly systems of
education.   An age which at least partially solved the vexed
question of land ownership, which gave expression to the
adventurous instincts of the race in forms consonant with
religion, which broke up empires to create nations of greater
independence, which successfully embodied its ideals in institutions of the most varied kinds, which gave birth to new
commercial enterprises as well as to universities and beautiful
cathedrals, an age which produced men like Alcuin, Pierre
Abélard, William of Champeaux, John Scotus Erigena, John
of Salisbury, and Thomas Aquinas, does not, when judged by
its contribution to civilization, seem to be the parent of an
inferior system of education.

[1] Cf. Adams : *Civilization during the Middle Ages*, p. 91 and footnote
p. 91.
[2] *Ibid.*   Cf. pp. 103, 128.

For our purposes we must neglect the process of development which this brief survey implies. Its detailed study would yield much of interest for our subject, but it could scarcely give us any other picture of general education than that of the Church, working upon elemental and primitive tendencies, producing results, at times poor from the point of view of scholarship, at times rich and deep in intellectual quality, but always considerable for the advancement of later civilization.

We may visualize the education of the Middle Ages at its best by reading the description of the Abbey of St. Gall in the ninth century given by the erudite historian of *Christian Schools and Scholars*. The author writes at length of the vast range of stately buildings which almost filled the valley. ' Churches and cloisters, the offices of a great abbey, buildings set apart for students and guests, workshops of every description, the forge, the bakehouse, and the mill, or rather mills, for there were ten of them, all in such active operation that they every year required ten new millstones ; and then the house occupied by the vast numbers of artisans and workmen attached to the monastery ; gardens, too, and vineyards creeping up the mountain slopes, and beyond them fields of waving corn, and sheep speckling the green meadows, and far away boats busily plying on the lake and carrying goods and passengers—what a world it was of life and activity ; yet how unlike the activity of a town ! It was, in fact, not a town, but a house—a family presided over by a father, whose members were all knit together in the bonds of a common fraternity. I know not whether the spiritual or the social side of such a religious colony were most fitted to rivet the attention. Descend into the valley, and visit all these nurseries of useful toil, see the crowds of rude peasants transformed into intelligent artisans, and you will carry away the impression that the monks of St. Gall had found the secret of creating a world of happy Christian factories.' [1] Every type of useful occupation seems to have entered into these monastic seminaries. Agriculture, forestry, wood, stone and metal work, alternated with the work of the scriptorium and the ritual of divine service. Some specialized in painting, others in the weaving of carpets and tapestries. In all some traces of the liberal arts remained,

[1] Drane, *op. cit.* p. 169. (Edition 1924.)

in many there was a deep love of ancient learning. The work of the monastery was, in short, an interesting example of a concentration scheme, which naturally related the whole round of activities to the elemental needs of life, and demanded a versatility and a knowledge of many things—by no means, as we shall see, unimportant conditions of freedom.[1]

A glance at the work of one or two of the most renowned mediaeval schools may enable us to estimate the strength of the chain that bound all their activities to the service of the Church. We shall first deal with the Royal School taught by Alcuin at the court of Charlemagne. Alcuin's early studies at York gave ample evidence of the liberal nature, as well as the orthodoxy, of his training. As a teacher he was ' patient, enthusiastic, indefatigable, careful not to load the mind of the learner by giving him too much to learn, striving literally to educate, to call out in each the latent intellectual power, as— to use his own simile—a man strikes out of the flint the fire which has all along been hidden in it.'[2] In his treatise on *Grammar* he explains to his pupils that what is sought from without is alien to the soul, and that they should be led by the steps of erudition from lower to higher things until they

[1] The union of incompatible qualities so characteristic of mediaeval life is strikingly evident in Irishmen of that age. ' That fierce and restless quality,' says Miss Waddell in *The Wandering Scholars*, ' which had made the pagan Irish the terror of Western Europe seems to have emptied itself into the love of learning and the love of God : and it is the peculiar distinction of Irish mediaeval scholarship and the salvation of literature in Europe that the one in no way conflicted with the other.' (*Op. cit.* p. 28.)

Compare with the text the interesting account of Irish schools given in *Ireland's Ancient Schools and Scholars* by Dr. Healy. There was a royal palace school in Erin five hundred years before that of Charlemagne and considerable literary culture in the Celtic Ireland of the third century. St. Patrick's policy of utilizing native customs and prejudices seems to have produced excellent results in later years. At an early date the ' knowledge of Greek, which had almost vanished in the West, was so widely diffused in the schools of Ireland that if anyone knew Greek it was assumed that he must have come from that country.' (Sir J. S. Sandys, *A History of Classical Scholarship*, i. p. 439.) Dr. Healy gives a description of the organization and daily life of the monasteries. It shows the close connection of education with the elemental needs of life. The monks raised their own corn, dried, ground, and baked it into bread. They milked their own cows, made their own cheese and butter, kept their own sheep, combed, spun, and wove their habits. They built their churches and cells, made their own furniture and kitchen utensils, cut and dried their own fuel, washed their own habits. ' When a monk died there was no need of an undertaker—his brethren made the grave, and he was simply buried in his habit with his cowl over his head.' (Healy, *op. cit.* p. 105.)

[2] C. J. B. Gaskoin, *Alcuin : His Life and Work*, p. 197.

gradually become stronger. He directly connects these steps with the ' Seven pillars of wisdom,' and sees in the seven ascents of theoretical discipline, grammar, dialectic, rhetoric, arithmetic, geometry, music, and astronomy, the real staircase of the soul. ' Let your youthful steps, my dear sons, run daily along these paths until a riper age and a stronger mind shall bring you to the heights of Holy Scripture.' [1] But many of his dialogues scarcely bear out the striking figure of the flint and spark :· ' They ramble without plan and allegorize without restraint.' Thus :—What is writing ? The guardian of history. What is language ? The betrayer of the soul. What is the winter ? The exile of summer. What is the spring ? The painter of the earth. Yet it cannot be denied that Alcuin had the gifts of a true teacher. To hold the interest of a class for a period of ten years is a severe test of teaching ability. But when it indulges in an almost continuous criticism and discussion, and has as one of its members an emperor so eager for learning that he sleeps with a slate under his pillow in order to work during the wakeful hours of the night, and becomes so interested in Jerome and Augustine that he must enquire why he cannot find twelve such men and is silenced only by the teacher's reminder that the Most High had to be content with two ; when the class includes father and son, princes, princesses, and courtiers ; when it has freedom to follow the argument whither it leads the fancy and to assume at its pleasure an attitude of levity or gravity, the test is extraordinarily severe ! In one respect Alcuin was more fortunate than most educational reformers : the State was a friendly critic of his schemes and had some inkling of its need for instruction. Had Pestalozzi or Tolstoy had the opportunity of teaching a royal pupil, their educational efforts might have been crowned with the success that came to Alcuin. His strange blend of conservatism and reform, of solid common sense and poetry, of scholarship and pedantry proved equal to the demands of his task. By his influence upon the Palace School he raised the standard of education and stimulated the desire for learning throughout Frankland.[2]

---

[1] A. F. West, *Alcuin*, pp. 97-8.

[2] Worthy of mention as showing Alcuin's concrete methods of approach to arithmetical problems is his set of puzzles for whetting the wit of youth (*ad*

Alcuin's pupil, Rhabanus Maurus, head of the School at Fulda, gives a picture of the course of studies in the monastic schools of the eighth and ninth century. He places first in order of studies the Holy Scriptures, then follow the unadulterated truths of history, the modes of speech, the mystical sense of words, the separate branches of knowledge, integrity of life as shown in morals and good taste, penetration in the explanation of doctrine, medicine, and the study of various forms of disease — an encyclopaedic programme, and in some respects fuller than that of the *trivium* and *quadrivium*, the subjects of which are considered in detail and in relation to the requirements of the sacred writings. *Grammar*, the science which teaches us to explain the poets and the historians and the art which qualifies us to write and speak correctly, is the source and foundation of the liberal arts. How could one understand language if one did not understand its elements, its letters and syllables, feet, accent, verses, figures of speech, laws of word formation ? A knowledge of prosody is not dishonourable since ... the Psalter resounds with iambics, and Alcaics and Sapphics and even catalectic feet. In Deuteronomy and Isaiah, in Solomon and Job, there are hexameters and pentameters. *Rhetoric* may seem to refer primarily to secular wisdom yet is necessary for ecclesiastical instruction. The preacher of the Divine law must present his ideas in an eloquent manner and

acuendos juvenes) : a book so similar to the Venerable Bede's work on the same subject that it must either have been a copy of that work, or an embodiment of problems and methods that were widely used at the time. It is the beginning of mathematics through puzzles and amusements, and although many of the exercises are crude and indicative of the writer's limited knowledge, some are models of concrete presentation. His method of finding the sum of an arithmetical series may be given as perhaps the best illustration of his teaching methods. There is a ladder with a hundred steps. One dove is on the first step, two on the second, and so on. How many doves are on the ladder ? On the first and ninety-ninth steps there are one hundred doves, and one hundred on the second and ninety-eighth steps. Proceeding thus through the pairs of steps we find forty-nine steps containing one hundred doves, with the fiftieth and hundredth steps omitted, which last contain jointly one hundred and fifty doves. The total is accordingly five thousand and fifty. Some of his puzzles are undoubtedly educational means of arriving at information, as when, for example, he requests three hundred pigs to be killed in three batches on successive days, an odd number to be killed each day. ' *Ecce fabula* ! ' he cries in glee. ' Here's a go ! There is no solution. This fable is only to provoke boys ' (West, *Alcuin*, p. 112). Such exercises show clearly enough that computation in the early Middle Ages was not entirely confined to calculations of church festivals.

clothe his exposition in adequate and impressive language. And who would dare to say that the defenders of truth should stand weaponless in the presence of falsehood so that exposition should make listening a burden, apprehension a weariness, and faith in the truth an impossibility? *Dialectic* is the science of sciences ; it teaches us to teach others, as well as to learn. Through it reason manifests itself according to its nature, and brings us to apprehend our being, our origin, and the origin of the Good ; it teaches us to discover truth and to unmask falsehood, to draw conclusions, to know what is valid argument and what is true, probable or false : by it we investigate everything with penetration, determine its nature with certainty, and discuss it with circumspection. *Arithmetic* turns the mind from fleshly desires and ' awakens the wish to comprehend what with God's help we can merely receive from the heart.' [1] Ignorance of number leaves many things unintelligible which are expressed mystically in Holy Scripture. *Geometry* proceeds from observation. The stars and the planets and every well-ordered arrangement obey its requirements. The Trinity makes use of geometry in bestowing manifold forms and images upon the creatures it has called into being ; circles, spheres, hemispheres, and quadrangles entered into the building of the tabernacle and the temple. *Music* is a science as eminent as it is useful. The stranger to it is not able to fulfil the duties of the ecclesiastical office in a suitable manner. It penetrates all the activities of our life ; all that makes our hearts beat faster is expressed through its rhythm and harmony. When we do what is wrong we do not feel ourselves drawn to music. Pythagoras testified that the world was created and ruled by it. *Astronomy*, if investigated with a pure heart and an ample mind, will fill us with a great love of study. That part of it which investigates natural phenomena, the course of the sun, of the moon and stars and the proper reckoning of time, the Christian clergy should learn with the utmost diligence, . . . so that they may fix the time for Easter and all other festivals and holy days and announce to the congregation the proper celebration of them.

Rhabanus concludes this interesting account of the liberal

[1] Selection from Rhabanus Maurus given in Painter, *Great Pedagogical Essays*, pp. 159-168.

disciplines with a sentence that shows clearly the attitude of
the Church to liberal studies. ' When philosophers have per-
chance uttered some truth which agrees with our faith we should
not handle it timidly but rather take it from its unlawful
possessors and apply it to our own use.' The subordination of
learning to ecclesiastical ends has been criticized as illiberal,
but it is clear that the mere transference to the religious field
of facts and ideas usually restricted to secular pursuits is not
intrinsically unsound. The presentation of early studies
through a specific life activity, like that of church ritual, may
have some advantages. But the *keeping* of ideas within the
circle of religious life is pedagogically unwise : it gives a
relatively specific, not a really liberal training—a training not
likely to spread to other activities of life.

It may be pointed out that the monastic life compensated for
the canalization of its educational aims by providing a wide
range of activity which was more or less vitalized by its
ideals. But the compensation is more apparent than real.
There was comparatively little flow of educational ideas beyond
the confines of the monastery. The monk distrusted human
nature. Acutely aware of his own personal defections and
unable to satisfy the needs of his spiritual nature through the
normal activities of communal life, he could scarcely regard as
part of his duty that opening out of the pupil's aspirations to
the demands of the community which the teacher usually
regards as his first responsibility. His distrust of the world
and his mistrust of himself led to an extreme submission of the
self to the demands of religion. This had weak as well as
strong points. Its strength lay in perceiving that some things
supremely worth having are not to be gained by strife, self-
assertion, or pride of place, that, on the contrary, passive
virtues and gentle lives may be full of power.[1] Its weakness
lay in seeking gentleness and power mainly for their effect upon
the *individual* self : in hiding under a professed self-abasement
the aggrandisement of the self that sometimes accompanies a
morbid desire to save one's own soul.[2] Some monks, no doubt,

[1] Cf. Adams, *Civilization during the Middle Ages*, p. 132.

[2] The limitations of the monastic view of life were occasionally stated in
very plain language. Thus Theobald of Étampes states (between 1119 and
1135) : ' A church is an assembly of the faithful, but a monastery is a place

recognized the truth that in seeking to save one's life one might lose it, but, in general, the monastic system was not only self-centred but distrustful of others as well as of self.   In Benedict's rule idleness was stated to be the great enemy of the soul, *therefore* the monks were to be always occupied in manual labour or in holy reading—a view that had both good and bad results.   It led to an immense amount of practical activity directly useful to the outside world ; for the monks excelled in most of the crafts.   More important still, it led to the preservation of manuscripts which otherwise would have perished. But it gave a perverted view of work, inasmuch as it found the value and dignity of labour neither in the result of that labour nor (as in the case of play) in the mental and physical processes that produce and sustain it, but in the attitudes which were *repressed* because of the activity.

A myopic view of the values to be presented to the pupil was united with a very austere conception of discipline.   Even here, however, it is well to remember that the Middle Ages were by no means ages of unmitigated severity.   The early traditions of the monasteries gave abundant evidence of a paternal regard for the children under their care.   St. Pachomius had a deep affection for childhood ; St. Basil, like Quintilian, advocated the idea of discipline through consequences closely related to the child's own action ; Alcuin observed the natural dispositions of his pupils and distributed studies according to their gifts ; Ekkehard I, arguing that Nature was an economist in her gifts and that often a slow head was accompanied by skilful fingers, alternated mental and manual activity : St. Ethelwold allured his pupils to study by cheerful and encouraging words ; the pupils of St. Gall were sufficiently free to capture the Bishop of Constance and hold him as a prisoner until he promised a handsome reward.[1]   As we shall

and prison of the damned, that is of monks, who have damned themselves to avoid eternal damnation.   They are, however, more profitably damned by themselves than by someone else.'   Leach, *Educational Charters*, p. 105.

[1] A custom of the school ordained that any stranger might be captured and not released until he had offered a ransom.   The Bishop was conducted to the master's chair and informed that he could not leave until he had made an acceptable promise.   ' Very well,' he said, ' as you have put me in the master's chair, I shall exercise the master's authority ; prepare all of you to be flogged.'   The boys agreed, but claimed to redeem themselves in return, on the same terms as their master usually gave them—' by making verses.'   The

see, there is also abundant evidence of attempts to make the work of learning pleasant. But there are also dismal accounts of educational methods in the Middle Ages.

In the tenth century Ratherius' book was addressed to pupils in the suggestive terms *Serva dorsum*.[1] In the twelfth century the autobiography of Guibert, Abbot of Nogent, gave a picture of his own early education that deepens the suggestion. It is the story of an ignorant and brutal teacher and a sensitive and painstaking boy. Guibert tells us that almost every day he was pelted with a hail of blows and hard words whilst his teacher was forcing him to learn what he himself could not teach. ' He took vengeance on me,' says Guibert, ' for not knowing what he knew not himself ; he ought certainly to have considered that it was very wrong to demand from a weak little mind what he had not put into it.' Six years of this fruitless struggle passed with no reward worth the expenditure. . . .
' For by the strain of undue application the natural powers of grown men, as well as of boys, are blunted, and the hotter the fire of their mental activity in unremitting study, the sooner is the strength of their understanding weakened and chilled by excess and its energy turned into sloth.' [2]

The supervision of the oblates and novices at Canterbury School is described in great detail in the *Constitutiones Lanfranci* [3]

Bishop was so pleased with their improvisations that he allowed three whole-day holidays after the Feast of the Holy Innocents and certain luxuries from the kitchen. See Drane, *Christian Schools and Scholars*, pp. 276-7 ; cf. also pp. 22, 24, 85, 137, 170, 216.

[1] Or *Spara dorsum*—' a little book on the grammatical art which he called by the pleasant name of *Spara dorsum* . . . to the end that young children making use of it might be preserved from scourges.' From Folcuin's *History of the Abbots of Lobes*. (Quoted from Drane, *Christian Schools and Scholars*, p. 256.)

[2] *The Autobiography of Guibert* (trans. by C. G. S. Bland), pp. 20-23.
The autobiography is also of interest because of its attempt to find an explanation of Guibert's boyish feelings towards his teacher. ' As for me considering the dull sensibility of my age and my littleness, great was the love I conceived for him in response, in spite of the many weals with which he marked my tender skin, so that not through fear, as is common in those of my age, but through a sort of love deeply implanted in my heart, I obeyed him in utter forgetfulness of his severity.' And with great frankness he adds . . . ' Clearly the impulses that constrained me then were not religious feelings begotten by thoughtfulness but only a child's eagerness.' There is here a direct recognition of the fundamental receptivity which is the basis of that *willing* obedience to which we have referred in a previous chapter.

[3] Leach, *Educational Charters*, pp. 65-7. Compare also : Maître, *Les Ecoles Episcopales et Monastiques en Occident*, pp. 129-136.

(*c.* 1075). After providing that, with certain exceptions, no one may make signs or even smile at the younger boys the *Constitutions* consider the disciplinary arrangements for the young men. . . . ' They shall, as is above said, sit separate from each other ; shall never leave the place in which they are kept, except with the monk who has charge of them ; shall carry lanterns in pairs ; and shall make confession to no one but the abbot or prior, unless by special arrangement. At the midday rest they shall not read or write, or do any work ; but cover themselves up and keep quiet ; they shall have their beds before or between their masters' beds. If they have to get up, they shall first wake their master, then light a lantern, if it is night, and go to the Necessarium with their master. No one shall be allowed to sit in the place assigned to them except the abbot, the prior, and their masters : nor make any communication to them by words or signs, except with the leave of the abbot or prior ; and when leave is given the master ought to sit between the youth and the one who is talking to him. No youth is to talk to another, except so that the master may hear and understand what is said by both of them. The masters ought to sit between them or in front of them, so as to be able to see them, if they want to. When they go to bed the masters ought to stand in front of them until they lie down and are covered over, and at night, with lighted candles.' This excessive concern for the minutest details of conduct arose, no doubt, from the feeling of responsibility and the sense of the sacredness of childhood ; it led the monk to banish from the child's world the temptations and trials from which he himself had sought to escape. It must be judged according to the standards of the age and viewed in the perspective of monastic life. [1]

We have already seen that some effort was made to render instruction palatable to the children of the Middle Ages. A markedly successful teacher of the tenth century, Gerbert of the Cathedral School at Rheims, succeeded in making difficult studies easy and delightful. In particular, he popularized the sciences of astronomy and mathematics, making use in his

---

[1] It must be remembered that the relation of the abbot to the monk resembled that of the master to the slave, and that the monks were mainly recruited from a servile class. Even as late as the Council of Frankfort (794) there is a reference to the blinding and mutilating of monks by abbots.

lectures of the terrestrial and celestial globes, and if not introducing, certainly popularizing, the use of the abacus.   Anselm, too, a leader of the intellectual movement of the following century, may be regarded as an advocate of freedom.   His conversation with a neighbouring abbot regarding the best methods of educating young children is a witness to the existence of enlightened, as well as of benighted, methods in the eleventh century.   The abbot explained that his pupils were perverse and incorrigible.   ' We do our best to correct them,' he added ; ' we beat them from morning till night, but I own I can see no improvement.'   ' And how do they grow up ? ' inquired Anselm.   ' Just as dull and stupid as so many beasts,' was the reply.   ' A famous system of education, truly,' observed the Abbot of Bec, ' which changes men into beasts.   Now, tell me, what would be the result, if, after having planted a tree in your garden, you were to compress it so tightly that it should have no room to extend its branches ?   These poor children were given to you that you might help them to grow, and be fruitful in good thoughts ; but if you allow them no liberty their minds will grow crooked. Finding no kindness on your part, they will give you no confidence, and never having been brought up to know the meaning of love and charity, they will see everything around them in a distorted aspect.' [1]

Worthy of note, too, are the early attempts to make linguistic instruction interesting to children.   The two Latin primers that served as text books for many centuries—the works of Donatus and Priscian—were revised and presented in a new form by Aelfric, a monk of Winchester.   Aelfric had been the pupil of Aethelwold, of whom it was said that ' it was ever sweet to him to teach youths and little ones, to explain their Latin books to them in English, to instruct them in the rules of grammar and prosody, and allure them by cheerful words to study and improvement.' [2]   Aelfric expressly says in the Preface to his Grammar that his lessons follow the practice of Aethelwold, ' who taught many the elements to good purpose.'   His book aims at presenting material suitable for children.   In the preface he writes : ' I, Aelfric, as not being very learned,

[1] Quoted from Drane, *Christian Schools and Scholars*, p. 314.
[2] Drane, *Christian Schools and Scholars*, p. 219.

have taken pains to translate these extracts from the larger
and smaller Priscian for you tender children into your own
language, so that when you have gone through Donatus on the
Parts of Speech, you may be able to instil both languages,
Latin and English, into your youthful minds, by this little
book, until you reach more advanced studies. I am aware that
many will blame me, for being willing to devote my mind to
such a pursuit as to turn " The Art of Grammar " into English.
But I destine this lesson-book for little boys who know nothing,
not for their elders.' [1]

Another work of Aelfric—*The Colloquy*—makes the attempt
to introduce Latin in the form of an interesting and amusing
dialogue dealing with the scenes of every-day life and presenting
a rather wide range of vocabulary. Were it not for an interlinear
gloss in Anglo-Saxon it might be considered the first example
of a really direct method of teaching Latin. It is probable,
however, that the translation is for the teacher's and not for
the pupil's use, and that it is a testimony to the teacher's
ignorance of Latin at the end of the tenth century. Monks,
ploughmen, shepherds, cowherds, hunters, fishermen, hawkers,
merchants, shoemakers, salters, and bakers speak in turn and
describe their occupations. In the course of the conversation
the master asks : ' Will you be flogged while learning ? ' which
brings the reply : ' We would rather be flogged while learning
than remain ignorant ; but we know that you will be kind to
us and not flog us unless you are obliged '—a tactful response
which is scarcely in keeping with their frank (and probably
truthful) hint that their master is occasionally too deep for
them. Both these works use simple language and appeal to
every-day experience. The variety of occupations has raised
the question whether the *Colloquy* implies a wide dissemination
of education, or whether it is a translation of an earlier Latin
description of the Roman School.[2] Its comprehensiveness is
probably due to the desire of an enlightened teacher of modern
languages to provide variety of vocabulary.

A similar wide range of words collected into a continuous
discourse is found in the *De Utensilibus* of Alexander Neckam

---

[1] Leach, *Educational Charters*, p. 49.

[2] Cf. Leach, *Educational Charters*, xvii. Adamson, *Short History of Education*, p. 16.

(twelfth century).   Neckam begins with the kitchen, its furniture and utensils, and passes on to articles of food and methods of cooking.   He next deals with the man of the house, his dress and his accoutrements, then the chamber-maid and her employments.   The poultry-yard invites a dissertation on the cooking of poultry and fish.   Then we are taught how to build a feudal castle, fortify it, store it and defend it, and by a natural transition we talk about war and arms and armour and soldiers. Soon we go back to the barn, the poultry-yard, and the stable. The important mediaeval occupation of weaving is next considered : then country life invites attention.   The construction of carts and waggons, the implements and occupations of the farmer, the construction and use of the plough, navigation and the duties of the Scribe follow, and finally there is an extensive list of ecclesiastical furniture.   A similar treatise of John de Garlande belongs to the earlier half, and a French text (with an interlinear gloss) written by Walter de Biblesworth belongs to the end of the thirteenth century.   The subjects in the latter work are arranged in ' an order considered suitable for the class for which it was intended.'   It begins with the child new-born and tells how it is nursed and fed !   Grammatical distinctions are emphasized in the sentences chosen for illustration.   By the fifteenth century pen and ink drawings, probably designed to fix the attention of the scholar on his task, are found in the margins of vocabularies and grammatical treatises.   They show us ' how little of novelty there is in most of the plans for simplifying school-teaching in more modern times, for in these mediaeval treatises we meet with the prototypes of almost every scheme that has been proposed from the more recent Hamiltonian system to the *Orbis Pictus* of Comenius.' [1]

Professor Adamson reminds us that the education of the clerk was not the only form of mediaeval education.[2]   As we have seen, the Palace School of Charlemagne was a school of

---

[1] *A Library of National Antiquities* (B. M. copy published by Joseph Mayer, edited by Thomas Wright).   See Drane, *Christian Schools*, pp. 546 ff. for an account of mediaeval primers.   Versified geography and grammar books are common in the fourteenth and fifteenth centuries.   The ' horn book ' dates from about the middle of the fifteenth century.

[2] *A short History of Education*, ch. iii.

noblemen, and the author of the *De Rebus gestis Aelfredi* describes a similar school in England. In the twelfth, thirteenth, and fourteenth centuries the castles of the leading nobles became centres of instruction for the boys and girls of noblemen. The knight's education was thoroughly utilitarian and aimed at producing knightly rather than cultural qualities. From the age of seven to fourteen he was taught mainly by the ladies of the household; later, physical training, outdoor and indoor games, graces,[1] and accomplishments were added. From fourteen to twenty-one the ' squire ' served as a soldier, waited and carved at table. In Chaucer's words :

> ' He coude songes make and wel endyte
> Juste and eek daunce, and wel purtreye and wryte.'

This interesting type of education had its advantages and also its disadvantages. It worked mainly upon fundamental dispositions like pugnacity, self-assertion, imitation, suggestion, and the play impulse. It gave a carefully graded and efficient training within a limited and rigidly defined social environment. But so specific was the training and so limited the environment that the training proved ineffective when the social and other conditions were even slightly changed. The knight went to battle in defence of the weak, but failed to recognize his own

---

[1] Instruction in courtesy formed an important part of mediaeval education. It may be illustrated by the following couplets from Richard Weste's *School of Virtue*, which, though published at the beginning of the seventeenth century, is fairly typical of mediaeval prescriptions of manners. See *The Babees' Book* (Done into English from Dr. Furnivall's Texts by Edith Rickert), pp. 162 ff.

> ' With steadfast eye and careful ear, remember every word
> Thy schoolmaster shall speak to thee as memory shall afford.

> ' Let not thy brows be backward drawn, it is a sign of pride,
> Exalt them not, it shows a heart most arrogant, beside.

> ' Nor let thine eyes be glumly down cast, with a hanging look,
> For that to Dreamers doth belong, that goodness cannot brook.

> ' Let forehead joyful be and full, it shows a merry part,
> And cheerfulness in countenance, and pleasantness of heart.

> ' Nor wrinkled let thy countenance be, still going to and fro,
> For that belongs to hedgehogs right ; they wallow even so.

> ' Nor imitate with Socrates to wipe thy snivelled nose
> Upon thy cap as he would do, nor yet upon thy clothes.

> ' But keep it clean with handkerchief provided for the same,
> Not with thy fingers or thy sleeve ; therein thou art to blame.

> ' Observe in courtesy to take a rule of decent kind :
> Bend not thy body too far forth, nor back thy leg behind.

weakness in face of danger. He respected scrupulously the claims of inferiors but regarded their persons with scorn and contempt. His gallantry did not extend to women beneath a certain rank. Like the training of the clerk, the knight's education adjusted to the environment of the moment, forgetful of the wider liberty that tends to supply a principle of adjustment to varied environments and diverse conditions of life.

The closing centuries of the mediaeval period escaped the shackles of specific adjustment. As Professor Adamson points out, a moment in the twelfth century gave promise of anticipating the literary revival of the fourteen and fifteen hundreds. For the moment men turned back to the old Greek and Roman culture. The study of philosophy and law, the assimilation of ideas from newly discovered treatises of Aristotle, the rise of universities, the keen and subtle disputations of scholasticism, the influence of Byzantine and Arabian knowledge, the quickening of emotions and intellect by the Crusades ; the opening of new markets and trade routes, the revolts of men like Pierre Abélard and Roger Bacon, voices though they were in the mediaeval wilderness of authority—all these are the manifestations of human forces that would not suffer even the highest spiritual values to forge chains for human reason. The Middle Ages were an anticipation on the grand scale of Rousseau's negative education. They aimed at keeping the heart from vice and the mind from error. They were wonderfully efficient within a narrow field, but the lesson they teach us is the impossibility of keeping the mind in leading strings. The soul, as Gregory and Origen taught, cannot be coerced ; the body may be shackled but thought must be free or it ceases to be.

CHAPTER VII

FREEDOM AND HUMANISM

BURCKHARDT depicts mankind in the Middle Ages as dreaming or half-awake beneath a veil of faith and childish illusion which clad the world in strange hues. At the end of the thirteenth century man awoke. A new love of learning soon appeared and with it a clearer appreciation of the aim and value of classical culture. A deeper sense of the joy, beauty, and dignity of the present life quickened the minds of men. New emotions and new sympathies began to surge. Forces hitherto confined to one mode of expression found studies and pursuits that satisfied the aspirations of human nature. The wider view of life gave an enhanced sense of individuality. It is therefore to be expected that a deepened sense of freedom would appear in education.

In studying the period we may pass lightly over many of the Renaissance writers prior to Erasmus. Their writings are not unimportant, but their main threads are gathered together in Erasmus and in the works of Vives and Sadoleto. A review of the three will bring the problem of freedom into close grips with the study of the pupil's nature and capacity and also show freedom in its practical bearing on schoolwork. Glimpses of its actual operation in the school are to be found in Cordier's *Colloquies*. The relation of the educational views associated with Martin Luther and with Ignatius Loyola will give a further point of contact with actual schemes of education. Finally, we shall briefly consider the new forms of education that appear in the works of Ascham, Elyot, and Mulcaster, and sum up the old and the new views by glancing at their satirical presentation in the works of Rabelais.

The pioneer in the educational movement of the Renaissance is Vergerius. Like Plato, he attempts to base education on the human tendencies that sustain it.[1] Two of these, emulation

---

[1] Vergerius, *De Ingenuis Moribus*. Trans. Woodward in *V. da Feltre*, p. 98.

and obedience, have already been discussed ; a third, shame, will be considered in its fuller presentation in Sadoleto. The fourth, alertness or industry, is the medium of Vergerius' main contribution to freedom—the recognition of education through individual tendencies, or rather in spite of some of them, for the general tone of the treatment is mildly repressive. The faults of youth are hindrances to that full devotion to liberal studies which expresses the writer's aim of education.

' We call those studies *liberal*,' says Vergerius, ' which are worthy of a free man ; those studies by which we attain and practise virtue and wisdom ; that education which calls forth, trains, and develops those highest gifts of body and of mind which ennoble men, and which are rightly judged to rank next in dignity to virtue only. For to a vulgar temper, gain and pleasure are the one aim of existence ; to a lofty nature, moral worth and fame. It is, then, of the highest importance that even from infancy this aim, this effort, should constantly be kept alive in growing minds. For I may affirm with fullest conviction that we shall not have attained wisdom in our later years unless in our earliest we have sincerely entered on its search.' [1] Education is at last recognized to be the development and guidance of the gifts that ennoble humanity ; liberal studies those which are consonant with the dignity of the free man ; moral worth and virtue the only pursuits which bring freedom ; education through liberal studies a concern of the *present* life and co-extensive with it.

Although passing in review the traditional course of liberal studies and regretfully pausing to notice the decadence of learning in his own day Vergerius does not agree that a liberal education is necessarily the product of the complete curriculum of disciplines prescribed by the Greeks. He even suggests that we should pursue the study which we find most suited to our intelligence and tastes, and that boys have such varying aptitudes that the choice of studies will depend to some extent upon the character of their individual minds. Some pupils have peculiar facility in dealing with abstract truths but are defective on the side of the particular and the concrete. They make good progress in mathematics and metaphysics, while others are apt in natural science and practical affairs.

---

[1] Vergerius, *De Ingenuis Moribus*. Trans. Woodward in *V. da Feltre*, p. 102.

' The natural bent should be recognized and followed in education.' But if education develops the *strong* powers of the
personality the pupil must be taught the value of humility.
' Any exercise by which we may learn to distrust our own
attainments, and so increase our diligence and our modesty, is
to be prized. . . . It is perhaps the first essential of real progress to be sceptical of our own powers, and to discard that
presumption of our own ability or knowledge which tempts us
to make light of the need for thoroughness.' In the concluding
remarks to Ubertinus (the son of the Lord of Padua) he gives the
key word to his whole treatise : ' Follow the instincts of your
best self and you will be found worthy.' In our final review of
the meaning of freedom we shall see that this is a maxim of
first importance. It expresses the new faith in man which
accompanied the humanist point of view.[1]

The same faith appears in the headmaster of the famous
classical school at Mantua, who, in the words of his critics,
' refused after fair trial made, to force learning upon an unwilling scholar, holding that nature had not endowed all with
taste or capacity for study.' [2] With a clear perception of the
human values embodied in liberal studies, and with a keen
desire to impose only humane rules and regulations upon his
pupils, simple, direct, and forceful in his explanations and
illustrations of classical literature, Vittorino da Feltre seems to
have combined the qualities of a Quintilian and a Pestalozzi.
A similar faith in the pupil's ' desire to learn ' appears in many
writers of the period. Thus Aeneas Sylvius insists that ' a boy
must be won to learning by persuasive earnestness, and not be
driven to it like a slave '; [3] Guarino that ' there can be no
proficiency in studies unless there be first the desire to excel '; [4]
Alberti that the innate force of curiosity will, by suitable instruction, find attractive material in arts, sciences, and letters which
will thus become an object of spontaneous interest when the

[1] Against this view Giovanni Dominici strongly protested in his *Cura della
Famiglia*.

[2] Woodward, *Vittorino da Feltre*, p. 34.

[3] *De Lib. Ed.* par. 1 (Woodward, *op. cit.* p. 137).

[4] *De Ord. Doc.* par. 1 (Woodward, p. 162).

stage of pupilage is past.[1] The Greek παιδεία and the Roman
studia humanitatis find a concrete setting in Alberti's *Trattato
della Cura della Famiglia*, where he develops the view that the
mutual interests of family life are the most fitting of all social
environments for the realization of true individuality.

Almost a century after Alberti's *Trattato* the great Erasmus
wrote his satire on the imitation of Cicero into which the
humanistic movement in education had then degenerated. He
makes the devotee of Cicero boast that for seven years he has
read no other author. He has even compiled an ' alphabetical
lexicon of Cicero so huge that two strong carriers well saddled
could scarcely carry it upon their backs ; a second volume, even
larger than this, in which are arranged alphabetically the
phrases peculiar to Cicero ; and a third, in which have been
gathered all the metrical feet with which Cicero ever begins or
ends his periods, and their sub-divisions, the rhythms which
he uses in between, and the cadences which he chooses for each
kind of sentence, so that no little point could escape.' [2] Thus
does Erasmus illustrate the decadence of the school curriculum
of his day with its meticulous attention to grammatical subtlety,
its appeal to memory, and its divorce from the human values
which the earlier literary studies made central.

No writer gave himself more willingly to the cause of freedom
in education than Erasmus. He drew attention to the tena-
cious, the curious, and the imitative tendencies of the mind
and its natural susceptibility to guidance. He urged that the
first task should be to secure the pupil's affection, the second
to secure it for the subject taught. Pleasure could be aroused
by appealing to the play motive, to ambition, to emulation,
and to varied activities. Formal grammar, into which teaching
had degenerated, should yield place to conversation bearing
on the boy's own interests, play, and social life.

In his *De Pueris Instituendis* Erasmus states the case for the
individual choice of subjects.[3] His watchword is to observe and
follow Nature.[4] Three conditions determine individual pro-

---

[1] Woodward, *Education during the Renaissance*, p. 61.

[2] Trans. from *Dialog. Ciceronianus* quoted from Graves : *A History of
Education*, vol. ii. p. 136.

[3] Erasmus, *De Pueris*, 498-499 (Woodward, pp. 195 ff.)

[4] *Ibid.* 499.

gress : (1) the ' nature,' innate capacity, or native bent towards
excellence ; (2) training ; and (3) *the free exercise on our own
part of that activity which has been implanted by nature and is
furthered by training.*[1]   Observation of animal life shows that
' each creature learns, first of all, to perform those things which
preserve life and to avoid those things which make for pain and
destruction.   This is true not less of plants, as we can see when
we contrast the close-knit tree of the exposed sea-coast and its
fellow spreading luxuriantly in warmth and shelter.   *All living
things strive to develop according to their proper nature.'* [2]
' Nature claims the help of the schoolmaster in carrying forward the special gifts with which she has endowed the child.
By following the path which she points out the toil of learning
is reduced : whilst on the other hand nothing can be well
accomplished *invita Minerva.'* [3]

These passages recognize the pupil's spontaneity as an active
force of education and at the same time draw attention to the
teacher's positive functions in directing and aiding it.   A firm
union of three factors, practice, training, and nature is desired.
Nature leads the way, training is to be adapted to the ' age and
taste of the scholar,' practice is to be indistinguishable from
play and a source of enjoyment to the child.   Instruction is to
be simple, and to take the form of recreation.   The sense of
effort is to be lost in the pleasure of natural exercise : insensibly
the mind will become equal to harder tasks.   Wholly wrong
are those masters who expect their little pupils to act as though
they were but diminutive adults, who forget the meaning of
youth, who have no standard of what can be done or be understood except that of their own minds.   Such masters will up-
braid, exact, punish as though they were dealing with students
as old as themselves.   They forget that they were ever children.[4]

Erasmus deals at length with the right relationship of the
teacher to the pupil.   A gentle and sympathetic manner, a
knowledge of attractive methods, ability to win the pupil to
find pleasure in his task are emphasized.   The man of manners
so uncouth, of expression so forbidding, of speech so surly, that
he repels even when he wishes to attract, is declared wholly
unfit to be the teacher of children.   A lover of horses would

[1] *Ibid.* p. 191.   *Italics* mine.   [2] *Ibid.* p. 191-2.   *Italics* mine.
[3] *Ibid.* p. 213.   [4] Cf. Woodward, *Erasmus,* p. 211-12.

hardly put such a person in charge of his stable, yet there is no hesitation in allowing him to ' break in ' the young child. Fear, says Erasmus, is of no avail in education : not even parents can train their children by this motive. Love must be the first influence. It must be followed and completed by a trustful and affectionate respect, which compels obedience far more surely than dread can ever do.[1] There is a painfully vivid sketch of the teacher of the time. He is too often uncouth and intemperate. He may be an invalid, or a cripple, or mentally deficient. He finds himself dressed in a new authority. He cannot teach but he can flog. The school is a torture chamber. Blows and shouts, sobs and howls fill the air. ' It is, indeed,' proceeds Erasmus, ' the mark of the servile nature to be drilled by fear : why then do we suffer children (whose very name imports free men, *liberi*—those born fit for a " liberal training ") to be treated as slaves might be ? ' *Yet even slaves, who are men like the rest of us, are by wise masters freed from something of their servile state by humane control.* Let a father stand towards his son in a more kindly relation than that of a master towards his serf. If we put away tyrants from their thrones, why do we erect a new tyranny for our own sons ? Is it not meet that Christian peoples cast forth from their midst the whole practice of slavery ?

The fear of just reproach and the desire for praise are the two chief weapons of the schoolmaster, and Erasmus, as if aware that he is inspired by Quintilian, proceeds to add another weapon suggested by another source—' Unwearied pains conquer all things.' ' Let us watch, let us encourage, let us press and yet again press, that by learning, by repeating, by diligent listening, the boy may feel himself carried onward towards his goal. Let him learn to respect and to love integrity and knowledge, to hate ignorance and dishonour. Bid him regard those who are lauded for their virtues, be warned by those who are denounced for their ill-doing. Set before him the example of men to whom learning has brought high praise, dignity, repute, and position. Warn him of the fate of those who by the respect of high wisdom have sunk into contempt, poverty, disgrace, and evil life. These are your instruments of discipline, my Christian teacher, worthy of your calling and

[1] Cf. 503E–504A *De Pueris Inst.* Trans. Woodward, *Erasmus*, p. 203.

of your flock. But should none of these avail, then, if it must be so, let the rod be used with due regard to self-respect in the manner of it.' [1]

Equally wise is his discussion of concrete and pleasurable methods of teaching. He has ' no patience with the stupidity of the average teacher of grammar who wastes precious years in hammering rules into children's heads. For it is not by learning rules that we acquire the power of speaking a language, but by daily intercourse with those accustomed to express themselves with exactness and refinement and by the copious reading of the best authors.' [2] He sees that there is no intrinsic virtue in difficulty. He remembers how his own childhood was tortured by logical subtleties which had no reference to anything that was true in fact, or sound in expression.[3] He wishes to change all that. Narrative, illustration, appeal to objects rather than words, vivid descriptions, picture-methods, even the use of the boy's wilder nature are of service in the first stages of teaching. He asks the teacher for *the kind of effort that people are willing to bestow upon training a parrot to talk*.[4] Lack of attractiveness in the teaching of grammar arises not a little from the teacher's lack of judgment. The beginner is worried about the names of the letters before he knows one of them by sight, or about the case of *Musae* or the tense of *legeris* before he has learnt his accidence. The master's ' shallow mind parades its thin layer of knowledge before the class ! ' Three principles underlie a right use of method. First, do not hurry : learning comes easily when the proper stage is reached. Second, avoid a difficulty which can be safely ignored or postponed. Third, when difficulty must be faced make the approach to it gradual, and interesting. (Lucretius tells us that doctors sweeten the rim of the medicine glass with honey.) ' Lead the beginner to face unfamiliar matter with self-confidence, to attack it slowly but with persistence. We must not under-rate the capacity of youth to respond to suitable demands upon the intelligence. Youth indeed lacks that sheer force which marks the bull, but, on the other hand, Nature has given it something of the tenacity and industry of the ant. The child, like every other creature, *excels in the*

---

[1] *Op. cit.* pp. 208 ff.   [2] *De Rat. Studii* (Woodward, p. 163).
[3] Woodward, p. 221.   [4] Woodward, p. 215.

precise activity which belongs to it. How else could he race about for hours and not be tired ? But such exercise is instinctive ; it is only play to him ; there is no sense of toil about it, no compulsion. *Follow Nature, therefore, in this, and so far as is possible take from the work of the school all that implies toilsomeness and strive to give to learning the quality of freedom and of enjoyment.'* [1] Perhaps this is the first *explicit* recognition of the spontaneous activities as the most *efficient* method of education.

Juan Luis Vives, the pupil of Erasmus, not only counsels us to ' follow the child's nature,' but attempts to find what that nature is. As Professor Foster Watson points out, he anticipates the method of investigating nature usually associated with Francis Bacon's writings.[2] His contribution to our subject lies in his effort to ascertain the facts of mental development and to determine school work in the light of the ascertained facts. ' Every two or three months,' he advises, ' let the masters meet together and deliberate and judge with paternal affection and grave discretion concerning the minds of their pupils, and send each boy to that work for which he seems most fit. If that is done incredible advantage will ensue to the whole human race. Nothing would then be done badly and perversely by those who now do it under compulsion and against their desires.[3] Vives has dreams of basing education on the innate tendencies. He argues that the human mind has a certain bias towards the fundamental and most simple truths, and a tendency to realize

---

[1] Woodward, p. 217. *Italics* mine.

[2] In a remarkable passage of his *De Tradendis Disciplinis* (trans. by Foster Watson in *Vives on Education*, p. 87), Vives states more clearly than most modern writers the foundations of a science of education : ' In teaching the arts, we shall collect many experiments and observe the experience of many teachers, so that from them general rules may be formed. If some of the experiments do not agree with the rule, then the reason why this happens must be noted. If the reason is not apparent, and there are some deviations, they must be noted down. If there are more deviations than agreements or an equal number a dogma must not be established from that fact, but the facts must be transmitted to the astonishment of posterity, so that from astonishment— as has been the case in the past—philosophy may grow. All the arts connected with doing, or making things, are best acquired from observing the actions and work of those who have been best instructed in them by nature, study, and habit. From such inventors, as we have shown, the arts were born.'

[3] *Ibid.* p. 82.

the aims that are most clearly good, just as the earth has the power of growing herbs, and the eye of noting differences of colour. But idleness destroys or enfeebles these powers or ' anticipations and premonitions of truth.' Exercise on the other hand develops and improves them. It follows, therefore, that, as different individuals have different gifts and different views of the good there must be various types of instruction. He distinguishes many types of mind—the analytic and synthetic, the perceptive and reflective, the steady, flighty, dim, clear, quick, slow, stubborn, equable, light and solid, the person who thinks with his hands as well as he who thinks with his head. He tends to envisage education as a discipline, and to assign suitable studies to varying types of mind —though no one is ' incapable at least of learning languages.'

Vives shows the signs of mal-adjustment that usually mark times of transition. He has at times the zeal of Vittorino for ancient culture, teaching his pupils to regard it as a gift from God to the human race ; at times he has something of Rhabanus Maurus' love of ecclesiastical studies and wishes to impress the authority of Holy Scriptures with great awe on the hearts of children ; at times the desire of Erasmus to hasten slowly, and to spare punishment ; at times the impatience of a schoolmaster who will punish the boy who refuses to speak Latin after a year's tuition ; at times a clear vision of the human values of subjects ; at times, as in his treatment of grammar, he is wedded to formalism ; at times he emphasizes disciplinary values, and in the next paragraph the appeal of studies apart from discipline. He is something of a humanist, a realist, a naturalist, a disciplinarian ; a compound of Plato and Erasmus, of Roger Bacon and Locke, of Vittorino and Pestalozzi. On the whole he is a good representative of the empirical idea of freedom. Boys must not be pressed too much or driven to study ; they must be allowed relaxation ' lest they should begin to hate work before they begin to love it.' Yet they must not glide into mean pleasures. ' The human mind is wonderfully inclined to freedom. It allows itself to be set to work, but it will not suffer itself to be compelled. We may easily gain much by asking, but very little by extortion and that little with difficulty.' [1]

[1] *Ibid.* p. 121.

We do not propose to dwell upon the controversies which the new learning provoked in the fifteenth and sixteenth centuries. The conflict of Humanism and Christianity raised essentially the same problems as we found in the adjustment of Christian and pagan values in the early centuries of the Christian era. The opposition between the two in fifteenth century Italy was due to the over-emphasis of one or other of two fundamental tendencies. Christianity, as we have seen, made its main appeal to self-submission. In Professor Adamson's words, ' it preached sacrifice, self-effacement, humility, dependence on a higher power.' Humanism, on the other hand, ' strong in its faith in human perfectibility, taught self-reliance and exalted magnificence and personal distinction.'[1] The intolerant Christian interpreted Humanism as a worship of intellect and a pursuit of pleasure ; the more ignoble of the Humanists advocated a narrow and rather aggressive solipsism. Writers like Erasmus and Vives tried to find a principle of adjustment. But even within the ranks of the Humanists there were different views of the function and value of authority, and these were reflected in the methods of the schools. The *Colloquies* of Erasmus and the *Linguae Latinae Exercitatio* of Vives [2] are examples of attempts to find interesting material for the practice of Latin conversation. They are concrete and realistic, and aim at didactic appeal rather than literary value.

A clearer recognition of the claims of classical purity as compared with superficial knowledge of the rudiments of a living language is found in Cardinal Sadoleto's *De Pueris Recte Instituendis*. In his opening pages he insists that human beings are ignorant and need the light of law by which they may be

---

[1] Adamson, *A Short History of Education*, p. 117.

[2] Cf. the appeal of the following conversation (quoted from Foster Watson's *Tudor Schoolboy Life*, p. 4) with the grammatical exercises condemned by Erasmus. *Beatrice awakens the pupils, complains of their sloth, and super-intends their dressing operations* :—

Emanuel to Beatrice : ' You think you are clothing not a boy but a bride.

Beatrice. Eusebius, bring a washbasin and a pitcher. Raise it to a fair height : let the water drop out rather than pour it from the stopple. Wash thoroughly that dirt from the joints of the fingers. Cleanse the mouth and use water for gargling. Rub the eyelids and eyebrows, then the glands of the neck under the ears vigorously. Then take a cloth and dry yourself. Immortal God ! that it should be necessary to admonish you as to all these things, one by one, and that you should do nothing of your own thought.

Emanuel. Ah ! you are too much of a boss and too rude.'

guided or even constrained against their inclination. Nature supplies what is central and fundamental, but in a rough and unfinished form. It is the function of letters to bring this central element of individuality to its highest perfection and to work it out in a beauty comparable to its divine original. We may distinguish two factors in development and two types of habit resulting from it. One is impressed upon us by the careful teaching of others ; the other is acquired by the purposive effort of our own minds. One is the phantom of a real habit, a mere picture pencilled on a tablet ; the other is the true offspring and product of reason, conscious of its own function and duty, and capable of maintaining its existence. The first is discipline, obedience to the authority of another's virtue ; the second is virtue in obedience to its own authority. Sadoleto's further exposition is so akin to the Platonic view of the absence of reason in childhood and the necessity of submitting the early passions to external constraint that it may fairly be represented by a single quotation : ' Habit impressed by careful government from without is not real virtue, but only the semblance and image of virtue, yet, as the legend and story tell of Pygmalion's statue of a woman, by the kindness of heaven, it comes about in the course of time that this image takes on the spirit and life of true virtue.' [1]

The subsequent development of the way in which the statue takes on the spirit and life of virtue shows that Sadoleto made at least as much use of the internal as of the external elements. He emphasizes equally the ' seeds and germs ' of virtue naturally implanted in the mind, and the force of good example and of fitting environment. The union of the two appears very clearly in his treatment of the sense of *shame* in youth. We shall consider Sadoleto's exposition at some length, for it, rather than his view of classical training, makes a contribution to the meaning of freedom, although he does not himself explicitly connect the two ideas.

Sadoleto takes the blush to be ' the pledge of a good disposition,' and the ' chief grace of youth,' the ' averter of crime,' and the ' bulwark of temperance and virtue.' He urges

[1] *Op. cit.* (trans. Campagnac and Forbes), p. 20. Cf. pp. 12, 18. This excellent version shows by means of footnotes the many points of agreement of Sadoleto with Plato, Aristotle, Cicero, Quintilian, and contemporary and later writers.

parents not to delay to cherish and increase in their children this chief support of virtue, this stern and vigilant guardian of virtue, this ' kind and divine timidity,' a phrase which expresses its real nature.   ' All other terrors, fears, and apprehensions, of death or of dangers, which cast down and all but destroy the spirit, we rightly deem in general empty and profitless and always disgraceful, for the very aspect they induce is unseemly and ignoble—the ghastly pallors of the cheek, the trembling and shrinking limbs.   The soul retreats to the citadel of life, the heart, and calls in thither all its forces ; it seems to desert the outer circuit of the city and to retreat before the foe. Now, shame, on the other hand, boldly sallies forth (for the danger is without, springing from the estimation and regard for others) ; and by setting a blush in the face, like a mask against its fault, seeks cover in the very act by which it reveals itself ; and yet it proves less that it has been guilty of a fault than that it is aflame with vexation at having committed it.   And it does this withal in so charming a fashion that the very confession confers a kind of grace upon the fault confessed.' [1]

Four points seem worthy of notice in this remarkably clear and concise statement.   First, shame is aroused by something closely connected with the positive achievements of the self. It is not, like fear, caused by something external to it. Secondly, the self is recognized as failing to achieve what others might reasonably expect it to achieve.   Thirdly, a feeling of inferiority is evoked by the presence of others who are recognized to be superior to the self in respect of the particular matter at issue.   Fourthly, the self asserts its supremacy over the delinquent self.   As Sadoleto notes, it is both active and passive, sallying forth to confront the object and to pass judgment upon it and aflame with vexation at its deeds, on one hand, on the other masking itself and taking cover.   Shame is thus a deeply self-conscious state aroused within a set of values actively and positively associated with the self, characterized by a keen sense of the self's defection, intensified by the presence of superiors and by a consciousness of the self acting as the judge of its own actions.

If we remove from this analysis the consciousness of defection we have in a concrete form the conditions for that close adjust-

[1] *Op. cit.* pp. 54-5.

ment of the individual to values partially expressed and partially unexpressed in his life which we have associated with freedom. The conditions which arouse shame are likely to be conditions that tend to remove the consciousness of it, and give a new sense of freedom, a fact which shows the close connection of Sadoleto's exposition with our subject. And Sadoleto sees that the very vehemence of the passions of boyhood and youth serves to stamp upon the mind the disapproval of a parent who has with fairness and patience set himself to the task of guiding and directing the slippery steps of youth. Let such an one ' take his son alone and gently reproach him, revealing his care and anxiety, disclosing to him his fault, and earnestly beseech him not to seek to ruin the hopes of his father and his family, nor to sacrifice the reputation and the position which he himself desires and hopes to win. And he need say but little— unless I am mistaken—for the early training and discipline will hold good. The boy himself will be a sterner critic of his own action than his father, will have less mercy on himself, and will feel much pain at the prayers and admonitions of the parent whom he dearly loves.' [1] But all this is the very antithesis of an external reason, or the implanting of good habits which are the mere shadow of virtue. It is the appeal to reason itself and to virtue through a wise use of concrete situations and the ties of parental affection. It is, moreover, a concrete picture of one aspect of freedom in education.

In Sadoleto's teaching of the liberal arts the same use and directive restraint of tendencies are noticeable. He reminds us that the Greek road to wisdom lay through these arts. Although the Greeks appointed teachers of oratory and philosophy who never left their pupils' sides, yet they provided teaching in mathematics, music, astronomy, so that children might gain something which the other studies did not give. ' They knew that boyhood and still more adolescence, is impetuous and aflame, incapable of repose, always restless, and in movement, unable to set bounds to its appetite for talking, running, shouting, and accordingly prescribed first of all those arts which they thought the most suitable for controlling that age and fashioning it to a certain mould of habit—the arts, I mean, of gymnastic and music, of which the one should bring

[1] *Op. cit.* p. 62.

beneath the sway of certain laws the impulses of the body, the other the impulses of the mind, both alike by nature, unbridled and unrestrained. So that in giving free expression to natural instincts and impulses, art and training should nevertheless be employed to invest those movements with grace, and make the body healthy, while they secured the balance of the mind.' [1]

The *Colloquies* of Mathurin Cordier illustrate the efforts of the fifteenth and sixteenth centuries to bring Latin within the range of youthful interests, and thus to unite in practice the two types of habit and training which Sadoleto distinguished in theory. So impressed was Cordier by the defects of the instruction of his day that he set himself to find a method less superficial than that of Erasmus and more interesting and concrete than those of the mediaeval schools. His own method, detailed in his *De Corrupti Sermonis Emendatione Libellus*, is interesting because of his attempts to utilize the corrupt, though natural, forms of the pupils' Latin speech as a first step, and the mother tongue itself as a further aid, to a correct version. He seems to have been rather inconsistent in his use of direct methods, the *Colloquies* presumably being written as a basis for conversation on topics naturally arising out of the boys' lives at home, in school, at church, and emphasizing, again and again, the necessity for 'ever speaking in Latin.' It is the content of the *Colloquies* that is of most interest for us. They show that almost continuous interfusion of learning and religion— *eloquens et sapiens pietas*—which, present in most of the earlier humanists, becomes a prominent feature in the writings of educationalists after the time of Luther. What is of still more interest is the delegation of nearly all the duties of the master to monitors. Elected once a month, they had disciplinary and house duties : they supervised studies and games, as well as attendance at school and church. Cordier seems to have had the qualities which beget confidence and trust, and to these qualities he added a modest self-reliance. He was an Arnold before Arnold's day.[2]

[1] *Op. cit.* p. 111.

[2] Charles Hoole writes of him in his *Epistle Dedicatory* of his translation of the Colloquies (*Maturini Corderii Coll. Scholastica Anglo-Latina* by C. Hoole, M.A., published London, 1657) : 'He underwent and performed the defatigating task of a Schoolmaster . . . he spent many private hours (stolen as it

The use made of the *Colloquies* by Cordier was decidedly educative. After explanation of a passage the boys were encouraged to act the various parts in turn and around them a living conversation developed which probably ' transferred ' much more readily to the outer world than do most of our ' direct ' lessons of to-day. That Cordier understood youth is evident from many of his lighter touches. Haggi,[1] for example, can't lend Simeon his Vergil because Gerard pawned it for threepence ! Castrensis avers that he knows more than might be expected from three Popish priests—a boast that would seem to be justified if he really performed all the actions which form the subject of conversation in Cordier's book ! Many modern teachers would wish for pupils of such commendable diligence as the following dialogue indicates : [2]

' PU. Master, may I speak a word with you ?

PAE. Speak boldly.

PU. I and my school fellows have been fast at our Books almost this three days together. May we refresh ourselves with a little play ?

PAE. Say some sentence, then.

PU. Interpone tuis interdum gaudia curis
Ut possis animo quemvis sufferre laborem.

PAE. Say the English verses, too, if you remember them.

PU. Mirth with thy labour sometimes put in ure
That better thou thy labour mayst indure.'

seems from his time of sleep and recreation) in providing such helps for his children as might ease himself and encourage them in the difficulties of learning, and though he knew well enough many jeered to see a man of his parts and years thus to busy himself in such boyish matters, yet he so far addicted himself to teach little ones that for their sakes he condescended to any, even the meanest, undertaking.' Hoole gives the right setting for labours of this kind in ' An advertisement touching Cato (*Disticha de Moribus*) and some other schoolbooks translated by him ' : ' For I know very well that the proportioning of things taught to the learner's just capacity, and the ordering of present documents in relation to the past and future, so as to help the memory to retain the one and prepare the understanding for receiving the other, still carrying on his affections to covet more is a mere slight, and yet a master-piece in our profession, which indeed it is very difficult to discourse on, if not impossible to discover. . . . *Scire quid deceat est caput artis, quod nulla arte docetur* is very true in school-teaching.'

[1] *Ibid.* p. 42. [2] *Ibid.* p. 13.

And for monitors like the following : [1]

> M. 1. ' Now that the master's absent, boyes, forbear
> To talk such words as God may much offend.
> Treat rather of your books, and honest things
> And use such words as thereto fitly tend.
>
> 2. ' Run often over what you are to say,
> *The Master cannot very like be by*,
> Learn well to trace the steps of honest men,
> I with sweet pleasures draw you not away.
>
> 3. ' Lo ! I forewarn you, trifle not your time :
> Lest you for doing so be whip't full sore,
> See, I the Monitor give you warning fair,
> Let none that's whipt lay th' blame on me, therefore.
>
> BRISCANTEL. ' Say you no more, here's none but will obey
> For God himself's a monitor to us :
> And his dear son, whose name is Jesus Christ
> And that good Spirit, which daily keeps us thus.

The Master's speech to his ' five publick monitors ' reads like an ordination service ! [2]

' You are not ignorant with how great feare of the Lord, I chose you yesterday in our common-hall.   We began with devout prayers ; our admonition followed, and our exhortation to all the company of scholars touching the fear of the Lord, and touching manners which become scholars which are daily at the school ; and then I chose you five not without the approbation of the best youths, whom I thought fit for this employment ; at last of all we came to the later prayer and a thanksgiving.   Do not, therefore, think that action, in which the name of the Lord hath been called upon so seriously to be a play or a jest.   And although this function seem both base and abject with them that are unskillfull and proud ; yet do we think that service of yours to be both honourable and holy. But if you shall think otherwise, it cannot be that you should rightly discharge your office. . . .'

An exhortation follows in which the monitors are warned against partiality, hatred, favour, revenge, and threats.   After which one of the monitors returns thanks, prays that Christ would always increase his gifts ' in the most kinde maister,' and earnestly desires a written copy of the exhortation so that by reading it often they may fasten it the better in their memories.

---

[1] *Maturini Corderii Coll. Scholastica Anglo-Latina* by C. Hoole, M.A., published London, 1657, p. 96.

[2] Hoole, p. 222.

These and similar methods [1] show the humanist's substitution of educative authority for the submission to ecclesiastical authority characteristic of the Middle Ages.

The influence of the great religious movements of the period upon the problem of freedom must now be briefly considered. Guizot characterized the movement initiated by Luther as ' a vast effort made by the human mind to achieve its freedom.' Its direct effect upon educational theory and even upon educational practice, apart from methods and systems of school organization, seems however to have been negligible. On this point Professor Adamson writes : ' The ecclesiastical revolution was the first step towards general liberty of thought ; but it was a very short step. It amounted to no more than this, that in Protestant regions it was permissible to deny the opinion which had been current for centuries and, under very strict limitations, to hold a different opinion. But in itself the new doctrine was as intolerant as the old.' [2] The short step was short because of the issues involved. For, however the Reformation worked out in practice, its underlying principle was ' freedom to obey the dictates of a conscience illuminated by the Word of God,' and the illumination involved pulpit instruction and Bible study. Thus the new freedom, so far as it existed, expressed itself mainly through a system of linguistic teaching, and the history of education at this time is a witness to the difficulty of relating the teaching of languages to the pupil's *free* powers of thought. Most modern methods of teaching languages are, indeed, to be found in Erasmus' suggestions for the reform of linguistic education in his day, but the time for carrying them into effect had not yet come. Perhaps it has not fully come in our own day.

As a rule the Reformers were in sympathy with humanism. Their first concern, however, was to give instruction that would make a man really ' wise unto salvation.' The times

---

[1] Cordier was not alone in anticipating the monitorial system of the nineteenth century. One of the Reformation leaders, John Sturm, rector of the Gymnasium at Strasburg, made use of a tutorial system by which the elder pupils taught the younger. Cf. Schmidt : *Jean Sturm*, p. 301. Valentin Trotzendorf, another of Luther's followers, introduced an extensive system of self-government on the plan of a Roman republic. Each class was divided into tribes ; there was an elective system of senators, censors, and questors. (*Mon. Ger. Ped.* Bd. lvii).

[2] *A Short History of Education*, p. 136.

demanded efficient methods. It is, therefore, to Luther's
credit that he recognized the value of liberal arts ' not only as
harmless but . . . of benefit for understanding the Holy Scriptures and carrying on the civil government,' that he saw the
value of ' schools where pupils would hear the history and
maxims of the world, and see how things went with each city,
kingdom, prince, man, and woman,' where, ' in a short time,
they would be able to comprehend, as in a mirror, the character,
life, counsels, undertakings, successes, and failures of the whole
world from the beginning.' It is still more to his honour that
he recognized the ' natural desire ' of children for learning, and
interpreted their delight in acquiring knowledge, whether
language, mathematics, or history, as a ' gracious arrangement
of God.' [1]

The society founded by Loyola is of particular interest for
our problems. Its breadth of studies, the efficiency of its
teaching, and the charm and learning of its teachers were
admitted even by its enemies. Men of intellectual distinction,
united by a vow of religious devotion to a common aim, and
sacrificing everything to the attainment of it, the Jesuit Fathers
gave the utmost care and thought not only to problems of
method and organization, but to the gaining of their pupils'
affections. Obedience was strictly enjoined, but the Prefects
of studies were to secure the pupils' love and confidence along
with it. Even in the earliest records there is evidence of
individual treatment and of a wise choice of means and methods
of influence.[2]

The underlying concept of the Jesuitical system is *religious
obedience.* Any freedom that the teacher or the pupil enjoys
is to be found within this conception. Its relation to freedom

[1] Luther, *A Letter to the Mayors and Aldermen of all the Cities of Germany*
(1524). In the later Puritan movement the short step of the Reformers
becomes an advance with liberty as part, at least, of the marching orders.

[2] Cf. Bader, *Mon. Ger. Ped.* ii. (Pachtler, p. 411) . . . . ' in defectibus eorum
sint longanimes et patientes ; noverint prudentes quaedam dissimulare vel
certe differre in tempus commodius.' The reasons for insisting upon intellectual capacity in the class room rather than upon merely intellectual abilities
include one of the earliest and best points in favour of a professional training
of teachers. ' There is no describing how much amiss Preceptors take it, if
they are corrected, when they have already adopted a fixed method of teaching.' Cf. *Mon. Ger. Ped.* v. p. 154, n. 6.

must therefore be considered at some length. Four main reasons are assigned for its central position. Three of these, unity of administration, permanent association of teachers, and unity of purpose are ultimately dependent upon the uniformity implied in the fourth. This uniformity is thus stated by the Rev. T. Hughes in his book on *Loyola and the Educational System of the Jesuits* : ' The truly obedient man is most prompt to execute whatever duty is assigned to him by one, whom, as by a religious act, he regards as being in the place of God and signifying to him God's will : wherefore obedience and heroism go together.' [1] This is an alluring proposition and as stated it is indisputable. But when one brings it down to the concrete facts of education, to the growing mind of a pupil in contact with values partially outside his experience, doubts arise.

Do the teacher's presentations really signify to the pupil God's will ? Has the teacher *quâ* teacher any credentials that lead the pupil to regard him as taking the place of the Deity ? Socrates was once faced with these questions and his honest scepticism found only one answer to them.

On the first point the Jesuits join issue with those who think that God reveals himself in many ways. ' Nothing can imperil more the harmony and efficiency of an educational organization than disagreement of opinion on the function and act of teaching.' The educator has a definite object, ' the equipping of fresh young spirits with principles of thought and habits of life to enter fully appointed on their paths of duty.' The professor in his chair ought not to mistake himself for the author in his study. He may test his private opinions in conference with equals but not on pupils. No one may follow new opinions in matters which pertain to religion without consulting the Superior or Prefect of Studies. ' The sifting of many opinions by the varied and multiplied activity of many minds leaves a residue of matter quite solid enough to support a compact and reliable system of teaching.' [2]

This argument assumes a ' residue ' of accepted didactic material which our survey of the history of education scarcely justifies. Where it is really found (as for example in mathematics) the will of the Deity does not seem to be very relevant.

---

[1] *Op. cit.* p. 49.
[2] *Op. cit.* p. 228.   Cf. also pp. 143, 148.

Where differences of opinion exist the presentation of compendious views does not seem to be the most efficacious means of reaching the truth about reality. A residue of learning without the emotional background of differences which give it actuality is likely to be a lifeless mass of ideas coherent and logically connected, no doubt, but without any really vital influence on a developing mind. The lack of real motive in early studies is admitted by the Jesuits. Its place is taken by an appeal to emulation. Rivalry disguises the aridity of school work. As Father Hughes puts it : ' In the dry course of virtue and learning, satisfaction of this kind is not excited in the young without a sign, a token, a badge, a prize. Then they feel happy in having done well, however little they enjoyed the labour before.' [1]

In opposition to this view we would venture to cite, as a later established fact of educational history, the existence of ' pleasurable ' schemes of early education, which do not appeal to signs, tokens, and prizes, and also to suggest that emulation is not a panacea for the inherent dryness of educational work. It is rather a means of arousing the pupil's deepest desires for excellence in the performance of pleasurably toned tasks. To appeal to it merely as a solvent of drudgery is likely to withdraw the pupil's attention from his task and to focus it upon an unhealthy comparison of the self with others. In the prosecution of agreeable tasks these results are not so likely to be found, for the energies are directed to the doing of something worthy of the self as well as of others. A system that makes abnormal appeal to emulation is one that forgets the truth of Erasmus' contention that all living things develop according to their own nature.

In considering the teacher's claim to the religious obedience of his pupils it is fair to appeal to Origen's view of the reason or intelligence as a self-directive as well as a submissive faculty. Where it is, it is of its *own* nature. A *teacher* has no other title to obedience than that which he gains by appealing to his pupils' reason and intelligence. It is in the harmony of the pupils' reason *and* obedience that freedom is found. No matter, therefore, how solid and final the ' residue ' of accepted knowledge may be, the wise teacher will present it as at least

[1] *Op. cit.* p. 90.

partially fluid and plastic. This is admitted by the Jesuit
Fathers. ' They hold that, upon a basis of concord, there is
always room and liberty for the exercise of talent : first, in
those questions which are manifestly indifferent ; secondly, in
thinking out new distinctions and reasons, whereby truths
already certain may be made more secure still ; thirdly, in
attacking the same, either when publicly disputing, or also
when actually teaching, if what they acutely urge against a
position, they more acutely refute ; fourthly, in proposing new
opinions and questions, but after they have sought the approval
of the responsible authorities, lest the labour be spent amiss.
The most learned men have always been persuaded that there
is more subtlety shown, more applause merited, and comfort
enjoyed, in pursuing the lines of approved and received thought,
than in a general license and novelty of opinion.' [1]   These are
very important admissions but their reservations are also very
striking. It is not merely that they confine the freedom of the
intellect to a carefully defined circle of ideas, for in practice
everyone's freedom has to be found within some circumference.
The restrictions lie in the fixation of the *results* of thinking.
The details of the pattern are allowed to vary but the broad
design must remain the same. The emphasis is placed on
subtlety in disputing and refuting propositions that are brought
forward to be disputed and refuted. There is no clear place
for the intelligence that is there of its own nature, or the search
for truth, *coûte que coûte*. The denial of these in the interests
of religious obedience would for many souls be the death both
of obedience and religion. Not that human reason is to be
placed on a pedestal : the Fathers are on sure ground in
encouraging the individual to bring the efforts of his mind to
the touchstone of authority and to the human formulations of
truth. They are wise in requesting their teachers to consult
responsible authorities before offering personal opinions. But
before the consultation and after it there is only one thing
that convinces any man of error or truth—the light of his own
reason. Whether this converges to, or diverges from, the
reason of his fellow men, it is the only light that can show
up the final path of religious obedience. He may sometimes
wander from the path taken by other men and yet not really

[1] Hughes, *Loyola*, p. 229.

err. The Aristotelian maxim, *Perfectum est quod generat simile sibi*, may have great force in a system of education convinced of its direct continuity with the source of perfection, but plain men may be forgiven for noting that God's perfection did not lead Him to create what William James called a ' block ' universe. The idea of perfection through individual differences has a safer historical sanction than that of a religious uniformity.

Michelet's phrase ' the discovery by man of himself and of the world ' has been quoted as peculiarly relevant to the Renaissance. The works of Castiglione, Ascham, Elyot, and Mulcaster bear testimony to a conception of individuality in some respects fuller and richer than that of the early Humanists. All agree in extending education so as to include the fine arts and courtesy along with learning and scholarship. Two main reasons are given for the extension : Castiglione, in particular, is the advocate of a larger freedom than mere humanism or accomplishments could provide. Ascham and Elyot are keenly aware of the deleterious effect of school studies. The first complains that they mar men's wits, ' change men's manners over sore,' ' make them unfit to live with others and unapt to serve in the world ' ; [1] the second that many ' good and clene wittes of children be nowe a dayes perisshed by ignorant schole maisters,' [2] and that a ' noble childe by his owne naturall disposition and not by coertion ' [3] may be induced to receive perfect instruction in such studies as music, painting, and sculpture. Mulcaster, at a later date, insists that one of the proofs of a good *Elementarie* is to resemble nature in the multitude of abilities and to follow her lead in teaching—for as she

---

[1] *The Scholemaster* (Arber Reprint), p. 34.

[2] *The Governor* (Everyman Edition), p. 69.

[3] *The Governor* (Everyman Edition), p. 31. Compare the extension of the curriculum suggested by Ascham (*The Scholemaster*, pp. 64, 66) : ' To ride cumlie ; to run faire at the tilte or ring : to plaie at all weapones : to shote faire in bow, or surelie in gon : to vaut lustely : to runne : to leape : to wrestle : to swimme : to daunce cumlie : to sing, and playe of instrumentes cunnyngly : to hawke : to hunte : to playe at tenness, and all pastimes generally, which be ioyned with labor, used in open place, and on the daylight, conteining either some fitte exercise for warre, or some pleasant pastime for peace, be not onelie cumlie and decent, but also verie necessarie, for a Courtlie Ientleman to use.'

is ' unfrindlie, wheresoeuer she is forced, so is she the best gide
that anie man can follow, wheresoeuer she fauoreth.' The main
argument is that ' natur makes a childe most fit to excell in
manie singularities, so theie be furthered and aduanced by
elementarie train in the younger years.' [1]

In 1575 a rather remarkable book was published by Dr. Juan
Huarte. It was entitled *Examen de Ingenios*, and although it
was not translated into English until a century later, it must
have influenced the educators of that time, many of whom
would have been prepared for its point of view by the writings
of Erasmus and Vives. It anticipates Rousseau's exposure of
the uselessness of school studies. Learning is a snare to the
feet of the fool and as manicles to his right hands.[2] Arts and
sciences are also chains to fetter the minds of fools rather than
to dispose them to be more free. The main point of the book,
as the title indicates, is the need for ' trying the wits ' of children before prescribing their studies—a view re-stated seven
years later by Mulcaster in the proposition that it is more
important to settle who is to learn than what is to be learnt.
' If I were myself a master,' says Huarte, ' before I received
any scholar in my school, I would sift him narrowly, to find if
I could what kind of Genius he had.' If the pupil passed the
test he would be accepted willingly ; [3] if not, Huarte would
implore him for God's sake to waste no more pains but seek
out some other ' way to live ' that requires not such abilities as
learning. When the inclinations and tendencies had been discovered the pupil would be required to apply himself wholly to
the study most agreeable to his capacity. But there would be
no undue haste. The beginnings of the negative attitude to
education appear in references to Hippocrates' analogies between the development of ' wits ' and the growth of seed. The
husbandman must wait the proper seed-time.[4] Periods of
development and studies appropriate to them are discussed at
some length. Galen's experiments on the newly-born kid that
refused ' wine, water, vinegar and oyl ' and accepted milk are
reviewed, and at the conclusion of a discussion which reveals

---

[1] Mulcaster's *Elementarie* (Ed. by Professor Campagnac), p. 30.
[2] *The Tryal of Wits* (Trans. by Bellamy, 1698), p. 25.
[3] *Ibid.* p. 35.
[4] *Op. cit.* p. 38.

Huarte as seeking for the bearing upon education of what we should now call reflexes and instincts, he records the conviction that underlies many conceptions of freedom in education. ' Souls are directed what to do without the Teaching of any Master.' [1] The naturalistic tendency usually attributed to Rousseau, begins here if it did not really begin with Erasmus and Vives. The divisions of the mental operations into memory, imagination, and understanding, the subdivisions of these functions, and the classification of studies according to the functions they involve [2] are not unlike the *general* treatment of the *Emile*.

We have already referred to Mulcaster's ' choice of wits most fit for learning.' In his *Positions* he states the natural powers or abilities of children, finding in them also ' an ability to discern what is good and what is ill which ought forthwith to be made acquainted with the best by obedience and order and dissuaded from the worse by misliking and frown.' Then he adds the empirical rule which for so long expressed the view of the practical schoolmaster with regard to freedom. ' But for the best waie of their good speede, that witte maie conceive and learne well, memorie retaine and hold fast, discretion chuse and discerne best, the cheife and chariest point is, so to plie them all, as they may proceede voluntarily, and not with violence, that will may be a good boye, ready to do well, and lothe to do ill, never fearing the rod which he will not deserve. For wheresoeuer will in effecting, doth ioyne with ability to conceive and memorie to retaine, there industrie will finde frute, yea in the frowne of fortune.' [3]   Mulcaster does not think his use of the voluntary principle will banish the rod. It ' may no more be spared in schooles than the sworde may in the Prince's hand.' A ' sharp maister ' who will make boys learn

---

[1] *Op. cit.* pp. 106, 112 ff. The translation, however, is rather ' free.' The text of *Examen de Ingenios*, cap. 7, edition 1640, p. 7, gives *erudita est natura licet recte facere non dediscerit*, without any reference at that point to Hippocrates, but with a reference to Galen. The text of Galen (*de locis affectis*, lib. vi. p. 135) reads : *Hippocratem vere dixisse animalium naturas esse indoctas.*

[2] Those acquired by the memory are Grammar, Latin and all other Languages, Theory of Law, Positive Divinity, Cosmography and Arithmetic ; by the Understanding, School Divinity, Logic, Natural and Moral Philosophy, Practice of Law ; by the Imaginative (or inventive) powers, studies that depend upon Figure, Correspondence, Harmony, *e.g.* Poetry, Rhetoric, Music, Mathematics, Astronomy, etc.

[3] *Positions*, by Richard Mulcaster (ed. R. H. Quick), pp. 27, 28.

what will afterwards be of service even though they are unwilling at the time, is to be preferred to the ' vaine shadow of
a curteous maister.' . . . ' It is slauish sayeth Socrates to be
bet. It is slauish then to deserve beating sayeth the same
Socrates. If Socrates his free nature be not found, sure
Socrates his slauish courage must be cudgelled, euen by Socrates
his owne confession. . . . A wise maister . . . will helpe all,
either by preuenting that faultes be not committed, or by well
vsing whensoeuer they fall out, and without exception must
have both correction and curtesie committed unto him beyond
any appeal.' [1] If Mulcaster retains the rod he uses it only for
''lewdness ' and laziness.

The need of a principle that would ensure efficiency may be
illustrated by a brief reference to one of the early books of the
seventeenth century, the *Ludus Literarius* of John Brinsley.
It gives the usual lip-service to the school as a place of play,
but the detailed discussion of the matter and methods of
linguistic teaching show the operation of a ' meet and loving
feare, furthered by wise severitie to maintain authoritie.' In
truth, the Grammar School of the day was a ' *Ludus a non
ludendo*, a place void of all fruitlesse play and loytering ' if
Philoponus fairly represents its teaching. But the period had
glimpses, at least, of a more courageous freedom. Some seventy
years before the publication of Brinsley's book, at the time
when Sadoleto's and Elyot's views were given to the world
Peter Ramus had shocked the universities by declaring that
all Aristotle's teachings were false, and, true to his principle of
freeing education from authority, had sketched a new organization of school work which in our days we should probably
describe as a modified Dalton plan.[2] Lectures, individual
study and discussions alternated. One hour's work by the
teacher to five hours' work by the pupil briefly describes the
method by which Ramus sought to free school children from
the fate of the guests of Heliogabalus.

We have described the period covered in this chapter as
one of mal-adjustment. Its labour and futility, as well as its

---

[1] *Positions* (Quick), p. 277.
[2] Cf. F. P. Graves, *Peter Ramus and the Educational Reformation of the
Sixteenth Century.*

imperfect fusion of old and new elements are well depicted in Rabelais' kindly, if satirical, chapters on education.   Pantagruel's education is relatively prosaic.   He has time for play, for the chronicles of his ancestors, for law, and tennis, and the seven liberal arts.   He makes good progress, for he has a memory capacity ' equal to the measure of twelve oyle budgets or butts of olives.'   He is, therefore, fitted to become the 'abysse and bottomless pit of knowledge,' which not inaptly expresses the aims of the Renaissance.   He is to know Greek, Latin, and Hebrew for the Holy Scripture's sake, Chaldee and Arabic likewise.   All history is to be in his memory, and books of Cosmographie, as Elyot advocated.   The influence of Erasmus and Vives appears in the study of Nature in addition to the usual liberal arts.   Through it the ' abysse ' receives all the material to be found in the heaven above, in the earth beneath, and in the water under the earth !   The learning of warfare and chivalry and other exercises, representative both of the Renaissance and of mediaeval education, form part of Pantagruel's programme.[1]

Some critics suggest that *Gargantua* was an afterthought : Rabelais, finding that *Pantagruel* was well received, set himself to write a still more satiric introduction to his earlier satire of the encyclopaedic education of his day.   His aim may have been to suggest that the encyclopaedic programme of studies, so energetically administered by Ponocrates, necessitated an even closer supervision of the pupil than the older systems represented by Sophister Master Tubal Holophernes and the coughing Jobelin Bride.   Ponocrates is monk and sophister in one.   He cleanses the perverse habits of the brain and dissolves the memory masses which the earlier treatment had crystallized.   But the new treatment is almost as cloistral and is much more exacting.   Four o'clock in the morning brings the masseur and the reading of the Holy Scriptures.   Prayers, explanations, repetitions ;   dressing to the accompaniment of a lecture upon the estate of man ;   three hours' lecture—so interesting that it is the sole topic of conversation in the following play hour.   Rabelais cannot refrain from crystallizing the Renaissance view of liberty into a single pregnant sentence.

[1] *The Works of Rabelais* (1653 trans. Navarre Soc.), book ii. chaps. 5, 6, 7, 8 (pp. 188-207).

' All their *play*,' he writes maliciously, ' was but in liberty for they left off when they pleased, and that was commonly when they did sweat all over their body.' Rehearsal of lectures in the changing room ; the history of warlike deeds as an aid to digestion ; ' object ' lessons with quotations from classical authors showing the virtue, propriety, efficacy, and nature of everything that was served. . . . Cards not for amusement but as a means of learning a thousand tricks of Arithmetic, Geometry, and Astronomy. . . . Singing in five parts and the playing of half a dozen instruments, writing, riding, and some hundreds of games. . . . Further walks, with the inevitable reference to the views of the ancients on tree and plant and meadow. . . . Dinner to the accompaniment of another reading lesson. . . . Games and astronomical observations—then recapitulation of everything learned during the day ! And all this, says Rabelais, in his mildest way, although at the beginning difficult, became a little after ' so easie and so delightful that it seemed rather the recreation of a king than the study of a scholar ! ' [1] Did Rabelais despair of reform in education or did he think it unnecessary ?

Some see in the Abbey of Thelema Rabelais' view of a really free society. It had no abbot, no statutes, no laws. Its one regulation may have suggested to Rousseau the idea of education sketched in *Emile* : ' In all their rule and strictest tie of their order there was but this one clause to be observed : Do what thou wilt. (*Fais ce que vouldras.*) Because men that are free, well borne, well-bred, and conversant in honest companies, have naturally an instinct and spurre that prompteth them unto vertuous actions, and withdraws them from vice, which is called honour. Those same men, when by base subjection and constraint they are brought under and kept down, turn aside from that noble disposition by which they formerly were inclined to vertue, to shake off and break that bond of servitude, wherein they are so tyrannously inslaved ; for it is agreeable with the nature of man to long after things forbidden, and to desire what is denied us.' [2] It is worthy of note that Rabelais did *not* transfer this idea to his educational schemes.

[1] *Op. cit.* book i. chaps. 14, 15, 21, 22, 23, 24.

[2] *Op. cit.* book i. chap. 57.

Rabelais' chapters are a true epitome of the Renaissance movement in education. It began, as with Pantagruel, in an appeal to human values and with the attempt to 'follow nature.' It tried, like Ponocrates, to vitalize the old methods of grammatical study by the substitution of living for inert ideas. It soon showed the dependence upon authority and formal methods characteristic of the mediaeval period. It professed to fit the curriculum to the individual capacities : in reality it increased rather than diminished the number of studies. There was much discussion about their order but it resulted in a more closely filled time-table. There was a clearer perception of the futility of *mere* learning. Grammatical and other exercises were related to the living wholes into which they naturally entered, but the result was often as ludicrous as Ponocrates' concentration of study upon the breakfast table and his correlation of Vergil with country walks. There was some perception of the natural means of self-expression, but the vernaculars and the studies which utilized them were regarded as excitations and recreations of the mind,[1] accessories which must not be allowed to stand in the way of linguistic studies. There were laudable attempts to connect education with the activities of the outer world, but the union of the old and the new was imperfect and it appeared only in the person of a king, a prince, a governor, or a courtier. Men were groping after a combination of ' real ' and ' linguistic ' studies but timorous of crystallizing the union into a new and substantive form of universal education. There was an array of learning without the real depth and unity of vital knowledge. Physical, aesthetic, and even moral forms of education found a place, but they were not closely related to the main educational scheme. There was the same vagueness in the conception of the teacher's attitude to freedom. Severity and even minute supervision were seen to have baneful effects upon the native desires for learning and upon the moral nature of the pupil. Gentleness and courtesy and a degree of liberty were, however, regarded as the best means and guarantors of an enhanced efficiency in education. There was, as in Rabelais, an attempt to utilize the native tendencies so as to expedite the

[1] Cf. A. Coutaud, *La Pédagogie de Rabelais*, p. 98 : ' Chez les Jésuites on accordait une demi-heure par jour au français et aux études accessoires.'

process of learning, and to make the natural impulse to play, and even some forms of repulsion, real factors of development. But, as we have also seen in Rabelais, there was no clear and explicit recognition of freedom as a guiding and directing principle of an educational activity designed to produce free men. This idea appeared in the writings of Michel de Montaigne.

CHAPTER VIII

MONTAIGNE'S FREEDOM THROUGH MILD SEVERITY

MONTAIGNE, like Rabelais, is a keen critic of the futility of education. 'Whence it may proceed, that a minde rich in knowledge, and of so many things, becommeth thereby never livelier nor more quicke-sighted ; and a grose-headed and vulgar spirit may without amendment containe the discourse and judgment of the most excellent wits the world ever produced I still remaine doubtfull.'[1] As plants are choked by excessive moisture and lamps dimmed by too much oil, so the mind seems to be overwhelmed by continued study. It loseth the means to spread and clear itself and its surcharge keepeth it low-drooping and faint. 'We labour, and toyle, and plod to fill the memorie and leave both understanding and conscience emptie. Even as birds flutter and skip from field to field to pecke up corne, or any graine, and without tasting the same, carrie it in their bils, therewith to feed their little ones; so doe our pedants gleane and picke learning from bookes, and never lodge it further than their lips, only to disgorge and cast it to the wind.'[2] We may become learned by other men's learning but we can never be wise but by our own wisdom. 'Except our mind be the better, unless our judgment be the sounder, I had rather my scholler had imployed his time in playing at Tennis.'[3] Thus does Montaigne insist that learning and knowledge must be not merely joined to the mind but incorporated with it.

In another essay he shows how he would exercise the judgment. The mistake lies in supposing that the pupil's task is to repeat what had been told him before. ' I would have a

---

[1] *Essays*, i. 25. Florio's trans. (1908 Ed. with Introduction by Thos. Seccombe), p. 151.

[2] *Essays*, i. 25. p. 155. [3] *Essays*, i. 25. p. 157.

148

tutor to correct this part, and that at first entrance, according to the capacitie of the wit he hath in hand, he should begin to make shew of it, making him to have a smacke of all things, and how to chuse and distinguish them, without helpe of others, sometimes opening him the way, other times leaving him to open it by himselfe. I would not have him to invent and speake alone, but suffer his disciple to speake when his turne commeth. *Socrates*, and after him *Arcesilaus* made their schollers to speak first, and then would speake themselves. *Obest plerumque iis qui discere volunt, auctoritas eorum qui docent.* (Cic. De Nat. I.). *Most commonly the authoritie of them that teach, hinders them that would learne.'* [1] For the first time the pupil really leads the way in education. Montaigne invites the tutor to make him ' trot on before him, whereby he may the better judge of his pace, and so guesse how long he will hold out, that accordingly he may fit his strength : for want of which proportion, we often marre all. And to know how to make a good choice, and how far forth one may proceed (still keeping a due measure) is one of the hardest labours I know. It is a signe of a noble, and effect of an undaunted spirit, to know how to second, and how far forth he shall condescend to his childish proceedings, and how to guide them. As for myselfe, I can better and with more strength walke up, than downe a hill. Those which according to our common fashion, undertake with one selfe-same lesson, and like maner of education, to direct many spirits of divers formes and different humours, it is no marvell if among a multitude of children, they scarse meet with two or three, that reap any good fruit by their discipline, or that come to any perfection.' [2]

It will be noticed that these passages anticipate Rousseau's negative ' education and that Montaigne raises the fundamental problems of education if he does not solve them. The pupil's spontaneity is taken as the starting point of education ; the teacher's offices are primarily determined by the pupil's reactions. Not that the teacher has an entirely negative rôle assigned to him. He has to trot along with the pupil and will, in the long run, be as breathless as his charge. He has sometimes to supply the motive for the race, and occasionally he may direct the race into paths which, without the teacher's

[1] *Essays*, i. 25. pp. 176-7.   [2] *Essays*, i. 25. pp. 176-7.

suggestion, would never be taken. But the activity must be the pupil's. ' It is a signe of cruditie and indigestion for a man to yeeld up his meat, even as he swallowed the same : the stomacke hath not wrought his full operation, unlesse it have changed forme, and altered fashion of that which was given him to boyle and concoct.' To change the figure once more : ' The Bees doe here and there sucke this and cull that flower, but afterwards they produce the hony which is peculiarly their own.'

To his keen perception of the teacher's difficulty in keeping the pupil trotting on before him—still keeping a due measure— Montaigne adds a vivid appreciation of the baneful effects of pedantry. ' Our minde doth move at others' pleasure, as tyed and forced to serve the fantasies of others, being brought under by authoritie, and forced to stoope to the lure of their bare lesson : wee have beene so subjected to harpe upon one string, that we have no way left us to descant upon voluntarie : our vigor and libertie is cleane extinct.' . . . ' In barring the pupil of libertie to doe anything of himselfe, we make him thereby more servile and more coward. Who would ever enquire of his scholler what he thinketh of Rhetorike, of Grammar, of this, or of that sentence of *Cicero* ? Which things thoroughly fethered (as if they were oracles) are let flie into our memorie : in which both letters and syllables are substantiall parts of the subject. To know by roat is no perfect knowledge.' [1]

Montaigne's exposition is, however, by no means a plea for eccentricity. In his Essay,[2] ' Of custome and how a received law should not easily be changed,' he deals at length with the rightful place of conservative tendencies, as well as with their different forms in different peoples. He gives an important place to the acceptance of restraint. Men, even when with great difficulty they have shaken off the importunity of a tutor, ' run to plant a new one with semblable difficulties, because they cannot resolve themselves to hate tutorship.' [3] And even though divers things received with undoubted resolution ' have no other anker but the hoarie head and frowning wrimples of custome,' strange and particular fashions proceed rather of folly or ambitious affectation than of true reason. A wise man

[1] Cf. *Essays*, i. 25. pp. 177 and 179.   [2] *Essays*, i. 22.
[3] *Essays*, i. 22. p. 125.

ought to ' retire his minde from the common presse, and hold
the same liberty and power to judge freely of all things, but
for outward matters, he ought absolutely to follow the fashions
and forme customarily received.' [1]

Great emphasis is given to the force and place of authority.
In *An Apology of Raymond Sebond* [2] several aspects of divine
and human authority are under review.   Montaigne insists that
' onely humilitie and submission is able to make a perfect
honest man,' that ' the first law that ever God gave unto
man was a law of pure obedience,' that ' to obey is the proper
dutie of a reasonable soule, acknowledging a heavenly and
superiour benefactor.'   He finds little, if any, ultimate
value in knowledge for its own sake.   ' Christians have a
peculiar knowledge, how curiosity is in a man a naturall and
originall infirmity.   The care to encrease in wisdome and knowledge was the first overthrow of mankinde : it is the way
whereby man hath headlong cast himselfe down into eternal
damnation.'   He asks whether man's long search after knowledge has enriched him with any new strength or solid truth ;
he is persuaded that all man has got from the pursuit
is the knowledge of his own weakness.   Those who are truly
learned are, like the ears of ripe corn, humble and dropping
downward : it is the empty ears that raise their head aloft,
upright and stout.   He has little commendation for those who
are lavish and unbridled in opinions.   ' In his study, as in all
things else, man must have his steps numbered and ordered.
The limits of his pursuits must be cut out by art.   He is bridled
and fettered with, and by religions, lawes, customes, knowledge,
precepts, paines and recompences, both mortall and immortall ;
yet we see him, by means of his volubility and dissolution
escape all these bonds.   It is a vaine body that hath no way
about him to be seized on, or cut off ; a diverse and deformed
body, on which neither knot nor hold may be fastened.   Verily,
there are few soules, so orderly, so constant, and so well borne,
as may be trusted with their owne conduct, and may with
moderation, and without rashness, saile in the liberty of their
judgments beyond common opinions.   It is more expedient to
give some body the charge and tuition of them.' [3]

[1] Cf. *Essays*, i. pp. 127-9.   [2] *Essays*, ii. 12.
[3] *Essays*, ii. 12. pp. 334-5.

But this oversight of the tutor has, by the very nature of things, its own limits. ' Whatsoever is told us, and whatever we learne, we should ever remember, it is man who delivereth, and man that receiveth : It is a mortall hand that presents it, and a mortall hand, that receives it. . . . We should remember that whatsoever we receive in our understanding, we often receive false things, and that it is by the same instruments, which many times contradict and deceive themselves.'[1] Tutor and pupil alike can escape the fickleness and mutability of the reasoning powers and neither is justified in setting himself above, or in cutting himself totally adrift from his fellows. ' To make the handfull greater than the hand, and the embraced greater than the arme ; and to hope to straddle more than our legs length is impossible and monstrous : nor that man should mount over and above himselfe or humanity ; for he cannot see but with his owne eyes, nor take hold but with his owne armes. He shall raise himselfe up, if it please God extraordinarily to lend him his helping hand. He may elevate himselfe by for-saking and renouncing his owne means, and suffering himselfe to be elevated and raised by meere heavenly meanes. It is for our Christian faith, not for his Stoicke vertue to pretend or aspire to this divine Metamorphosis or miraculous transmu-tation.'[2]

Montaigne quarrels with the education of his day because it is divorced from the pupil's natural powers of judgment. ' In my country and in my dayes, learning and bookishness doth much mend purses but minds nothing at all.' ' If it chance to finde them empty, light and dry, it filleth, it over-burthens and swelleth them : a raw and indigested masse : if thinne, it doth easily purifie, clarifie, extenuate and subtilize them even unto exinanition or evacuation. It is a thing of a quality very neare indifferent : a most profitable accessory or ornament unto a wel borne mind, but pernicious and hurtfully domageable unto any other. Or rather a thing of most precious use that will not basely be gotten, nor vily possessed. In some hands a royall scepter, in others some a rude mattocke.'[3] Thus Montaigne admits that natural powers need direction. At the same time he sees them to be the surest and safest data upon

[1] *Essays*, ii. 12. p. 342.   [2] *Essays*, p. 342, pp. 184-5.
[3] *Essays*, iii. 8. p. 199.

which education can work. The greater part of our life may be a vanity : our knowledge may in the end be a delusion, to possess it may belong to a greater power but ' we are borne to quest and seeke after truethe.' [1] The individual's efforts may be relatively fruitless, but his natural tendencies demand exercise : his surest way of life is to lean upon God, to give as free and as honest an expression of his natural powers as he can, always remembering his natural weakness and imperfection and keeping in close touch with his fellow men. Such seems to be Montaigne's general view of life.

His plea for freedom in education follows very directly from this philosophy. ' True perfect liberty is for one to be able to doe and work all things upon himselfe. *Potentissimus est qui se habet in potestate* (Sen. *Ep.* ix.).' [2] In the light of the above exposition it will be clear that this does not mean, as many critics have held, a *laissez-faire* policy in education. The very figure that Montaigne used to describe the pupil's action— trotting on—might have served to dispel that illusion. Yet an eminent literary critic, Emile Faguet, who is usually more concerned with the form of a great writer's views of education than with the virility of his ideas,[3] accuses Montaigne of basing his treatise upon such a policy. He writes in words which would inevitably suffer by translation :

' Aussi bien, voyez son traité de l'éducation. Il est séduisant comme tout ce qu'il écrit ; mais cassez donc l'écorce des mots et voyons ce qu'il y a au fond de ces propos charmants. Ce qu'il y a ? Ce dialogue : " Que faut-il apprendre aux enfants ? Heu ! mon Dieu ! ce qu'il faut apprendre aux enfants ? . . . Eh bien, rien du tout !—Hé ?—Oui, rien. Quand je dis rien. . . . Rien, comme vous pouvez penser, veut dire rien, ou peu de chose. Il faut les regarder apprendre ; les y exciter, un peu, oh ! très peu ; les guider insensiblement. Oh ! d'une façon tout-à-fait insensible. On n'est pas assez sûr que ce qu'on leur apprendra ne sera pas précisément ce qu'il aurait convenu qu'ils ignorassent ; et que la direction qu'on veut leur donner ne sera pas celle que leur nature d'esprit leur défend précisément de prendre. Aussi y faut-il une prudence extrême, et une circonspection qui doit aller presque jusqu'au laisser-faire et quasi jusqu'à ne faire rien. Laissez-les trotter devant vous. Je vous assure qu'ils trottent bien." '

[1] *Essays*, iii. 8. p. 200.   [2] *Essays*, iii. 12. p. 372.
[3] Cf. the comparison of Montaigne with Rabelais in Faguet's Preface to Guizot's *Montaigne : Études et Fragments*, pp. 14 ff.

Such a statement is unfair to Montaigne's general position. It omits all reference to his discouragement of eccentricity, to his disapproval of undue ' natural kindnesses ' on the part of parents, to his profound respect for law and custom, to his emphasis of obedience, to his recognition of the authority of the tutor, ' who should be soveraigne over the pupil,' [1] to his desire for instruction that should ' rule the pupil's manners and direct his sense,' [2] to his general view of the function of studies as giving the pupil a true knowledge of himself. ' This great universe,' he insists, ' is the true looking-glass wherein we must looke, if we will know whether we be of good stamp, or of the right byase . . . I would have this world's frame to be my schollers choise booke : So many strange humours, sundrie sects, varying judgments, diverse opinions, different lawes, and fantasticall customes teach us to judge rightly of imperfections and naturall weaknesse, which is no easie an apprenticeship.[3] This does not read like an education based upon a simple *rien*, nor does the following view of the scope of studies indicate a policy of *laissez faire* : ' What it is to know, and not to know what valour, what temperance and what justice is ; what difference there is betweene ambition and avarice, bondage and freedome, subjection and libertie by which markes a man may distinguish true and perfect contentment, and how far-forth one ought to feare or apprehend death, griefe, or shame.' [4]

Montaigne, it is true, does not give us any well thought-out or comprehensive scheme of studies but the positive and distinctive features of his pedagogy include the direction of the judgment, of the practical reason, and of the conscience. Although the extent and variety of his educational programme tend at times to suggest the training of the ' jeune seigneur,' he is insistent that his aim is not to produce a grammarian or a logician, but a complete gentleman. In agreement with other writers of the Renaissance period he selects from the liberal sciences those which make men free. They all serve for instruction, but he wishes to make especial choice of those which may directly and pertinently serve the purpose of freedom. This freedom, as we have seen, is not attained without

[1] *Essays*, i. 25. p. 182.   [2] *Essays*, i. 25. p. 191.
[3] *Essays*, i. 25. p. 189.   [4] *Essays*, i. 25. p. 190.

obedience, submission, restraint, and adaptation of the individual's values.[1]

In line with this broad view of freedom is Montaigne's view
that education should be directed by 'a sweet-severe mildnesse.'
Violence and compulsion are to be removed. ' There is
nothing that doth more bastardize and dizzie a wel-borne and
gentle nature. If you would have your pupil stand in awe of
shame and punishment, doe not so much enure him to it :
accustome him patiently to endure sweat and cold, the sharp-
nesse of the wind, the heat of the sunne, and how to despise all
hazards. Remove from him all nicenesse and quaintnesse in
clothing, in lying, in eating, and in drinking : fashion him to
all things ; that he prove not a faire and wanton-puling boy
but a lustie and vigorous boy.' Montaigne would away with
the severe discipline of the Colleges—' verie prisons of capti-
vated youth '—places in which one hears nothing but the bawl-
ing of tormented children and of masters besotted with anger.
' How wide are they, which go about to allure a child's mind
to go to his booke, being yet but tender and fearefull, with a
stearne-frowning countenance and with hands-full of rods !
Oh, wicked and pernicious manner of teaching ! ' He himself at six years old had ' gotten as pure a Latine tongue as
my Master could speake . . . without bookes, rules, or grammar,
without whipping or a tear.' He learnt Arithmetic and Geometry through play and exercise. By an unforced kind of will,
of his own choice, without compulsion or rigor he was brought
up in all mildness and liberty. His spirit was slow and sluggish, but when he left college he continued to read of his own
choice. Had his teacher been severe or dictatorial it is certain
he would have brought nothing from him but hate and contempt for books.[2]

So Montaigne is led ' to condemne utterly all manner of
violence in the education of a young spirit, brought up to
honour and liberty. There is a kind of slavishnesse in churlish-
vigor, and servility in compulsion ; and I hold, that that which
cannot be compassed by reason, wisdome and discretion, can
never be attained by force and constraint. So was I brought
up : they tell me, that in all my youth, I never felt rod but
twice, and that very lightly. And what education I have had

[1] Cf. i. 25. p. 190.   [2] Cf. *Essays*, i. 25.

my selfe, the same have I given to my children.' . . .   His
daughter, Leonora, had only gentle words as punishments, and
even had the results been less good Montaigne would have
considered his discipline just and natural.   If he had been the
father of boys he would have loved to store their minds with
ingenuity and liberty, for he had seen no other effect of the
rod than ' to make childrens mindes more remisse or more
maliciously head-strong.' [1]

In several ways Montaigne reinforces the claims of freedom.
He is the direct product of an education animated by it.   He
has noted at first-hand its value as a directive concept of early
instruction.   He has no hesitation in giving it a central place
in his philosophy of life and of education.   He realizes that the
authority of the teacher may be a hindrance.

His contribution to its meaning is worthy of note.   He emphasizes its essential reference to the self, to self-government,
to reason, to the operation of conscience.   He notes the
satisfaction that comes from the regulation of one's own
impulses, from the forming of one's own judgment, from the
testing and evaluation of opinions, and from persistent exercises in personal reflection.   He sees that to think rightly,
clearly, strenuously, persistently, is the surest means not only
to action but to right action ; not only the natural exercise of
the mind but the natural equilibrant of the passions.   His
emphasis of our proneness to error brings out the value of
the persistent search for truth : the free man is he who has the
power of continually testing the truth of his theories by applying them to himself.   To this end he pleads for direct contact
with reality, for the use of one's own senses and powers, for the
appeal to spontaneous effort.   He sees clearly that real freedom comes only through obedience to God and to man, that
it means neither licence nor eccentricity, that man left freely
to himself makes for himself a master and envisages for himself
an ideal which provokes him not only to further effort but also
to submission and reverence.   He sees the value of the teacher
who tries to place himself within his pupil's life, who is willing
to allow his pupil to speak, to think, and to act frankly and
naturally.   He sees that life is more than grammar or logic and
that, as he puts it, even Greek can be acquired at too great a

[1] *Essays*, ii. 8. p. 82.

cost, that the task of the teacher is not merely to form a mind, or a body, but a man. Finally, he looks from the height on the concrete tendencies of life, discerns their inner values, and focuses those which are central and essential. By emphasizing the vital forces in human activities he seeks to make the pupil more clearly aware of the fundamental aims of his being, and thus makes more and more possible that 'working of all things upon the self ' which gives a ' true, perfect liberty.'

CHAPTER IX

FREEDOM AND REALISM

THE earlier stage of the Renaissance movement was essentially a reinforcement of the human virtues and qualities as the central elements of education : in its own way an emphasis of realism. It degenerated into a formal study of language :

> ' . . . the trade in classic niceties,
> The dangerous craft of culling term and phrase
> From languages that want the living voice
> To carry meaning to the natural heart ;
> To tell us what is passion, what is truth,
> What reason, what simplicity and sense.' [1]

It is true that Latin was not an entirely ' dead ' language, but its disciplinary exercises often failed to give an adequate outlet for the *self*-expression of the pupil, or to influence his native impulses, or to guide his own gropings after truth. Teachers, like Mulcaster, aware of the defects of current practice, advocated instruction through the vernacular, and Rabelais and Montaigne, as we have seen, extended the scope of the curriculum so as to bring to the pupil a knowledge of himself and of the world, as well as of books. The Renaissance movement proper and the views of these reformers have at least one common characteristic. They stand for a more direct contact of the pupil himself with the educational material presented to him by a teacher. They are important steps towards freedom and have, therefore, been briefly treated in the previous chapters. In this chapter we are concerned with a further aspect of the pupil's contact with the means of his education : the directness which is usually associated with the term *sense realism*, and which, for our purposes, may be better designated

[1] Wordsworth, *Prelude*, Book vi. l. 109.

by Wordsworth's phrase—'the carrying of meaning' to the pupil—the direct appeal to his own sense of truth, to his own reason, to his own passions.

This movement was powerfully stimulated by the writings of Francis Bacon. In the *Novum Organum* he compares experimenters to the ant which collects the material it uses ; reasoners, like spiders, make cobwebs out of their own substance. Like Montaigne, he finds the oft-quoted reference to the transforming and appropriating powers of the bee an apt description of the union of the experimental and rational faculties. In his *Advancement of Learning* [1] he urges that direct activity of the mind increases both its receptivity and reliability. A blind man does not tread surer by a guide than a seeing man by a light. He is prepared to sanction the flights of imagination in the 'feigned history' which we call poesy, but sees in it 'a plant that cometh of the lust of the earth and spreads abroad more than any other kind.' The judicial place or palace of the mind 'where reason doth buckle and bow the mind unto the nature of things' deserves, in his opinion, more reverence and attention. [2]

Bacon suggested (in 1605) that if a man begins with certainties he will end in doubts, but if he is content to begin with doubts he will end in certainties. Descartes' *Discourse on Method*, published some thirty years later, elaborated Bacon's suggestion into a philosophy. Making up his mind to accept nothing as true that he did not see clearly to be true, Descartes sought for many years no other science than the knowledge of himself, and of the great book of the world. It occurred to him that he would find more truth in the reasonings of individuals in matters of personal interest than in the speculations of the learned. [3] After some years he resolved to make his own mind the object of study, and like one walking in the dark, to proceed cautiously so that any advance made would be sure and certain. To this desire to follow the truth whithersoever it led him Descartes united a sincere devotion to the authority of the church. He held, nevertheless, that neither his own intelligence nor that of any human being, should be the

[1] *Op. cit.* book i. especially § 2, 6, 7.
[2] *Op. cit.* book i. § 3.
[3] Cf. *Discourse on Method* (Everyman trans. p. 9).

object of external coercion, and that no one should be asked
to believe anything unless he were constrained to admit its
truth by the force and evidence of reason.[1] Man by his
very nature must reason : his innermost soul tells him that
his reasoning may be false, yet he may not abrogate the
exercise of his reasoning powers. This is Descartes' lesson to
the world.

Descartes' indirect influence upon education must have been
very great ; he definitely influenced the work of the Little
Schools of Port-Royal. There, in spite of a system of almost
complete surveillance, the animating conception was a direct
contact of the pupil with the problems of real life and a natural
union of the teacher's and the pupil's lives.[2] The Preface
to the Port-Royal *Logic* insisted, as Descartes did, that, while

---

[1] Cf. the final sentence of his *Principles*.

[2] The theological views of St. Cyran, the founder of the Little Schools, might
have led him to advocate a system of coercive education. He taught that the
devil possessed the soul of the child even before his birth and that, while
baptism restored him to a state of innocency, his corrupt nature made him
naturally prone to fall into deadly sin. Free-will was of no avail in the
salvation of the soul.   St. Cyran could not, therefore, have accepted Vergerius'
idea of following one's best instincts, or have agreed with Huarte that souls
are directed what to do without the teaching of a master. But the ideas of
Plutarch and Quintilian had by this time passed into the theory of education
and were beginning to exercise a vital influence on its practice. It was
recognized that freedom gave the most efficient conditions for the presentation
of any subject matter, sacred or secular.   The labours of such men as Erasmus,
Vives, and Vittorino da Feltre had done something to convince schoolmasters
that learning need not necessarily be an unpleasant task. Descartes and
Bacon had shown the efficacy of *individual* reason, and both had by implication, at least, found in it a responsiveness to the considered views of other
seekers after truth.   Thus it happens that teachers were led, like St. Cyran, to
advise praying rather than scolding, and speaking about their charges to God,
rather than talking about God to them.   Lancelot tells us that St. Cyran did
not like to weary children with precepts, but to confine their moral instruction
to the occasions and opportunities which God brings about, ' as indicated by
the impulses which He gives us and the willingness to hear which He shows us
in them ' (Barnard, *The Port Royalists in Education*, p. 115). Nicole urged
that moral instruction, though it should occupy the chief place in education,
should be imparted in a manner suitable to the age and ability of the pupils,
who, if possible, should know all the precepts of morality while scarcely knowing there is such a thing, for ' nothing makes less impression on the mind than
that which comes in the somewhat unwelcome guise of a lesson or instruction '
(Barnard, *op. cit.* p. 94).   The atmosphere of affection did not mean that the
pupil was relieved of effort.   Guyot's very sensible views seem to describe the
general practice of the Port Royal Schools : ' I cannot agree with those who
wish their pupils to become learned only at the expense of toil and trouble and
who, instead of relieving them, let them be weighed down by a thousand
unnecessary difficulties. I believe, on the contrary, that we ought to give

there is nothing contrary to reason in yielding to authority
in matters which are above reason, ' there is no ground whatever in human sciences, which profess to be founded only on
reason, for being enslaved by authority contrary to reason.' [1]
Mr. Barnard, in his interesting survey of the schools, describes
the Port-Royal system as a distinctly *moral* education based
upon the affection of the pupils. Yet it avoided direct lessons
on morality, being convinced of the efficacy of those incidental
appeals to reason which come from the contact of one personality with another in an atmosphere of confidence and
affection.

The combination of affection and directness of appeal, with
high religious motives, is also exemplified in the educational
schemes of Fénelon. Fénelon anticipates many of Rousseau's
ideas. He urges that there should be no haste in the early
years of education. It is better to strengthen the child's
organs than to press instruction upon him.[2] Reason develops
slowly, but the curiosity and restlessness of childhood if not
appropriately treated may be the occasion of a second ' original
sin ' which will impede the development of later life. Fénelon
notes the child's short span of attention. He compares the
youthful brain to a candle exposed to the wind. But although
he urges that we must be content with following and helping
nature [3] he does not think the teacher's function should be
negative. As the child's reason grows it must be exercised.
Encouragement must be given to his questions, and clear and
simple answers must be given to them. Further, appeal must
be made to the pupil's own perception of the value of reason :
the teacher will point out to him the greater strength of his
reasoning power this year as compared with last. Every effort
will be made to utilize youthful curiosity, this *penchant de la
nature qui va comme au-devant de l'instruction.* Without formal

them all the aid we can, and that we should make their work, if it is possible,
more pleasant even than their games and recreations. There will always be
enough other difficulties—whether they arise from our pupils' intellects or from
their inclinations and natural dislike for study—without our adding extra ones
of our own by the incompetent manner in which we set about teaching.'
(Barnard, p. 118).

[1] Bayne's trans. Discourse ii. p. 23.

[2] *Œuvres de Fénelon* (Ed. 1823, Paris, Label), tome xvii. p. 13.

[3] *Ibid.* p. 15.

lessons the most important facts of life may be pleasantly and naturally acquired. A country mill will serve for a series of lessons on food and harvesting. Fénelon's main prescription is to allow the child to play and to mingle instruction with his recreations.[1]

The directness and sincerity of Fénelon's general methods again suggest a comparison with the *Emile*. He insists upon absolute frankness in dealing with faults. He will even make out of the teacher's mistakes a means of instructing and edifying the pupil : he will take every precaution to show the reasonableness of the teacher's prescriptions, to make the pupil feel that pleasure will follow the drudgery of work, and that work will fit him for the duties of the world. Punishment will be the last of all expedients, and when it is necessary it will be administered in sorrow, as a last resort, and with commiseration for the pupil's lack of reason. Like Sadoleto before him and like Locke afterwards, Fénelon emphasizes the importance of the feeling of shame, but he has a really paternal affection for the child who is to suffer abasement. He makes use of the services of some reasonable person to dispose the pupil to return to the teacher and to repose confidence in him ; he tries to ensure that the pupil condemns his own wrong action. But the main emphasis is placed on the general pleasantness of the process of learning.

Here Fénelon anticipated the wisest and frankest moments of Rousseau. Formal lessons were to be replaced by ' *conversations gaies* ' ; everything that rejoiced the child's imagination was to be pressed into the teacher's service ; books were to be attractively bound and to be full of short stories. Writing was to be taught by simple and natural exercises. Free curiosity was to take the place of rules. Emulation and even jealousy were to be brought into play. From the earliest years a large measure of liberty was to be given so that the pupil might reveal his inclinations.[2] Before taking steps to correct children the teacher was to know them thoroughly.

Fénelon personally tested the worth of these theories in his attempts to educate the Duke of Burgundy, grandson of Louis XIV. The Duke was by nature a strong-willed, obstinate,

---

[1] *Œuvres de Fénelon* (Ed. 1823, Paris, Label), tome xvii. p. 21.
[2] *Ibid.* p. 38.

hot-tempered boy, but the *Dialogue des Morts*, the *Fables*, and the *Telemachus* gave such telling pictures of universal history, of an ideal state of society, and of the pupil's good and bad actions that he soon responded to their influence. They are noteworthy combinations of literary and pedagogical genius, remarkable both for their appeal to the play spirit and for their attractive presentation of abstract ideas in a concrete form. With these aids at his hand, Fénelon based all his lessons on the pupil's own conduct, anticipating in a very clear and convincing manner the discipline of natural consequences advocated later by Locke, Rousseau, and Spencer. But however much Fénelon's practice is in advance of previous advocates of freedom his conception of freedom adds little or nothing new. One sentence shows its aim and its depth : ' Let us change the (usual) order : let us make study agreeable ; let us hide it *under the appearance of liberty and of pleasure.*'[1] Directness of appeal, use of imagery, vivid presentation of abstract ideas, appeal to the imagination,[2] play and pleasurable activity are Fénelon's means of hiding study under the appearance of liberty.

Milton's *Tractate* may be regarded as the focus of the Puritan view of education. It is addressed to Samuel Hartlib, a Pole, who interested himself in philanthropic projects and in the views of English educationalists. Hartlib had persuaded Comenius to come to London, and the two, in conjunction with Hezekiah Woodward, John Dury, and Sir William Petty—one of the founders of the Royal Society—sketched a number of educational reforms mainly based on Baconian views. In these writers the influence of Comenius is clearly apparent, but our exposition must disregard the minor points of connection and influence.

It would have been strange if Milton, the defender of civil, ecclesiastical, and religious liberty, the advocate of domestic

---

[1] *Ibid.* p. 30.

[2] Cf. p. 50. Fénelon's use of ' *images sensibles* ' is borrowed from the methods of scripture, and is applied with a certain exuberance to the teaching of religion. Thus God is presented to children as seated on a throne; His eyes are compared to the rays of the sun and the flashes of lightning; His ears listen to everything; His hands support the universe; His arms are always raised to punish the wicked.

and personal freedom,[1] had not in some degree championed the cause of freedom in education.   His general view of freedom through obedience to a moral law apprehended by reason appears in *Paradise Lost*,[2] where he insists that true liberty

> ' . . . always with right reason dwells
> Twinned, and from her hath no dividual being.
> Reason in man obscured, or not obeyed,
> Immediately inordinate desires
> And upstart passions catch the government
> From reason, and to servitude reduce
> Man, till then free.'

In *Areopagitica* (written, like the *Tractate*, in 1644) he comments upon the restrictions of Plato's *Laws* and insists that freedom is part of God's plan for mankind.   When God gave man reason He gave him freedom to choose, for reason is but choosing. God left man free, set before him a ' provoking object ever almost in his eyes ' ; He created passions within and pleasures around him.   These rightly tempered are the very ingredients of virtue.   ' Banish all objects of lust, shut up all youth into the severest discipline that can be exercised in any hermitage ; ye cannot make them chaste, that came not thither so. . . . God sure esteems the growth and completing of one virtuous person more than the restraint of ten vicious.' [3]   In another of his writings he designates liberty as the best school of virtue and the man who is not content with equality of laws and rights as *ambitionis atque turbarum quam libertatis ingenuae studiosior*.[4]   Writing ten years after the *Tractate* he refers to his ' previous discussion of the principles of education . . . than which nothing can be more necessary to principle the minds of men in virtue—the only genuine source of political and individual liberty, the only true safeguard of states, the bulwark of their prosperity and renown.[5]   In the *Tractate*

---

[1] Freedom did entrust
  To his sure hand her two-edged blade :
  Which slays who wrongly asks its aid,
  And only serves the pure and just.
(From the *Plaint of Freedom* by an anonymous writer, 1852.)

[2] *Paradise Lost*, xii, 83-89.   Cf. also vi, 164-81, and *Comus*, 381-5.

[3] *Prose Works*, ii. pp. 74-5.

[4] *Second Defence of the People of England* (*ibid*. i. p. 294).

[5] *Ibid*. i. p. 259.

there is no *explicit* reference to that freedom of thought which Descartes and the Port-Royalists willingly conceded in secular subjects. Elsewhere he asks judges, law-givers, and teachers to note that he who would wisely restrain the reasonable soul of man within due bounds must first himself know perfectly how far the territory and dominion extends of just and honest liberty.[1] And, short as the letter to Mr. Hartlib is, it has several touches reminiscent of the ' smiles that flow from reason,' of the doctrine that even in learning :

> ' . . . not to irksome toil, but to delight
> He made us, and delight to reason joined.' [2]

The *Tractate* gives, just as in *Comus*,[3] two sets of pictures :

> ' How charming is divine Philosophy !
> Not harsh and crabbed, as dull fools suppose,
> But musical as is Apollo's lute,
> And a perpetual feast of nectared sweets,
> Where no crude surfeit reigns.'

On the one hand there is a view of the ' grammatic flats and shallows ' where pupils ' stick unreasonably to learn a few words with lamentable construction,' of the seven or eight years spent merely ' in scraping together so much miserable Latin and Greek as might be learned otherwise easily and delightfully in one year,' and of the ' tossing of unballasted wits in fathomless and unquiet deeps of controversy.' On the other, there is a picture of the ' right path of virtuous and noble education,' ' laborious at the first ascent yet smooth and green,' of pupils led and drawn ' in willing obedience,' ' inflamed with the study of learning and admiration of virtue,' ' despising their childish and ill-taught qualities,' and ' delighting in manly and liberal exercises.' [4]

The difference between the two is a difference of directness and utility. Errors lie ' either in learning mere words, or such things chiefly as were better unlearned.' ' A complete and generous education fits a man to perform justly, skilfully, and magnanimously all the offices both private and public, of peace

---

[1] *To the Parliament of England with the Assembly* (*ibid* iii. p. 175).
[2] *Paradise Lost*, ix. 242-3.
[3] *Comus*, 476-480.
[4] *Tractate* (*ibid*. iii. p. 465 ff.).

and war.'   But Milton does not merely state an aim of *education* in these objective terms.   Earlier in the *Tractate* he defines the end of *learning*—' to repair the ruins of our first parents by regaining to know God aright, and out of that knowledge to love Him, to imitate Him, to be like Him, as we may the nearest by possessing our souls of true virtue, which being united to the heavenly grace of faith, makes up the highest perfection.'   And as if he were conscious of the lack of contact of this idea with the natural life of the pupil, ruined as he sees it, he hastens to add : ' But because our understanding cannot in this body found itself but on sensible things, nor arrive so clearly to the knowledge of God and things invisible as by orderly conning over the visible and inferior creature, the same method is necessarily to be followed in all discreet teaching.' He follows up the advocacy of ' things first ' by showing the relation of linguistic to ' real ' studies.   ' And seeing every nation affords not experience and tradition enough for all kinds of learning, therefore we are chiefly taught the languages of those people who have at any time been most industrious after wisdom ; so that language is but the instrument conveying to us things useful to be known.   And though a linguist should pride himself to have all the tongues that Babel cleft the world into, yet, if he have not studied the solid things in them as well as the words and lexicons, he were nothing so much to be esteemed a learned man as any yeoman or tradesman competently wise in his mother dialect only.' [1]

---

[1] *Tractate*, pp. 52-3.   The details of Milton's Academy do not concern us ; it is sufficient to note the proposals for the teaching of such subjects as agriculture, natural philosophy, and physiology through classical authors, and for pressing into his pansophic scheme, ' the helpful experiences of hunters, fowlers, fishermen, shepherds, gardeners, apothecaries, architects, engineers, mariners, and anatomists.'   Bacon's works had stimulated the desire of men of his time to know all that was to be known of the world, and Milton's methods of giving a ' tincture of natural knowledge ' show that the pansophic idea was not so absurd as it may seem, at that, or indeed at a later, time.   An interesting account of an actual attempt to carry out some of Milton's ideas is to be found in a pamphlet appended to an edition of the *Tractate*, published in Edinburgh in 1819.   The author (Wm. Scott) describes the activities of an Edinburgh Academy close to the College in Lothian Street.   The students, having no director of studies and realizing the advantages of conversation and discussion, for the gaining of information and the acquiring ' of a certain degree of polish and good manners which a collision of gentlemen never fails to produce,' formed an association of young men preparing for the army, the navy, and other professions.   A detailed account of the method of studying

In Hezekiah Woodward's book[1] we have a good illustration of the union of puritanical conceptions of gentleness and affection with the direct appeal to the senses. The process of education is like the backing of a colt and the breaking of a skittish heifer, but calmness and gentleness are the best means of attaining its end. A marksman, says Woodward, does not hoot and bellow when he takes his aim. But the author would deal faithfully with the sins and faults of youth of which he seems to have a full knowledge. Pride and arrogance, ' the blowing up of this little bladder ' with prizes and ornaments are condemned. Idleness, ' the very rust and canker of the soul,' ' the Divel's cushion,' seems to be one of the characteristics of youth, but the exposition suggests that Woodward's views are based upon the current practice of the schools. He seems to have a keen sense of children's difficulties. ' In learning anything they seem to pull, as it were, at a dead thing. It is a great point of wisdom in the teacher to put some life into it that the child may see it stir, and coming onward, else the work may seem so hard to them that they can better bear the smart of the rod than the labour of the work ; then discouragements follow, such as make them hate the book before they know it.'[2] The suggestions for the enlivening of school work show the dual conception of directness at this time. In the first place, the teacher is advised to re-acquaint himself with a process of learning so that he may the better understand the pupil's difficulties and keep alive his own sense of ' unaptness.' Woodward's own plan of learning Hebrew while he taught Greek is forcefully if not very tactfully presented. He believes the teacher who goes too quickly for his pupil's understanding to be ' the verier childe ' and remarks that a man would ' hardly

several subjects is given. Electricity, for example, was taught by reading in Latin Dr. Gilbert's *De Magnete*, Beccaria gave a ' most clear and beautiful account of Dr. Franklin's theory.' The discoveries of Galvani and Volta were given as much as possible in the words of the original authors. This is declared to be the best and most logical way of teaching any science, for the student becomes acquainted with the original process of reasoning. Milton's note of caution at the end of his *Tractate* : ' This is not a bow for every man to shoot in that counts himself a teacher but will require sinews almost equal to those which Homer gave Ulysses,' makes the appropriation of the method by Scotsmen natural, if not inevitable.

[1] *A childes Patrimony laid out upon the Good Culture or tilling over His whole Man.*

[2] *Ibid.* p. 34.

think how it would calm a teacher ' to learn something new. Teachers forget how ' unapt ' they were when children ; learning something new would make their sense of it fresh again. The suggestion for ' calming ' the parent is to remind him that an elephant, or some imitating creature, may be taught more in a month than he hath learnt in a whole year.

In the second place, Woodward's ' good culture ' aims at ' tilling over the whole man by the well improving of the seed-time,' and the attainment of the aim is not in doubt if the right means are taken. His conception of direct contact with reality may be illustrated by a few of his aphorisms. . . . Speak to the senses. . . . They make report to the mind. . . . When you cannot carry the childe abroad to view the creatures, bring the creatures home to the childe. . . . Use illustrations. . . . Understanding and language are to develop along parallel lines. . . . Ask questions. . . . It will much enliven and quicken the childe's fancy to see it self joyned as a party in the work, though it is little it can do.

The problem of words *versus* things is one of the main topics of *Sir William Petty's Advice to Mr. Samuel Hartlib.* It is primarily a scheme for a Research College inspired, doubtless, by Bacon's works, but it deals at some length with the education of children. Petty would not have the ' educands ' wearied with ' hard Hebrew words in the Bible ' or with the ' repetition of heteroclitous nouns and verbs.' He would have them taught ' to observe and remember all sensible objects and actions,' whether natural or artificial, and would have the ' history of Faculties ' expounded so that before they become apprentices to a trade they may know ' what will and strength they have to it and not spend seven years in repenting and in swimming against the stream of their inclinations.' One paragraph so fully states the advantages of instruction through ' things,' and especially through the activities of boyhood, that it may be quoted at length :

' As it would be more profitable to Boyes to spend ten or twelve years in the study of Things, and of this book of Faculties, than in a rabble of words, so it would be more easy and pleasant to them, as more suitable to the natural propensions we observe in them. For we see children to delight in Drums, Pipes, Fiddles, Guns made of elder-sticks, and bellows' noses, piped keys, etc., for painting

Flags and Engines with elder berries and corn-poppy, making ships with paper, and setting even Nut shells a swimming, handling the tools of workmen as soon as they turn their backs, and trying to work themselves, fishing, fowling, hunting, setting springs and traps for birds, and other animals, making pictures in their writing books, making Tops, Gigs and whirligigs, quilting balls, practising divers juggling tricks upon the Cards, etc., with a million more besides. And for the females they will be making pies with clay, making their babies clothes and dressing them therewith, they will spit leaves on sticks, as if they were roasting meat, they will imitate all the talk and actions which they observe in their Mother and her gossips. . . . By all which is most evident that children do most naturally delight in things, and are most capable of learning them, having quick senses to receive them and unpreoccupied memories to retaine them. As for other things whereunto they are nowadays set, they are altogether unfit for want of judgment which is but weake in them, and also for want of will, which is sufficiently keen, both by what we have said before, by the difficulty in keeping them at schools and the punishment they will endure rather than be altogether debarred from this pleasure which they take in things.' [1]

John Dury's [2] *Reformed School* has many ideas in common with the education given by the religious societies of France. The detailed supervision of the pupils—some of whom were later to be teachers—is almost monastic in its rigidity, but the chief rule of the establishment is that nothing is to be tedious or grievous to them. Seriousness of study, careful observation and treatment of each pupil, simple and direct measures of restraint, delightful and varied studies are all to be combined. Laws are to be drawn up regulating looks, angry words, hasty actions, and everything tending to a breach of Christian love ; rules concerning justice, equality, meekness, humility, love, etc., are to be hung up in the pupils' chambers ; monitors and ' spyes ' are to be appointed with disciplinary powers ; the laws of truth and faithfulness are to be inculcated, civility and courtesy to be encouraged, and a seemly carriage of the body is to be required.

---

[1] *The advice of W.P. to Mr. Samuel Hartlib for the advancement of some particular parts of learning. Op. cit.* p. 12. (The pagination is defective : it should be p. 24.)

[2] Also written Durie. The British Museum copy of Dury's work gives no date. *The Reformed Librarie Keeper* (a supplement to *The Reformed School*) is dated 1650.

The regulations of the actual work of learning are more liberally conceived. Faults of current education are noted—the learning of words and sentences before any notion of their meaning is acquired, the learning of rules apart from the matter to which they apply, the drawing of fine and subtle distinctions, whereby the mind is ' puffed up with a windy conceit of knowledge, and the affections are taken off from the plainness of useful truths, and the pupils are left incapable of receiving any truth in its simplicity.'

Some of Dury's ideas regarding the aim and means of education are of interest for freedom. The end of all human learning is, in his opinion, to supply the defects of our ignorance and to remedy the natural lack of order which characterizes our use of the natural faculties. Nothing, therefore, is true learning which is not serviceable to the individual. It follows that nothing should be taught until the pupil understands the purpose of learning it and the way in which he will use it when it is learnt. The sciences, or parts of learning, must be arranged in the order of their dependence upon one another and taught in that order. If Dury recognizes the possibility of conflict between these two principles he tries to avoid it by formulating a single, fundamental, undeniable maxim of all teaching: '*The whole way of understanding must be made answerable unto the nature of the end and proportionate unto the property of the means and parts of learning.*'[1] His discussion of these means and parts shows that he is more concerned with the way in which the mind adapts itself to them than with the logical dependence of the parts (or sciences) on one another. The three means are sense, tradition, and reason. Dury brings the movement towards ' directness ' to its logical conclusion by laying down as a general law that *any art or science that can be received through the senses should be taught in no other way, and further that whatsoever can be made obvious to the senses should be taught first.*

Three factors condition the teacher's work. The first is the capacities and natural powers of the pupil. Here Dury follows the main conceptions of writers like Huarte, but he insists more clearly on the senses as the first means of development. Sense is the servant of imagination, imagination of memory and memory of reason. The faculties of children ' break forth

[1] *Op. cit.* p. 40. *Italics* mine.

in them by degrees,' and ' are to be filled with objects whereof they are capable.'

The second conditioning factor is the nature and order of the subjects taught, and the third (which, as we have seen, is to remove any conflict between the first two) is the use of a method which is economical, orderly, easy of apprehension, and delightful to the pupil's affections. Success is assured if the capacities are filled with proper objects, if nothing capable of being received by the capacities is left untaught, if no time is lost in teaching, if nothing is presented before it is required, if everything is well joined with what follows, if the conjunction of all the lessons lead the individual without distraction to his true end. Finally, comes the condition which to Dury's mind must have been the test of the smooth working of all the others, and the condition of the single maxim of teaching quoted above: '*If no servile constraint is laid upon the inclination of him that is taught, by forcible means to break his spirits but his affections are raised by a delightful willingness to receive that which is offered by allurements and generous insinuations readily.*' [1] And Dury adds that if these conditions be all observed little or nothing will be wanting that can be supplied by rational endeavour and humane industry. This is a large claim, but with the exception of the earlier conditions (which receive a needed correction in the pages of Rousseau) there is no more adequate statement of the determinants of success to be found in the history of education. For the first time the pupil's freedom (in the sense of absence of servility) is explicitly stated to be one of the essential factors of success in the art of teaching.

The conditions enumerated above do not give the impression that Dury's *chief* concern was the ' filling of the capacities ' or the logical arrangement of subject-matter. This view is confirmed by a study of his method of teaching languages. For the pupil in the second of the three stages of education he advocates a concentric method of learning. Pupils of eleven traverse again the earlier subjects of study, adding Hebrew terms to objects already named and described in Latin and Greek. The close association of language with concrete objects is noticeable, but the development of the language lesson around the object is the noteworthy feature of Dury's method. A

[1] *Op. cit.* p. 50. *Italics* mine.

general notion of it is first given ; a study of its parts follows. A second stage draws attention to the properties of the parts in their relation to the whole ; a third ' looks upon the Action or Passion, or fitness to Action or Passion which ariseth from the frame and properties of the whole and its parts ' ; a fourth deals with the use, properties, and actions of the thing in relation to man.   Grammatical rules in relation to properties come still later, although appropriate linguistic exercises appear in the earlier stages.   The experimental study of children's methods of learning by Stern and others gives substantial confirmation of the psychological accuracy of the order suggested by Dury, and most modern methods of early linguistic teaching embody his suggestions.

Dury, in short, definitely prefers the psychological to the merely logical method of teaching and views his subject-matter in its life setting.   Both of these criteria of directness are illuminated by his writings ; the second may fairly be said to be his own idea.   Very few writers have succeeded in giving more valuable help in one paragraph than he gives in the following :

' Two things are fundamentally to be heeded in the manner of proposing everything.   First, that the scholars before the thing is proposed be made sensible of the End, wherefore it is taught them, and they ought to learn it, viz. what the necessity, use, excellency and perfection thereof is in the life of Man, etc. Secondly, that the way of offering it unto them be the same at once to all, by all alike perceptible, common, plain, distinct and orderly in every part.   And to these two fundamentals whereof the first relates unto the will, the second unto the understanding, a third may be added relating to the memory which is that in the method of proposing everything this Rule be observed : Let the generall notion of every object or the shape of the whole be first offered to the imagination and then the parts which are contained under it to be represented unto the thought by way of division and this being done, let the mind afterwards be led retrograde to review the parts as they look toward another and make up the whole by collection.   And at the conclusion of every lesson a brief and summary Recapitulation of that which hath been offered unto them is to be proposed and the Question should be asked whether any hath a doubt of anything, or would have something repeated, or further explained that they should speak.'[1] Finally, a suggestive list of ways and means of 'entertaining the things taught '—through writing, painting, and drawing exercises, and translations is offered.

Although Comenius deservedly holds a high place among educationalists of the seventeenth century his contribution to freedom has little of distinctive value. He synthesized and elaborated the views of his predecessors, gave them practical shape, partially anticipated the lines of advance of succeeding thinkers, but added little that was really new. His views and Ratich's, for example,[2] are very similar. There is the same emphasis of everything according to the order and course of nature, of teaching everything without tears or violence, of uniformity in method, of graded studies, of the use of the senses ; of everything through induction as these writers misconceived it.

Two inconsistent sets of ideas seem to exist side by side in Comenius' pages. His great desire of ' teaching all things to all men ' is responsible for a certain magnification of the teacher's office and a consequent emphasis of the pupil's passivity. Thus he writes : ' The teacher should never step up to any one scholar or allow any one of them to come to him separately, but should remain in his seat where he can be seen and heard by all, just as the sun sends forth its rays over all things. The scholars, on the other hand, must direct their ears, eyes and thoughts towards him and attend to everything that he tells them by word of mouth or explains by means of his hand or of diagrams.'[3] Again he writes : ' With a little skill it will be possible to arrest the attention of the pupils, collectively and individually, and to imbue them with the notion that (as really is the case) the mouth of the teacher is a spring from which streams of knowledge issue and flow over them, and that whenever they see this spring open, they should place their attention like a cistern beneath it, and thus allow

---

[1] *Op. cit.* p. 72.

[2] Cf. the summary of the two writers' views given (after Schmidt and Von Raumer) in Laurie : *J. A. Comenius*, pp. 35 ff.

[3] *The Great Didactic* : trans. by Dr. Keatinge, p. 166.

nothing that flows forth to escape.' [1]   Here it is assumed that attention is a capacity which can be filled with streams of knowledge, just as Dury conceived each of the capacities to be filled with appropriate objects.   Attention is essentially passive, and so with the other capacities.

On the other hand, the main idea of the *Magna Didactica* is to ' follow the footsteps of nature ' in presenting knowledge to the pupil.   The intellect is not to be forced to any study ' to which its natural bent does not incline it in accordance with its age and the right method.' [2]   Comenius elaborates the idea of the ' little skill ' that arrests attention and formulates a number of excellent rules of teaching, amongst others the entertaining and interesting of the pupils, the connection of new knowledge with previous teaching, the importance of making the pupil realize his lack of knowledge, the practical application of what is learnt, the use of sense material, the questioning of the whole class, the effective treatment of the inattentive pupil.   In this ' daily training of attention ' there is an appeal to the active powers of the mind, to the pupil's interests and desires, to his instincts and bodily activities.   On the whole, however, Comenius has little sympathy with the individual difficulty or the individual question.   He is so obsessed with the idea of *all* things for *all* men that he loses sight of the actual pupil confronted with a specific task.

Is Comenius an advocate of formal or disciplinary education ? In the *Great Didactic* he writes thus :

' Such a daily training of the attention will not only be of momentary use to the young, but will stand them in good stead throughout their whole lives.   For if this training last for some years, and they get into the habit of concentrating their minds on whatever is being done at the time, they will continue to do so of their own accord without any external pressure.   If schools are organized on this principle, surely we may look forward to a considerable increase in the number of clever and intelligent men ! ' [3]

The answer seems to depend on the amount of ' *external* pressure ' that enters into the daily training.   Mental discipline assumes a certain mental receptivity in virtue of which external pressure produces definite or fairly definite results.

[1] *The Great Didactic :* trans. by Dr. Keatinge, p. 166.
[2] *Ibid.* p. 127.   [3] *Ibid.* p. 168.

One of these is the adoption of a mode of expression which is not primarily initiated by the self. But when we enquire into the conditions under which the external pressure begins to be really operative in the individual we are forced to admit that there can be no other starting point than the native or already acquired tendencies of the mind. They are the only possible springs of growth and the only forces upon which a disciplinary exercise can work. Their existence is often forgotten by the advocates of disciplinary education.

Daily exercises that provoke the pupil's interests, desires, curiosity, and spontaneity will undoubtedly tend to concentrate his mental activity on the task of the moment. Repeated and continuous acts of concentration may lead, under favourable circumstances, to the formulation, or the unconscious operation, of an ideal of industry. In this way, as Professor Bagley [1] has shown, there may be a ' spread ' or ' transfer ' of training from one school activity to another, and from school exercises to the tasks of later life. But the possibility of transfer depends upon the extent to which the full *spontaneous*, self-directed activity of the pupil enters into the items of his daily training. The ' external pressure ' that ' gives the habit of concentrating ' upon the task of the moment is merely a means of arousing *some* impulse in the mind that without pressure will remain dormant. If the impulse aroused is sufficiently vital, and if it is capable of finding further expression in the other exercises which enter into the pupil's training, it will tend to 'spread.' These conditions are very unlike those suggested by Comenius' idea of the cistern.

In other passages the conditions seem to be stated in very different terms. Thus :

' Now no discipline of a severe kind should be exercised in connection with studies or literary exercises, but only where questions of morality are at stake. For, as we have already shown, studies, if they are properly organized, form in themselves a sufficient attraction, and entice all (with the exception of monstrosities) by their inherent pleasantness. If this be not the case, the fault lies, not with the pupil, but with the master, and if our skill is unable to make an impression on the understanding our blows will have no effect. Indeed, by any application of force we are far more likely to produce a distaste for letters than a love for them. Whenever,

[1] *The Educative Process*, pp. 210 ff.

therefore, we see that a mind is diseased and dislikes study, we should try to remove its indisposition by gentle remedies but should on no account employ violent ones. . . . Such a skilful and sympathetic treatment is necessary to instil a love of learning into the minds of our pupils, and any other procedure will only convert their idleness into antipathy and their lack of interest into downright stupidity.' [1]

In this passage the pupil's mind and powers are active, and ' external pressure ' is recognized to result in a ' spread ' that is by no means calculated to increase the number of clever and intelligent men.

So far, in this discussion, we have made little reference to the natural unity of the powers of the mind—a quality likely to be overlooked by writers, like Comenius, concerned with the parcelling out of the elements of pansophy.   Both in subject-matter and in mental activity Comenius emphasizes ' elements.' ' A carpenter,' he insists, ' does not begin by teaching his apprentice to build turrets, but first shows him how to hold the axe, to cut down trees, to shape planks, to bore holes, and to fasten beams together.   A painter does not make his pupil commence by painting portraits, but teaches him how to mix colours, to hold the brush, and to make lines ; then to attempt rough outlines and so on.' [2]   But this ' step by step ' advance is certainly not the ' order of nature ' unless the relation of each step to the whole is, in some measure, apparent to the pupil. Comenius, like many of his successors, fails to see the importance of *meaningful* elements.   Dury's exposition of the point is much more sound.   The following paragraph shows that the idea of a serial development of faculties, so prominent in Rousseau's *Emile*, was also beginning to exercise the minds of educational writers :

' Our faculties are best developed in the following manner. The object should first be placed before the organs of sense on which they act.   Then the internal senses should acquire the habit of expressing in their turn the images that result from the external sensation, both internally by means of the faculty of recollection and externally with the hand and tongue.   At this stage the mind can begin to operate, and by the processes of exact thought, can compare and estimate all objects of know-

---

[1] *Magna Didactica*, p. 250.　　　　[2] *Ibid*. p. 196.

ledge. In this way an acquaintance with nature and a sound judgment may be obtained. Last of all, the will (which is the guiding principle in man) makes its power felt in all directions. To attempt to cultivate the will before the intellect (or the intellect before the imagination, or the imagination before the faculty of sense-perception) is mere waste of time. But this is what those do who teach boys logic, poetry, rhetoric, and ethics before they are thoroughly acquainted with the objects that surround them. It would be equally sensible to teach boys of two years old to dance, though they can scarcely walk. Let our maxim be to follow the lead of nature in all things, to observe how the faculties develop one after the other, and to base our method on this principle of succession.' [1]

On the other hand, it must be pointed out that Comenius, in many passages, emphasizes the value of natural wholes. He thinks that children should, for the sake of amusement, be given tools, be allowed to imitate different handicrafts, and to play at farming, at soldiering, at politics, at architecture, etc. They should be taken into the country in spring and taught the various species of plants. The titles of doctor, licentiate—of field marshal, general, captain—of king, minister, chancellor, etc.—might be given them as an encouragement to play.[2] This recognition of elements as they exist in life situations is far removed from the idea of a succession of faculties exercised by appropriate material. Comenius argues, too, that every language and science should first be learnt in its simplest rudiments or elements; afterwards rules, examples, exceptions, and irregularities may be presented. But he tends to think of the elements as principles which should carry meaning to the pupil just because they are fundamental parts of the meaning of the whole for the adult.

On the whole, Comenius does not seem to have been an advocate of disciplinary or formal training, but his pages show very clearly the conflicting ideas which underlay the educational theory of his day. It had shaken itself loose from the shackles of a compulsory and perfect system of political values, from the rigid ecclesiastical control of the mediaeval period,

---

[1] *Magna Didactica*, chap. xxvii. 7 (Keatinge, p. 257).

[2] *Ibid.* chap. xix. 49 (Keatinge, p. 179). Cf. also the condemnation of ' words ' apart from things (p. 177).

and from the broader and narrower views of a universal or liberal education associated with the humanist movement. But these compulsions had merely yielded place to the compulsion of learning all things. With the latter came the idea of capacities to be filled, a notion which is, in essence, much more utilitarian and specific than formal or disciplinary. But the pansophic idea is probably the root and origin of the extreme views of education which are supposed to exemplify the fallacy of formal training. It was destined to be an illusion. When seen to be a dream, it was likely that the idea of capacities to be filled should be supplanted by that of faculties to be sharpened. Formal training originated not, as some suppose, when linguistic studies could no longer be justified as subjects of school instruction on the ground of their value for the dissemination of knowledge,[1] but when the active notion of pansophy was realized to be impossible, and when the underlying idea of passivity implied by Dury's and Comenius' doctrine of capacities no longer found the sympathetic ministrations of equally affectionate teachers. It was supported by early views of the mind as a succession of faculties, and by the pedagogical maxim of following nature, found in such writers as Erasmus and Comenius. But Comenius' view of nature is really a view of freedom. He sees her enthroned side by side with the schoolmaster on the elevated platform which he considers so essential to the teacher's success. She is really the invisible teacher that turns the pupil's 'cistern' of attention to the visible teacher's words. The latter may greatly dare when he has this unseen aid. And if Comenius shows a childlike simplicity in materializing his vision of nature we must remember that he is not the first or the last writer to imagine that nature's way of forming a mind is simpler and plainer than it actually is.

In this chapter we have a clearer definition of the rôles of teacher and pupil. The teacher's is much more negative, the pupil's much more positive than in the previous periods. The experimental investigation of nature is followed by an honest attempt to investigate the pupil's nature and to state the main facts of his development. To these facts the teacher is com-

[1] Cf. Monroe, *History of Education*, p. 505.

pelled to bow. The conception of nature as a teacher deepens
the desire to understand the aims and methods of her teaching.
Three results are noteworthy :

(1) The relationship of the pupil to his studies becomes more
    direct and personal. He himself is brought directly
    into sensory contact with the outer world, and his
    further studies are developed out of this contact.

(2) The content of his studies is presented not, as before,
    almost entirely in definite terms of human aspiration
    —activities fit for a philosopher or a king, a governor,
    or a prince—but as truths gleaned directly from nature,
    collected and synthesized by the operation of men's
    minds upon the facts of experience, and concretely
    presented to the senses of a *human* being. Nature
    makes all men brothers in a new sense.

(3) Emphasis is placed on the pupil's *mental* activity, and
    particularly on his reasoning, and language is recog-
    nized to be not an end in itself but the vehicle and
    the incarnation of thought.

The teacher appears as a mediator between the pupil and
nature (in the Baconian sense of the term). The results of
psychological analysis and of the study of youthful development increase rather than diminish the affection for the pupil
advocated for various reasons by preceding writers. The study
of nature itself gives a new view of education which, as it is
interpreted by a writer like Comenius, induces an attitude of
respect for the gradual maturing of the child's powers. Liberty
is definitely stated to be *one* of the conditions of successful
teaching. But men's minds are groping towards these truths
rather than possessed of them.

CHAPTER X

LOCKE'S FREEDOM FOR 'INDIFFERENT ACTIONS.'

LOCKE's writings reinforce the claims of realism set forth in the previous chapter. As they have been somewhat fully discussed we propose in this chapter to concentrate directly upon his doctrine of liberty. To this subject he gives considerable attention in his *Essay on the Human Understanding*, and in his two pedagogical works : *Thoughts Concerning Education* and *The Conduct of the Understanding*.

The view of liberty in the later editions of the *Essay* is of secondary interest for education. The object of Locke's discussion is an enquiry into the notion of the term *power*. Although he admits the idea of ' passive power ' or the capacity to receive impressions from external agents,[1] he limits his exposition to the active use of the term. The exclusion makes his view of liberty applicable to only a part of education. It is, however, an important part, for, sooner or later, the reception of ideas must be followed by the activity of which Locke writes.

In the *Essay* both liberty and the will are *powers*, but they have different functions. (1) By the will he means the power which directs the operative faculties of the mind to the producing, continuing, or stopping of any action in so far as that action is dependent on us. This is not a free power : the will is determined by some ' present uneasiness ' which is, or is accompanied with, that of desire. Total deliverance from pain is the *main* determinant of desire and a necessary part of our happiness. Every good, nay every greater good, does not always affect desire, the satisfaction of which may be suspended until we have examined whether it is consistent or inconsistent with our happiness. The result of our judgment upon that

---

[1] Cf. *Essay*, xi. 21. The above account follows the treatment of Locke's second and subsequent editions. See Fraser's edition, vol. i. p. 367, for the quotations in the text.

examination determines the will. (2) Liberty is the power to act or not to act according as the mind directs. A man is not free if his will is determined by anything but his own desire, guided by his own judgment. . . .

'I consent to say,' writes Locke, 'that liberty is placed in indifferency ; but it is an indifferency that remains after the judgment of the understanding ; yea, even after the determination of the will ; and that is an indifferency not of the *man* (for after he has once judged which is best, viz. : to do or forbear, he is no longer indifferent) ; but an indifferency *of the operative powers of the man* which remaining equally able to operate or to forbear operating after as before the decree of the will, are in a state which, if one pleases, may be called " indifferency," and as far as this indifferency reaches a man is free and no further. *E.g.* I have the ability to move my hand, or to let it rest ; that operative power is indifferent to move or not to move my hand ; I am, then, in that respect perfectly free. My will determines that operative power to rest ; I am yet free, because the indifferency of that my operative power to act or not to act, still remains . . . the indifferency of that power to act, or not to act, is just as it was before, as will appear if the will puts it to the trial, by ordering the contrary. But if during the rest of my hand it be seized by a sudden palsy, the indifferency of that operative power is gone and with it my liberty ; I have no longer freedom in that respect, but am under a necessity of letting my hand rest.' [1]

The notion of an 'indifferent' ability, it will be observed, is supported by examples of actions like the opening and closing of the hand, which are relatively speaking of little value for intellectual or moral development. The real significance of liberty, however, lies *not* in the power to do or not to do something, but in the more explicit *ability of doing what one wills*, the important actions of life being willed actions, the indifferency or reversal of which cannot be contemplated with so great equanimity. Locke seems to admit this in some of his passages. Thus he asks : 'How can we think anyone freer than to have the power to do what he will ? . . . In respect of actions within the reach of such a power in him a man seems as free as it is possible for freedom to make him.' [2] Thus expressed, Locke's idea of freedom has important bearings on education. It is, as Pro-

[1] *Essay*, ii. 21. 73. Fraser, vol. i. pp. 368-9. (See note 2 at end of this chapter.)

[2] *Essay*, ii. 21. 21. Fraser, vol. i. p. 325.

fessor A. C. Fraser points out, ' the necessitarian idea of a free agent . . . that of freedom from obstruction in executing what we have willed.' [1]   For the present, we may keep an open mind as to its sufficiency.   We may feel with Leibniz : ' Quand on raisonne sur la liberté de la volonté, on ne demande pas si l'homme peut faire ce qu'il veut, mais s'il y a assez d'indépendance dans sa volonté même ; on ne demande pas s'il a les jambes libres ou les coudées franches, mais s'il a l'esprit libre et en quoi cela consiste,' yet recognize in it a suggestive theory for freedom in education.

The main point of the definition is the reference to ability or power, and Locke's treatment is valuable in so far as it draws attention to a fundamental, negative condition of freedom.   If the pupil is unable to perform the actions we require, we tend to arouse in him not only a most acute sense of unfreedom but one also of antagonism.   It is the conjunction of impotency and antagonism that makes the failures of education.   As Locke insists : ' Wherever restraint comes to check power, or compulsion takes away indifferency of ability on either side to act, or to forbear acting, there liberty and our notion of it presently ceases.' [2]   When restraint is recognized to be due to personal inability, a peculiar sense of unfreedom results, as Adler and others have recently shown.   If it is aggravated by forms of compulsion which do not allow the pupil to express the dictates of his own will, we have conditions that inevitably lead either to servility or to active opposition.

Again and again in the *Thoughts*, Locke draws attention to the mistake of commanding pupils to do what they can not do. The charging of their memories with rules and precepts [3] which they cannot understand is one of the most glaring forms of this mistake.   What is required must be suited to ' the child's natural genius and constitution.' [4]   ' He that is about children should well study their natures and aptitudes, and see, by often trials, what turn they easily take, and what becomes them ; observe what their native stock is, how it may be improved, and what it is fit for ; he should consider what they want, whether they be capable of having it wrought into them by industry and incorporated there by practice, and whether it

[1] Fraser, vol. i.   Footnote to p. 329.   [2] *Essay*, ii. 21. 10.   Fraser, pp. 317-8.
[3] *Thoughts*, 64.   Ed. J. W. Adamson, p. 44.   [4] *Ib.* p. 46.

be worth while to endeavour it. For, in many cases, all that we can do, or should aim at, is to make the best of what nature has given, to prevent the vices and faults to which such a constitution is most inclined, and give it all the advantages it is capable of. Every one's natural genius should be carried as far as it could ; but to attempt the putting another upon him, will be but labour in vain ; and what is so plastered on, will at best sit but untowardly, and have always hanging to it the ungracefulness of constraint and affectation.'

In the *general* exposition of the *Thoughts* Locke gives equal prominence to the pupil as an active *agent* and as a *recipient* of the ideas of others. In the early sections he firmly insists that the ability to govern the appetites must be acquired. Like Plato, he believes that he who does not submit to the reason [1] of others in youth will not be likely to submit to his own reason when he grows up. The principle of all virtue is to deny ourselves the satisfaction of desires unauthorized by reason. ' Children should, therefore, be used to submit their desires and go without their longings even from their very cradles. The first thing they should learn to know should be that they were not to have anything because it pleased them but because it was thought fit for them.' [2] The authority of the father is to be early established. ' Liberty and indulgence can do no good to children : their want of judgment makes them stand in need of restraint and discipline.' [3] But this strictness is to be relaxed gradually ; fear and awe are to yield place to love and friendship, which alone enable us to hold power over minds. ' Every man must some time or other be trusted to himself and his own conduct, and he that is a good, a virtuous, and able man must be made so within. And, therefore, what he is to receive from education, what is to sway and influence his life, must be something put into him betimes, habits woven into the very principles of his nature ; and not a counterfeit carriage, and dissembled outside, put on by fear, only to avoid the present anger of a father, who perhaps may disinherit him.' [4]

It will be noticed that Locke brings together two partially conflicting ideas—submission, ' something put into the pupil,'

[1] *Thoughts*, p. 30.   [2] *Thoughts*, p. 31.
[3] *Thoughts*, p. 32.   [4] *Thoughts*, p. 34.

awe and fear on the one hand ; on the other, liberty, the expression of natural abilities and powers, love and friendship. How does the external force produce the internal effect ? Locke does not answer the question. On a necessitarian view of freedom it is not difficult to answer. Compulsion is merely an addition to the number of determinants of the will. All that Locke's theory requires is that the external determinants should be effective in delivering the pupil from some pain or uneasiness, or that they should arouse some strong desire. Amongst the sources of uneasiness he includes instincts, such as anger, and appetites such as hunger and thirst. In the early stages of education the parent and the teacher have many opportunities of alleviating uneasiness, and they are therefore likely to influence very strongly the directions in which the will is determined. It is for reasons like these, no doubt, that Locke early begins to exercise compulsion and inflexibly maintains it until awe and respect, submission and ready obedience become habitual. When these are established a certain indulgence may be granted.

The later pages of the *Thoughts* are a plea for freedom unusually strong and sustained for a markedly unemotional writer like Locke. He states fairly the dangers of compulsion and of too great liberty. ' *To avoid the danger that is on either hand, is the great art ; and he that has found a way, how to keep up a child's spirit, easy, active, and free ; and yet at the same time to restrain him from many things he has a mind to, and to draw him to things that are uneasy to him ; he, I say, that knows how to reconcile these seeming contradictions, has, in my opinion, got the true secret of education.*' [1] Freedom is here—by implication at least—regarded as a fundamental concept of education. Its dangers are regarded as difficulties to be solved, and the solution is to be found in a view of freedom that unites activity, ease, a measure of restraint, and a measure of sympathy with the values of others. It is still in harmony with the idea of the *Essay* (power to do what we will) but it indicates the means by which the will is to be influenced.

Locke, however, gives only an indication. He explains why the usual measures are abortive. Corporal punishment fails to add any motives that can vitally influence will. It merely

[1] *Thoughts*, pp. 35-6. *Italics* mine.

makes corporal pleasure or the avoidance of pain into a principle of determination. It sets up an opposition to the very
means of influence which we wish to establish. It increases
the appeal of forbidden things. It breaks the spirit. Rewards
flatter and feed inclinations that should be starved or controlled. To have *educational* influence, rewards and punishments must be *moral* consequences of the pupil's actions.
They must form part of a coherent whole permeated by
reasonableness.

Here we reach the nerve of Locke's theory of education. In
the earlier sketch of his view of liberty we found that ' freedom '
is really a determination of will by desire, or by a feeling of
uneasiness guided by judgment. Locke, perhaps inconsistently
with this view, urges that free agents may *suspend* volition
during deliberation. The ' suspense ' of will is an attempt to
ensure that judgment is more and more rational. In the
Thoughts and the *Conduct* the writer's main concern is to make
the pupil resort to reason and thus to make reason the
influential determinant of the will. But in his enthusiasm for
this view Locke parts company with Plato's theory of the late
appearance of reason and encourages us to treat children as
rational creatures, to appeal to their sense of shame, to utilize
their natural desire for esteem, and, so far as we can, to leave
them perfectly free and unrestrained in their play and their
childish actions.[1] In *The Conduct of the Understanding* he pleads
eloquently that reason is the light that lighteth every man.
The will itself, however absolute and uncontrollable it may be
thought to be, never fails to obey its dictates. The ideas and
images in men's minds are the invisible powers that constantly
govern them, and to these they all pay a ready submission.
In the *Thoughts* Locke seems almost compelled to sketch conditions of education that enable the pupil to use his own free
reasoning powers. Therefore he argues that children ' should
be allowed the liberties and freedom suitable to their ages, and
not be held under unnecessary restraints. . . . They must not
be hindered from being children, or from playing, or doing as
children, *but from doing ill* ; all other liberty is to be allowed
them.' [2] In a later passage he tells us, in words reminiscent of
Comenius, that it is in childish or ' indifferent ' actions that his

[1] *Thoughts*, p. 43. [2] *Thoughts*, pp. 48-9. *Italics* mine.

son is to have his liberty.[1] Locke's contribution to liberty lies in a bold and reasoned advocacy of restraint from ill doing and in the doctrine of *no compulsion in learning*.

Thus Locke virtually draws a definite circle inside which he consistently keeps to the idea of ability to do what one wills. All subjects (even Latin) can be taught to children without recourse to disciplinary methods. 'The right way to teach them those things is to give them a liking and inclination to what you propose to them to be learned, and that will engage their industry and application.'[2] Locke expounds the value of each of these three educational forces : 'Children have as much a mind to show that they are free, that their own good actions come from themselves, that they are absolute and independent, as any of the proudest of you grown men, think of them as you please.'[3] 'They should seldom be put upon doing even those things you have got an inclination in them to, but when they have a mind and disposition to it.'[3] Order a child to whip his top at a certain time, whether he has or has not a mind to it ; require it as a duty ; make him spend so many hours at it ; he will soon weary. Allow him to work at a subject when he so wills ; he will learn three times as much when he is in tune, as he will with double the time and pains when he is dragged unwillingly to it. Learning, under right conditions, might be made as much a recreation to play as play is to learning. This doctrine is by no means a 'soft pedagogy.' Locke thinks it is a great matter ' to teach the mind to get the mastery over itself, and to be able, upon choice, to take itself off from the hot pursuit of one thing and set itself upon another with facility and delight ; or at any time to shake off its sluggishness and vigorously employ itself about what reason or the advice of another shall direct.'[4] He would, therefore, call upon the pupil to combat laziness and to buckle to a proposed task. But he joins with it the admission of the child's willingness to work. ' If the things they see others do, be ordered so that they are persuaded it is the privilege of an age or condition above theirs, then ambition and the desire still to get forward, and higher, and to be like those above them, will give them an inclination which will set them on work in a way wherein they

---

[1] *Thoughts*, p. 67.   [2] *Thoughts*, p. 56.
[3] *Thoughts*, p. 57.   [4] *Thoughts*, p. 58.

will go on with vigour and pleasure, enjoying in it their dearly
beloved freedom ; which if it brings with it also the satisfaction
of credit and reputation, I am apt to think there will need no
other spur to excite their application and assiduity as much as
is necessary.' [1]

Thus Locke's main substitute for the ' rough discipline of the
cudgel ' is to reason with children. Forgetful of his earlier
advocacy of submission to another's reason he suggests that
even in the tender years appeal may be made to their reasoning
powers. Mildness, composure, and gentleness of treatment will
give an atmosphere of reason. The tutor can take steps to
show that studies are useful and necessary, and that his actions
do not proceed from caprice or passion or fancy. He can study
the pupil. Even the negligent and lazy child may for a time
be given full liberty so that his natural inclinations may be
observed. Novelty and variety of exercises are recommended
on psychological grounds, for, with youthful minds, ' a lasting
continued attention is one of the hardest tasks that can be
imposed on them,' and therefore he that requires their application should endeavour to make what he proposes as grateful
and agreeable as possible. [2]

The use of reason, and the limiting of free agency to the
power of suspending volition, are perhaps responsible for the
disciplinary idea of education in Locke's writings. The
severity of the early education, the use of submission and
obedience, the attempt to instil habits friendly to reason, are
measures taken to ensure the fully operative direction of judgment, and, like most reinforcements of active ideas, assume
an underlying passivity. Locke, it is true, attacked the current
doctrines of innate ideas, ' characters as it were stamped upon
the mind of man which the soul receives in its very first being
and brings into the world with it,' [3] but he asserted in turn that
the mind at birth was white paper,[4] or wax ' to be moulded
and fashioned as one pleases.' [5] He was thus led to exaggerate
the part played by external agents and substances in early
education, and either to neglect the native tendencies, or to
suppose that they were so feeble, in comparison with the
activity of the ideas supplied through sensation, that a suit-

---

[1] *Thoughts*, p. 59. [2] *Thoughts*, p. 131. [3] *Essay*, i. 2. 1.
[4] *Essay*, ii. 1. 2. [5] *Thoughts*, 216 (p. 179).

ably impressive and uniform authority would weaken their force as determinants of volition. Even when he writes of the pupil's inclinations he writes as if they were *acquired* by the treatment of the tutor. In considering his disciplinary views, then, it must be remembered that he assumes an almost unlimited receptivity of the mental powers. When the pupil is active he is active because of the use of reason, which is the real agent of the mind, the will being merely an executive officer with powers of suspension determined by reason. The purpose of Locke's discipline is either to ensure that the pupil exercises his judgment or that he suspends action until reason has time and opportunity to make its influence felt.

Locke's freedom is both genuine and well-regulated. It is, however, not free from the objection of imposition, and its emphasis of reason and suspended judgment suggests that freedom is confined to the intellectual and volitional aspects of life. But these defects are more apparent than real. The general argument leaves no doubt of Locke's desire to find even in early years some form of incipient reason which might be regulated and strengthened by appropriate treatment. A careful reading of his works will show that reason, as he conceived it, entered into all aspects of practical importance in life, and however exaggerated may be his conception of its function in the life of the average man, its significance for some of the greatest moments of life is undeniable. His rejection of pansophic schemes of learning is perhaps responsible for his emphasis of disciplines but, here again, his conceptions are neither formal nor merely disciplinary,[1] and he shows clearly that disciplines are not necessarily inconsistent with the pupil's inclinations and interests. He recognizes that freedom is the great secret of education. The development of that idea, and of Locke's view of liberty as being able to do what one wills, is the work of Jean Jacques Rousseau.

[1] See Note 1 to Chapter X.

NOTES TO CHAPTER X

(1). LOCKE AND FORMAL TRAINING

Locke has been held to be the father of formal discipline. (See *inter alia* Monroe, *History*, pp. 512-9, and Graves, *History*, vol. ii. pp. 306-10.)   He is supposed to advocate a view of education which assumes that specific types of training may produce results ' out of all proportion to the effort expended and give a power that may be applied in any direction ' (Graves, p. 309 ; cf. Monroe, p. 508).   If this is a serious definition then all educators who aim at vitally influencing the pupil's moral disposition through school work are advocates of formal training.   If by the term we mean the specific training of a ' faculty ' (such as reason) in the belief that a general, all-round ability to reason may be developed in consequence, or that a general influence may be exerted upon the whole mind, it may be difficult to acquit Locke of the charge.   The point at issue is of importance for freedom.   If general effects flow from specific disciplines the case for education through activities that arouse individual interests may seem to be appreciably weakened.   Subjects will be selected because of their suitability from the disciplinary point of view—one to give exercise in reasoning, another in imagination, and so forth—and these will be prescribed for all pupils.   But if general effects, such as the sense of freedom or unfreedom, diversion or delight (effects which are not supposed to be the products of the exercise of faculties but which undoubtedly arise from that exercise) also follow from these specific disciplines we have the possibility of one and the same type of training leading to a ' transfer ' or ' spread ' towards other fields and being at the same time either powerfully helped by a general tendency to find delight in every extension of the training *or* being powerfully hindered by an aversion from every extension of it.   In the first case the product would be a genius, in the second a person whose inner unity is progressively destroyed by his training !   The disciplinary point of view can be maintained only if at one and the same time the discipline tends to be pleasurable.   This, we venture to suggest, is Locke's general point of view.

(1) In the *Thoughts*, at least, Locke does not *prescribe* any subject merely for its disciplinary value.   His selection is determined by the utility of a study for life, or (as in the case of Greek) by the pupil's inclination.   He objects to many of the disciplines prescribed in his day.

(2) He gives no support to the idea of disciplining faculties *as* faculties.   In the *Essay* (ii. 21. 6.) he denies that the two ' faculties of the mind,' understanding and will, are ' real beings in the soul

that performed actions of understanding and volition.' In the *Conduct* (29) he warns us against mistaking words for things, names in books for real entities in nature. The will, he insists, in the *Essay* (ii. 21. 17.) signifies nothing but an ability to prefer or choose; it is as reasonable to say that the singing faculty sings, or the dancing faculty dances, as that the will chooses or the understanding conceives. Faculty, ability and power are different names for the same thing. One power does not operate on another : the mind, or the man, operates and exerts these powers. It is clear that Locke does not urge the disciplining of a faculty because of any possible effect that the training may produce on another faculty.

(3) While there are many passages that suggest the *possibility* of a *general* effect of training upon the mind as a whole, nearly every word that Locke writes is a denial, or a doubt, of its actuality. Thus : (*a*) In his discussions of rote memory (*Thoughts*, 176) he doubts the power of exercise to improve the native retentivity of the mind, and even suggests that any improvement is due to the ' imprinting afresh ' of material that has made a strong impression. Impressions on bees-wax or lead will not last so long as on brass or steel, but if they are renewed they will last longer. Every new reflection is a new impression, and ' it is from thence one is to reckon if one would know how long the mind retains it.' The explicit denial of the possibility of ' transfer ' is made in the assertion that the ' learning of pages of Latin by heart no more fits the memory for retention of anything else, than the graving of one sentence in lead, makes it the more capable of retaining firmly any other characters.' He suggests that if learning by heart did help memory in this way we should expect to find actors or ' players ' most helped, and, as if anticipating later experiment on the point, dismisses the suggestion by remarking that ' experience will show.' He sees that life offers so many opportunities for the exercise of memory that there is little probability of its growing dull and helpless through lack of practice. Xerxes' ability to call every soldier by his name was not the result of memory exercises in boyhood. And the connection of ' training ' with the demands of life is clearly postulated in the following : ' What the mind is intent upon and careful of, that it remembers best, and for the reason above mentioned : to which if method and order be joined, all is done, I think, that can be, for the help of a weak memory ; and he that will take any other way to do it, especially that of charging it with a train of other people's words, which he that learns cares not for, will, I guess, scarce find the profit answer half the time and pains employed in it.' This is not disciplinary education, but an appeal to the discipline of life. It is not formal training but the natural exercise of the mental powers. His subsequent emphasis of content in the passages chosen for the exercise of memory shows that any general

effect obtained was that of ' turning the pupil's thoughts inwards '
—one of the best intellectual *habits* in his opinion.

(*b*) Monroe cites a passage from the *Thoughts* (94) as evidence of
Locke's disciplinary views with regard to habits.   Locke claims that
they will give ' little by little a view of mankind and work him (the
pupil) into a love and imitation of what is excellent and praise-
worthy.'   ' The studies . . . are but, as it were, the exercise of his
faculties and the employment of his time. . . .'   The context shows
that Locke is speaking of the ' safe and insensible degrees ' by which
the boy passes into the man and that his real aim is to give knowledge
of the world, and to encourage virtue and industry.   His close connection of the training with specific and direct exercises of life is
indicated by two sentences in the same paragraph : ' The only
fence against the world is a thorough knowledge of it.' 'Nobody ever
went far in knowledge, or became eminent in any of the sciences,
by the discipline and constraint of a master '—a sentence which
Professor Adamson selects as the keynote of *The Conduct of the
Understanding*.   This exercise of the faculties, and this view of the
formation of habits describe not *formal* but *direct* training.

(*c*) The severity of Locke's views of early education has also been
mentioned as evidence of his disciplinary leanings.   It must be
admitted that Locke speaks of repressive measures as discipline
(*Thoughts*, 35).   But the aim is to teach the pupil to subject his
appetites and impulses to reason, and on the whole he is an advocate
of reasoning *with* rather than *for* children.   The main idea is
that of a very definite, though widely operative and extremely
difficult, form of training.   It is not formal, but it has many contacts
with various aspects of life and is therefore likely to ' transfer ' to
later life.

(*d*) The clearest evidence of formalism is to be found in certain
passages of the *Conduct* referring to reason.   The object of the whole
book is to promote the freedom of reason, for thus Locke thinks
' the mind will be strengthened, the capacity enlarged, the faculties
improved ' (Par. 3).   But an attentive reading will show that this
general effect is to be obtained by an extensive exercise of different
types of reasoning.   Locke bewails the universal neglect of the
reasoning powers.   Some accept the reasoning of others ; some are
swayed by passion ; some confine reason to aspects and parts of a
question.   Even men of study love to ' canton out to themselves a
little Goshen in the intellectual world.'   So clearly impressed is
Locke with the specific effects of training that he points out how
alert a man may be in making a bargain and how stupid in theological reasoning.

The specificity of the results is due to three main causes.   Few
have any early training in *strict* reasoning—in tracing the dependence
of a long train of consequences to its remote principles and con-

nections. Few make effort to improve their powers of reasoning
even in their particular callings in life. Few reason about matters
not directly connected with their immediate concerns. Locke
wishes to remedy the neglect of reasoning. His prescription is
exercise. The faculties of the soul are improved just as the members
of the body are. Hence he writes (*Conduct*, Par. 6) : ' Would you
have a man reason well, you must use him to it betimes, exercise
his mind in observing the connection of ideas and following them in
train. Nothing does this better than mathematics, which therefore
I think should be taught to all those who have the time and opportunity, not so much to make them mathematicians as to make them
reasonable creatures.' . . .

Again the context shows that Locke uses reasonable in the sense
of *rational* ; nature intended us to be rational but it is only *use,
exercise, industry, application,* that make us so. He goes on to insist
that the mistake is often made of supposing that he who is found
reasonable in one thing will be so in all ; to think or to say otherwise
being thought to be so unjust an affront and so pointless a censure
that nobody ventures to do it. Then he writes : ' It is true, that
he that reasons well in any one thing, has a mind naturally capable
of reasoning well in others, and to the same degree of strength and
clearness and possibly much greater, had his understanding been so
employed.' The sting of this statement is in its tail, but, again,
the following sentence shows that Locke's ' transfer ' to other things
is intended to be conditional upon the actual exercise of reasoning
in other things. For he adds : ' But it is true that he who can reason
well to-day about one sort of matters, cannot at all reason to-day
about others, though perhaps a year hence he may. But wherever
a man's rational faculty fails him, and will not serve him to reason,
there we cannot say he is rational, how capable soever he may be
by time and exercise to become so.' And later on he again
records his conviction that industry, application, use, exercise,
practice are the real means of improving our minds and warns us that
' we must expect nothing from our understandings any further than
they are perfected by habits.'

In the next section, however, Locke cautiously suggests the
possibility of ' transfer.' ' I have mentioned mathematics as a way
to settle in the mind an habit of reasoning closely and in train ;
not that I think it necessary that all men should be deep mathematicians, but that having got the way of reasoning which that
study necessarily brings the mind to, they might be able to transfer
it to other parts of knowledge as they shall have occasion.' He
proceeds to state the characteristics of the mathematical ' way '
which he believes to be a model for all sorts of reasoning. His main
points are close connection and coherence of ideas, and certainty or
probability of proof. Algebra, for example, may give ' new helps

and views to the understanding.' In both cases he believes that mathematical studies will give glimpses of a thoroughness and rigidity of reasoning which will not leave men ' so apt to think their minds wanted no helps to enlarge them.' They will give a greater sense of the relevance of ideas to one another, and of ideas that should be omitted from a particular line of thought. In subjects other than mathematical these absolutely essential conditions of clear reasoning are not so easily observed nor so carefully practised. In other subjects ' men reason as it were in the lump ; and if, upon a summary and confused view, or upon a partial consideration they can raise the appearance of a probability, they usually rest content, especially if it be in a dispute where every little straw is laid hold on. . . . But that mind is not in a posture to find the truth that does not distinctly take all the parts asunder and omitting what is not at all to the point, draw a conclusion from the result of all the particulars which may influence it.' (*Conduct*, Par. 7.)

The above argument is a plea for the enlargement of the field of reasoning, and for its exercise upon a definite type of material. It is a careful statement of certain characteristics and qualities of mathematical reasoning, or of ' concepts of mathematical method ' which, in Locke's opinion, may transfer to other types of subject-matter. It is probable that if mathematics were taught so as to emphasize these qualities they would be found helpful in the way Locke suggests, but here, again, the training would be direct rather than formal. The nerve of Locke's discussion is that the study of mathematics gives a unique sense of thoroughness and certainty of proof. He is probably influenced by the work of Descartes and probably too sanguine of the results with ' men whose fortunes and time are narrower.' But the truth of his contention about reasoning has never been put to the test of rigid experimental inquiry. Experiment, however, does tend to show that if there is transfer it will be obtained most readily by the emphasis of ' concepts of method ' and of ideals of thoroughness and accuracy such as Locke suggests. His whole treatment is so clearly in line with the general position that a merely specific or specialized training gives merely specific results that it seems unfair to make him the originator of a doctrine that expresses the precisely opposite view. There is no doubt whatsoever that he would have counselled the mathematician to reason about non-mathematical problems. His main concern was to encourage all men to test the principles by which they were wont to reason, to keep an open mind (or indifferency as he loved to call it) for truth of all kinds ; to accept nothing as true until they were convinced of its solidity, truth and certainty. It was in this way that he conceived that freedom of the understanding which was the true mark of the rational creature. (Cf. *Conduct*, Par. 12.) His great fear was not so much of a dangerous ' little learning,' as of specialism. ' Those sciences which men are particularly versed in they are apt to value and extol, as if that part of knowledge which every one has acquainted himself with were that alone which was worth the having, and all the rest were idle and empty amusements, comparatively of no use or importance.' (*Conduct*, Par. 22.)   He saw clearly the dangers of a specialized study that did not lead the student outside the confines of his subject into contact with new modes of thought, that did not keep his reasoning powers both keen and receptive and make him at one and the same time more reasonable and more humble, more firmly fixed in some convictions but more tolerant of the views of others.   These are values very difficult to attain, but they are the conditions of a *true* intellectual freedom. In putting them forth as the ultimate aim of all teaching Locke was in truth thinking of results ' out of all proportion to the efforts expended,' but he was the exponent of a new ideal of education rather than the originator of an educational fallacy.

(2). LOCKE'S VIEWS OF LIBERTY

Three theories of freedom have been mentioned in the present chapter.   The review of Locke's appeal to reason has drawn attention to his *general* agreement with the doctrine of *necessity*— a doctrine which will be further discussed in the chapters on Watts, Rousseau, Priestley, and Godwin.   The conception of liberty as *the absence of external impediments to action* appears, as Priestley notes, in Hobbes' *Liberty and Necessity* (*c.* 1654), but its application to the education of children is Locke's own idea.   For educational work these views are of much greater importance than the idea of a *freedom of indifference,* which is subjected to trenchant criticism in Anthony Collins' *Inquiry concerning Human Liberty* (1715), and in Joseph Priestley's *Doctrine of Philosophical Necessity* (1777).   Both writers show that, *in a pure form*, the freedom of indifference is a *philosophical* doctrine incompatible with external influence of any kind.   It is not discussed in the text for, as Collins insists, ' it reduces liberty to almost, if not quite nothing.'

CHAPTER XI

WATTS' APPEAL TO REASON

THE seventy years that elapse between Locke's *Conduct of the Understanding* and Rousseau's *Emile* add few important ideas to the content of freedom. But two contributions of the period seem worthy of notice, that of Francke in the practice, and of Watts in the theory, of education. To understand the first, let us glance at the actual conditions of the schools. One authority tells us that elementary instruction in the German schools was practically nothing more than a catechism class, usually taught by the *Küster* in his spare moments, or by old soldiers, or servants, or others who could not find more congenial occupation.[1] Locke's pages give a very restrained account of the general methods and influence of English schools in his day; the *gymnasia* seem to have been even more severe in the treatment of their pupils. In 1726 we hear of the head of a school complaining that his deputy received pupils in his private room and supplied them with pipes and beer, a form of entertainment which was excused on the ground that the pupils were soon going up to the university ! Another harassed member of the school staff thought that pagans and Turks were angels compared with the pupils of his *gymnasium*, and justified a long list of abusive terms, which he was accustomed to hurl at them, on the ground that Christ called his enemies vipers and children of wrath !

To combat the universal ignorance of the poor and to strike a happy mean between the usual excesses of cruelty and of liberty in education A. H. Francke devoted some twenty years of his life. Like Milton and Dury and other Puritan writers, his main aim was to instruct children in the vital knowledge of God and to introduce them to the principles of true religion.

[1] A. Pinloche, *La Réforme de l'Education en Allemagne au 18e siècle*, pp. 4 ff.

In the elementary schools which he founded, one half of the day was devoted to religion and most of the remaining time to reading and writing, with the addition of occasional lessons in arithmetic, vocal music, and knowledge of common things. But in Francke's schools religious instruction was given through things rather than words. He did not ' permit children to learn to prattle words without understanding them, by which they are little or rather nothing profited.' [1] The government of the schools was mild and humane. In the *Pädagogium* he attempted to unite Milton's idea of an academy with the principles of the *Ritterakademien* which were then springing up in Germany. Religion and Latin had the places of honour, Greek and Hebrew were regarded as useful for Biblical studies, compositions and rhetorical exercises had a Biblical setting, and arithmetical exercises a scriptural background. The Pietist schools (as the institutions founded by Francke came to be known) were instances of a fairly rigid ' concentration ' scheme with religion as a ' core ' subject, and with an underlying utilitarian basis. Modern studies were introduced in the hope of lessening the ignorance of many who had been taught through the medium of Latin. Exercises in skill which every ' gentleman ' of that time was supposed to include in his education, and recreative exercises that remind one of the Rabelaisian plan also formed part of the curriculum. The Pietist movement was a strange combination of religious and utilitarian motives, of this and the other world, of humanity and austerity, of breadth of studies and of narrowness of view. In some respects it was in advance of its time. It employed individual, nay, even scientific methods. Its aim was irreproachable. It had the definiteness and coherence so much desired by Comenius. It failed. Its aloofness from the world in due time ' passed into blank sectarian formalism ; when that day arrived, it seemed that the educational impulse derived from Francke was exhausted. The Latin grammar and Luther's Catechism, it has been said, thereupon became the pillars of the German secondary school, where they remained the major objects of concern till the close of the eighteenth century.' [2] In the movement itself we witness a reversion to mediaeval

---

[1] Adamson, *Pioneers of Modern Education*, p. 249.

[2] Adamson, *op. cit.* p. 257.

education, the tincture of modern ideas introduced by the realists being unable to give the contact with real life which freedom demands. The harnessing of utility to personal religion did not prevent the methods, individual though they were, from degenerating into formalism.

The Dissenting academies organized on the lines of Milton's *Tractate* had a broader view of education. In some cases they embodied a virile conception of freedom. It would have been strange if they had not done so. They owed their origin to the fight for freedom of some two thousand clergy-men of the Church of England who were dispossessed of their livings by the Act of Uniformity of 1662, and compelled not only to seek a new means of livelihood but to provide educational facilities for their sons, virtually excluded, as they were, from the universities and grammar schools. Many of the non-conforming clergymen were graduates of Oxford or Cambridge ; for over a quarter of a century [1] they lived the lives of educational outlaws, and devoted themselves to the organizing of their own academies. They included amongst their staff and their pupils some of the most distinguished thinkers of the time, amongst others, Daniel Defoe, Samuel Wesley (who later became a bitter critic of their methods), Robert Harley, Earl of Oxford, Henry St. John Viscount Bolingbroke, John Hughes, poet and dramatist, Josiah Hort, Archbishop of Tuam, Matthew Henry, Isaac Watts, Philip Doddridge, Joseph Butler, Thomas Secker, Archbishop of Canterbury, Joseph Priestley, and David Williams. They followed, so far as their limited conditions permitted, the wide curricula suggested in the *Tractate* and in the writings of Locke. One of their number, Dr. Isaac Watts, was the author of two works on education, *The Improvement of the Mind*—a favourite book of the academies for many years—and a *Discourse on the Education of Children and Youth*. The *Discourse*, for some reason, has not received the attention it deserves. For our purposes it is of first interest, discussing, as it does at some length, the place and claims of freedom in education, and developing explicitly the notion of freedom implied in Locke's *Thoughts*. Even if it adds little to these views Watts' work has the dis-

[1] The Act of Toleration of 1689 partially relaxed the provisions of recognition.

tinction of insisting, twenty or thirty years before the
appearance of *Emile*,[1] on freedom as a directive concept of
education.

In an Essay on the Freedom of Will in God and in Creatures
Watts disagrees with Locke's view that freedom is a power of
action (or of non-action).   Freedom of volition is the liberty
of an intelligent being.   Types and degrees of freedom are distinguished.   Moral freedom, in the sense of freedom from all

---

[1] Watts tells us in the preface to the first part of the *Improvement* that the
book was ' twenty years a-writing.'   The second part, along with the *Discourse*,
was published posthumously by Jennings and Doddridge in 1751.   A MS. note
indicates that it was written in 1718.   See vol. viii. of Dr. Watts' works, footnote to p. 209.   The *Emile* was published in 1762.

Isaac Watts, as a boy of sixteen, entered the academy of Mr. Thomas Rowe
in the year in which Locke's *Essay* was published.   He seems to have been
fortunate in his choice of a tutor, for in later life he addressed to him a poem
entitled *Free Philosophy* (*Works*, vol. ix. p. 268.)

> I hate these shackles of the mind
> Forg'd by the haughty wise,
> Souls were not born to be confined
> And led like Samson, blind and bound,
> But when his native strength he found
> He well aveng'd his eyes.
> I love thy gentle influence, Rowe ;
> Thy gentle influence, like the sun,
> Only dissolves the frozen snow,
> Then bids our thoughts like rivers flow
> And chuse the channels where they run.
>
> Thoughts should be free as fire or wind,
> The pinions of a single mind
> Will thro' all nature fly :
> But who can drag up to the poles
> Long fettered ranks of leaden souls ;
> A genius which no chain controls
> Roves with delight, or deep, or high ;
> Swift I survey the globe around,
> Dive to the centre through the solid ground
> Or travel o'er the sky.

In *Freedom* (1697) some verses are to be found which give the key to Watts'
conception of liberty :

> . . . . but as for me,
> I can and will be free :
> Like a strong mountain or some stately tree,
> My soul grows firm upright :
> And as I stand and as I go,
> It keeps my body so :
> No, I can never part with my creation right ;
> Let slaves and asses stoop and bow,
> I cannot make this iron knee
> Bend to a meaner power than that which formed it free.

superior authority, belongs only to God.   In the liberty of will
he distinguishes (a) a liberty of spontaneity or voluntariness,
and (b) a liberty of indifference of choice.

(a) In the first, Watts recognizes some actions which so nearly
express our own inclination that the question of their *choice*
never arises.   Freedom of the will, in such cases, is merely an
act of the will.   In this sense, for example, human beings
necessarily pursue happiness, and God freely and necessarily
determines himself to act in an eternal and unchangeable
manner towards his creatures.   (b) Watts also pleads for a
' liberty of indifference ' (*libertas indifferentiae ad opposita*)
which is utterly inconsistent with all necessity of whatever
kind.   ' Whensoever the will is necessarily determined to any
act or object by any thing without or within itself it has not
a liberty of choice or indifference.' [1]   He would prefer that the
term freedom should be restricted to this definite conception, but
admits that to do so would strain the ordinary usage of speech.
In effect, then, he admits both types of ' natural ' freedom
(liberty of voluntariness and of indifference) and, further, he
recognizes that, in practice, liberty may be absolute and perfect
or imperfect and comparative.   Where it is absolute, there is
no constraint, no reluctance, no bias towards the contrary
act ; where it is imperfect the mind has some inward reluctance or hostility to actions which, nevertheless, it performs
for other reasons, or it has some desire or inclination to an
action which for some reason it wills not to perform.   The
malefactor, for example, walks freely to the scaffold ; the
sick man drinks a bitter potion ; a man refrains from saying
what he thinks to an enemy in whose power he finds himself.
Acts may thus be free or voluntary in presence of a measure of
constraint or necessity.   But the ' *will* cannot really be compelled ; natural freedom or liberty will still belong to it in all
possible actions ; though not always a liberty of choice or
indifference.'

Watts' contribution to freedom is two-fold.   (i) He examines
the relation of judgment to will, and indicates the help that
education can give to both of these faculties, and (ii) he shows
that free acts are compatible with reasonable constraint.

The relation of judgment to will is a particularly important

[1] Vol. iv. pp. 458 ff.

educational question, for the teacher usually aims at influencing the understanding. Watts admits that when we pass a judgment we are constrained in regard to it : we *must* judge things as they appear to us at the moment. But he insists (1) that although the understanding directs and illuminates the will when it is able to distinguish the fitness or unfitness, the good or evil of things, yet the will may be, and sometimes is, left without any guidance. In such cases ' we love many things which we have chosen and purely because we chose them.' (2) Though the mind cannot judge of things contrary to their appearance, yet the will has a great deal to do in our judgments concerning objects proposed to the mind. Here Watts anticipates the Freudian doctrine of rationalization. ' The will is sometimes led by appetite and passion, has an inclination to choose a particular object, and then it wishes that object to be fit and good : it readily yields to the prejudices that lie on that side, it fixes the mind on those arguments which tend to prove what it wishes and turns the thoughts away from those evidences which lie on the other side of the question, and does not suffer them to be brought into full view and comparison : and thus secretly it influences the soul to judge the thing it descries to be good or fit, that is, to assent to those arguments which are brought to prove its fitness, keeping the contrary arguments out of sight.' On such a view, the will is often a very defective instrument : hence the wisdom of Locke's insistence upon the suspension of volition until the understanding has fairly and accurately examined all sides of a question. The perfectly wise person always acts according to the reason and nature of things, but there are few people who are perfectly wise.

In actual practice the will may not only act without the help of the understanding, but even contrary to it. It may be negligent, or it may be swayed by humour, caprice, wantonness, appetite, or passion. The will, though director or adviser, is therefore not absolute lord or ruler. It is receptive as well as directive. The understanding, too, is prone to error. It apprehends something to be fit or good upon a slight view. All these defects are clearly capable of being influenced by education. Although Watts does not deal with the function of education in this essay, his educational works emphasize (1) a clear and full under-

standing as an aid to the direction of the will, (2) the subordination of impulse to reason, (3) the sense of voluntariness and the
appeal as far as possible to it by suitable methods, (4) in the
early stages the enjoyment of at least the imperfect type of
liberty.   He takes for granted Locke's concept of liberty—
ability to do what one wills—and is concerned to help the pupil
to exercise his will rather than to consider the factors that
prevent him from carrying out its behests.   He recognizes that
both adult and child are apt to pursue the shadow, to be content with the appearance of things.   Too often appearance
determines judgment, judgment determines will, and will
determines action.   In contrast, Watts paints the wise and
good man as one whose will, although self-determining and
capable of choosing contrary to the understanding and of
obeying the influences of appetite and passion, *yet suffers itself
to be directed*.   It makes its choice by the fitness or unfitness of
things as they are represented to the understanding after a due
examination and survey wheresoever this fitness or unfitness
appears.   The condition of full freedom is, then, dependent
upon an ' illumination and persuasion of the grace of God upon
the soul of man,' which perhaps without irreverence can be
translated into terms of human educational agency.

The distinctive note of Watts' theory of education is the
appeal to the pupil's understanding.   To do this and at the
same time to make the teaching of religion the central subject
and aim of education is no easy task.   But Watts sets himself
to it earnestly.   In order to help the teacher of religious subjects to take all pains to make children understand everything
that they learn, he compiles sets of catechisms graded according to the age and capacity of the pupils.   He writes a *Discourse
on the Way of Instruction by Catechisms* in which he affirms the
value of early appeals to the child's reasoning powers.   Thus
he writes : ' I am by no means of their opinion who let children
grow up almost to the age of manhood before their minds are
informed of the principles of religion.   Their pretence is that
religion ought to be perfectly free and not biased and influenced
by the authority of the parents or the power of education.' [1]

---

[1] Note that this view was held twenty years before Rousseau's doctrine
of ' negative education.'   That negative education was discussed at this
time in connection with freedom is clear from statements by a schoolmaster

In opposing this view he argues that God has made the soul of children capable of learning religion by the instruction of others long before it is capable of tracing out the knowledge of God and religion by its own reasoning powers. Why should parents not follow the order of God and nature? They have as much responsibility for furnishing their children's minds with the seeds of virtue and happiness as they have for the provision of food and raiment. As children grow up they may be taught that ' religion ought to be a matter of their rational choice.' They may be taught to examine their principles and to settle their faith on solid grounds, but in the meantime they ought to be led into that ' religion in which their parents hope to obtain acceptance with God and happiness in the world to come.'

But this responsibility cannot be fully discharged by compelling a child to memorize a catechism or a page of scripture which he does not understand. ' The business and duty of the teacher is not merely to teach words but things. Words written in the memory without ideas or sense in the mind will never incline a child to his duty nor save his soul.' He puts aside such values as completeness and perfection of system : he prefers an A B C of religion to the overwhelming of a little soul with a full and accurate discourse on the deeper points of Christianity. Why should religion of all things be taught in a way that is least suited to make the learner understand it ? Words which are not understood are the most difficult of all to remember, and the learning of them will not, by itself, lead to understanding. It will probably tend to prevent the grasp of meaning by creating a positive dislike of holy things. Finally, Watts shows how he would give a simple yet practical knowledge of the elementary facts of religion instead of a mass of words dealing with theological doctrines.

The same practical utility is shown in the *Improvement of the Mind*, a book well summarized by two sentences in Dr. Johnson's eulogy of the man who ' for children condescended to lay

named Butler who published an *Essay on Education*, the copy of which in the British Museum is dated 1750 (?). ' Some gentlemen,' says Butler, ' have thought that education must not be begun till a boy is 12 or 14 years and that he may then be taught as much by the time he is 20 as he would have learnt by being employed from his infancy ' (p. 96). The author urges that school should be made a pleasure, but ' too much liberty' should be avoided (p. 83).

aside the scholar, the philosopher, and the wit, to write little poems of devotion and systems of instruction adapted to their wants and capacities.' [1] The first part of the work deals with the *Improvement of Knowledge* and the second with *Communication of Useful Knowledge* : the two ideas are closely connected in Watts' mind, and even in the title utility is emphasized.

By many approaches and by many methods Watts strives to show ' the vast importance of a good judgment, and the rich and inestimable advantage of right reasoning.' He counsels his reader to contrive and practise methods which will make him acquainted with his own ignorance ; to take a wide survey now and then of the vast and unlimited regions of learning ; to exercise his own reason and judgment upon all that he reads ; to regard knowledge as always capable of improvement ; to review daily, especially in the early years of life, the new ideas and truths gained by reading and meditation ; to avoid dogmatism in all its forms. Observation he places first as a method of study, and by it he means ' knowledge gotten at first hand.' He would have the student gain an encyclopaedic knowledge from nature, from the vicissitudes of nations, from the virtues and the vices of others, from distress and calamity, from ' the natural powers, sensations, judgment, memory, etc.' He tells us how to read books and how to improve our minds by conversation. Even in talking with children ' we can mark the buddings of infant reason ' ; [2] in thirty other ways we may continue to fight against our natural ignorance. Watts' view of reason determines his conceptions of authority and of liberty. They are fully discussed, the first in the *Communication of Knowledge*, the second in the *Discourse on Education*. He recognizes the possibility of the abuse of authority, but states three cases ' wherein authority or the sentiments of other persons must or will determine the judgments and practice of mankind.' [3] Parents must judge for young children and in-

---

[1] Dr. Johnson further writes of this work : ' Few books have been perused by me with greater pleasure than his *Improvement of the Mind*, of which the radical principles may indeed be found in Locke's *Conduct of the Understanding*; but they are so expanded and ramified by Watts, as to confer on him the merit of a work in the highest degree useful and pleasing. Whoever has the care of instructing others may be charged with deficience in his duty if this book be not recommended.'

[2] *Improvement of the Mind*, 1. ix. 2. Lond. 1800 Edn. p. 78.

[3] *Communication of Useful Knowledge*, ii. 4. p. 229 (Lond. 1800 Edn.).

struct them what to believe and practise in civil and religious life. All must recognize the authority and testimony of men, wise and honest, in matters of fact. All must submit to the authority of God.

In dealing with the first of these, Watts urges : ' It is impossible that children should be capable of judging for themselves, before their minds are furnished with a competent number of ideas, before they are acquainted with any principles and rules of just judgment, and before their reason is grown up to any degrees of maturity and proper exercises upon such subjects.' He will not admit, however, that a child is to believe ' nonsense and impossibility ' or the obviously false opinions of the parents : the main point is that a child knows no better way *to find* out what he should believe than to run to his parents. Thus does Watts state the case for natural receptivity. Where there is native reasoning power, appeal to it ; where there is not, exercise authority sincerely, frankly, and kindly. This seems to be Watts' general practice, and it is not inconsistent with the general view of imperfect freedom. His appeal to play methods is virtually an appeal to the ' freedom of voluntariness or spontaneity.' He cannot find any definite time of life when a child should be cut off from the aid of his parents. It is a matter of development : ' When childhood and youth are so far expired that the reasoning faculties are grown up in just measure of maturity, it is certain that persons ought to begin to inquire into the reasons for their own faith and practice in all the affairs of life and religion ; but as reason does not arrive at this power and self-sufficiency in any single moment of time, so there is no single moment when a child should at once cast off all its former beliefs and practices ; but by degrees and in slow succession he should examine them, as opportunity and advantages offer ; and either confirm, or doubt of, or change them, according to the leadings of conscience and reason with all its best advantages of information.' And Watts affirms that ' there is no reason whatsoever that can prove or establish any authority as fairly as to give it power to dictate in matters of belief what is contrary to all the dictates of our reasonable nature.' God gives no revelation contradictory to reason. Things may be above our reason, or reason may fail to see the connection of ideas, or be unable to reconcile truths or facts of experience, but when they stand directly and plainly against all sense and reason, no divine authority can be pretended to enforce their belief and human authority is impudent to pretend to do so.

Consistently with this theory Watts attempts to make instruction transparent to the child's reason and to make as much use as possible of his reasoning powers. Both of these points have already been illustrated. In the *Discourse* he deals at some length with ' self-government.' [1] By this he means the child's government of his thoughts, the determination of his will by understanding and not by obstinacy or by bad temper, the subordination of his lower powers to reason, the regulation of his senses, imagination, appetites, and passions. This, he points out, is not merely an aspect or part of religious instruction but teaching which should form part of all subjects. Concentration upon a task, steadiness and reasonableness of conduct, the long-circuiting of impulse, the government of anger, the control of temper, are all mentioned as elements to be desired. It is the ' little man ' rather than the child that Watts depicts.

One would expect a poetical exponent of education to look kindly on what he calls ' the accomplishments of life.' He thinks that poesy is a ' proper ornament of youth,' yet hesitates to recommend verse-making to every young gentleman. He himself has been too far betrayed by an unguarded inclination into attempts of this kind, and he sometimes repents of having spent so many days and hours in writing verse. But he defends the exercise mainly on grounds of utility ! ' It brightens and animates the fancy with a thousand beautiful images, it enriches the soul with many great and sublime sentiments and refined ideas, it fills the memory with a noble variety of language, and furnishes the tongue with speech and expression suited to every subject. It teaches the art of describing well . . . assists us in the art of persuasion ; leads us into a pathetic manner of speech and writing and adds life and beauty to conversation.' [2] A similar assortment of reasons with as little perception of the value of self-expression states the case for the teaching of singing.

These utilitarian and rationalistic motives are combined in

---

[1] Sect. iii. p. 277.   [2] Sect. vii. p. 297.

two chapters dealing respectively with the ' proper degrees
of Liberty and Restraint in the Education of a son,'[1] and ' of a
daughter.'[2] The strict and severe education of earlier days is
contrasted with the licence of Watts' own time, and if one or
other extreme is necessary, preference is given to restraint.
' But,' asks the author, ' is there no medium between these two
extremes, excess of confinement and excess of liberty ? May
not young understandings be allowed to shoot and spread themselves a little, without growing rank and rampant ? May not
children be kept in a due and gentle subjection to their parents
without putting yokes of bondage on them ? Is there no
reasonable restraint of the wild opinions and violent inclinations of youth, without making chains for the understanding
and throwing fetters on the soul ? . . . Is it not possible for
the parent to indulge, and the child to enjoy a just liberty, and
yet neither encourage nor practise a wild licentiousness ? '
The answer to these questions is a sketch of Eugenio at
twenty years of age, virtuous, entertaining, philosophic, beloved by his superiors, affectionate and deferential towards his
parents. ' He was trained from the very cradle to all the duties
of infant-virtue by the allurements of love and reward suited
to his age, and never was driven to practise anything by a frown
or a hasty word where it was possible for kinder affections to
work the same effect by indulgence and delay.' As fast as his
reasoning powers developed they were diverted to easy tracks
of thought. Every departure from duty was shown to be contrary to reason. He was given elementary yet practical and
concrete notions of religion. Only twice did he suffer corporal
punishment. Learning was presented as a reward for some
domestic duty. Nothing was required of his memory but what
was first led into his understanding. Difficult and abstract
notions were postponed until a partial idea had been first
obtained. He had two or three catechisms composed by his
tutor. He was instructed to prove everything by natural or
moral arguments. ' After he arrived at fifteen he was suffered
to admit nothing into his full assent, till his mind saw the
rational evidence of the proposition itself ; or at least till he
felt the power of those reasons which obliged him.' His tutor
never imposed anything on Eugenio with a magisterial air ;

---

[1] Sect. x. pp. 317-330.   [2] Sect. xi. pp. 330-336.

he advised him upon studies and methods, he warned him against dangers, he pointed out to him the consequences of certain actions. He freely expressed his own views and sentiments but exhorted his pupil to choose wisely for himself. Though Eugenio did not accept all his instructor's opinions, yet he could not but love the man that indulged him in such a liberty of thought. Under guidance he enjoyed the unspeakable pleasure of being his own teacher and of framing his opinions himself. ' By this means he began early to use his reason with freedom and to judge for himself, without a servile submission to the authority of others ; and yet to pay a just and solemn deference to persons of age and experience, and particularly to those who were the proper and appointed guides of his youth and who led him on so gently in the paths of knowledge.' He was not kept a stranger to the errors and follies of mankind, nor was he let loose among them, either in books or company, without a guard and a guide. His teacher let him know the mistakes and iniquities of men, but informed them with principles of truth and virtue. He was allowed to enjoy the society of persons above the level of his own age and attainment ; his curiosity was gratified by new sights and scenes, but he was made patient of restraint and disappointment. Some things were absolutely forbidden, but in so kind a manner as to make their guilt or peril appear in the strongest light, and thereby they were rendered hateful rather than objects of wish or desire. Eugenio was taught to say ' No ' boldly and to maintain his principles. A similar sketch of Phronissa's education is given.

NOTE TO CHAPTER XI

WATTS AND FORMAL TRAINING

Watts considers the functions of attention and memory in his chapters on the improvement and enlargement of the mind. In the treatment there is little positive evidence of a fallacious view of formal training. The general theory is that greater facility (of attention) is dependent upon exercise, and upon inclination. ' Get a good liking,' he tells us, ' to the study or knowledge you would pursue . . . there is not much difficulty in confining the mind to contemplate what we have a great desire to know ; and especially if they are matters of sense or ideas which paint themselves upon the fancy. It is but acquiring an hearty good-will and resolution to search out and survey the various properties and parts of objects ; our attention will be engaged if there be any delight or diversion in the study or contemplation of them. Therefore mathematical studies have a strange influence towards fixing the attention of the mind and giving a steadiness to a wandering disposition, because they deal much in lines, figures, and numbers ; which affect and please the sense and imagination.' [1] In the same way ' histories ' help ; they engage the soul by a variety of sensible occurrences. This is not an explanation of transfer of training but an appreciation of the ' fixation ' of attention through sensible objects and, therefore, a reiteration of the primacy of sensation. His second rule for the improvement of attention shows his appreciation of the limitation as well as of the value of sensory appeal. ' Sometimes we may make use of sensible things and corporeal images for the illustration of those notions which are more abstracted and intellectual. Therefore diagrams greatly assist the mind in astronomy and philosophy ; and the emblems of virtues and vices may happily teach children, and pleasingly impress those useful moral ideas on young minds which perhaps might be conveyed to them with much more difficulty by mere moral and abstracted discourses. I confess in this practice . . . we should be cautious lest we so far immerse the mind in corporeal images, as to render it unfit to take in an abstracted and intellectual idea, or cause it to form wrong conceptions of immaterial things. This practice therefore is rather to be used at first in order to get a fixed habit of attention and in some cases only ; but it can never be our constant way and method of pursuing all moral, abstracted, and spiritual themes.' That way is through application to studies which involve a chain of connected and closely knit reasoning. Watts proceeds to argue that although the passions often cause distraction yet if we can enlist them on the side of a particular study, they are a powerful aid to concentrated attention. The subsequent chapters bear witness to his anxiety to make ideas clear to the understanding, to enlist the instinctive tendencies, to provide continued exercise for the faculties, and to increase mental receptivity. Thus in the study of geometry he sees a means of opening the mind to the existence of incommensurables, and in astronomy and geography means of extending individual conceptions of space and of distance.

The same emphasis of methods likely to arouse mental activity and of content likely to provide new forms of exercise appears in the treatment of memory, of which a remarkably sane and broad discussion is given. After stating four qualities of a good memory and suggesting that in respect of each the memory may be injured or improved Watts writes : ' There is one great and general direc-

[1] *Improvement of the Mind*, I. xv. I. p. 124.

tion which belongs to the improvement of other powers as well as of the memory, and that is to keep it always in due and proper exercise. Many acts by degrees form a habit and thereby the ability or power is strengthened and made more ready to appear in action.' [1] He points out various specific forms of exercise which give specific results. His rules for improvement are, in the main, rules for the better assimilation and association of ideas. Thus he mentions due attention and diligence, depth of study, clear and distinct apprehension of things, method and regularity of learning, division into distinct headings, observance of the mutual dependence of ideas, frequent reviews and careful repetition, concentration, practical use of material learnt—teaching or communication of knowledge, pleasure and delight in the things learnt, adoption of the play attitude, use of rhymes and other aids (of which Watts is a discerning critic), and various forms of association. Even the use of coloured inks—a cardinal principle of the early Montessori Method —is mentioned.

In a further discussion of the use of various sciences to the learned professions Watts again considers the claims of mathematics. He speaks of arithmetic and geometry as ' means to fix a wandering mind, to beget a habit of attention and to improve the faculty of reason.' But he makes it clear that he does *not* fall into the essential fallacy of the advocate of formal training—that of compulsorily prescribing these subjects because of the above disciplinary values. ' I would by no means be understood to recommend to all a pursuit of these sciences to those extensive lengths to which the moderns have advanced them. This is neither necessary nor proper for any students, but those few who shall make these studies their chief profession and business of life, or those gentlemen whose *capacities and turn of mind are suited to these studies*, and have all manner of advantage to improve in them.' [2] He recognizes that mathematics exercise and improve certain powers of the mind and that they do this more efficiently if there is a natural inclination for mathematical studies. But he also emphasizes the utility and service of mathematics for ordinary life and thinks that too deep a penetration into their abstruse difficulties may have certain very specific and un-desirable effects. He quotes with approval Dr. Cheyne's view that mathematics are but barren and airy subjects for a man entirely to live upon ; that for a man to indulge and riot in these exquisitely bewitching contemplations is only proper for public professors and gentlemen of estates ! . . . It is noteworthy that a quotation from Dr. Cheyne is the only passage in which the explicit claim of ' *ex-tending* ' the training or operation of a faculty is made ; but even then the quotation bears testimony to certain supposed effects of mathematical training which suggest the inadvisability of making

[1] I. 17. p. 148.   [2] I. 20. 11. p. 184. *Italics* mine.

mathematics the be-all and end-all of education.   The paragraph is worthy of quotation *verbatim*.

' But,' says he,[1] ' to own a great but grievous truth, though they (mathematics) may quicken and sharpen the invention, strengthen and extend the imagination, improve and refine the reasoning faculties, and are of use both in the necessary and the luxurious refinements of the mechanical arts ; yet having no tendency to rectify the will, to sweeten the temper, or mend the heart, they often leave a stiffness, a positiveness and sufficiency on weak minds, which is much more pernicious to society, and to the interests of the great end of our being, than all their advantages can recompense.   He adds further concerning the launching into the depth of these studies, that they are apt to beget a secret and refined pride, and over-weening and over-bearing vanity, the most opposite temper to the true spirit of the gospel.   This tempts them to presume on a kind of omniscience in respect to their fellow-creatures . . . nor are they fit to be trusted in the hands of any but those who have acquired a humble heart, a lowly spirit, and a sober and teachable temper.' [2]

One might suppose that Watts quoted Dr. Cheyne in order to reduce the notion of general disciplinary values to an absurdity. If the study of mathematics produces an unteachable temper as well as a concentration of mind, it can scarcely be said to produce any *general* effect at all.   It, like any mental activity, exercises the mind in specific ways which may be improved, within limits, as a result of exercise, and which either in their original or their improved state may annul one another.   That is all we are entitled to say. If we admit general effects it will be very difficult to draw a line at any point in the above paragraph and say that the disciplinary influence of mathematics ends here or there.   There is as much *logic* in arguing that stiffness and positiveness of mind are the result of mathematical training as in arguing that invention or imagination are its products : if mathematics ' extends the imagination ' it may extend ' the positiveness, stiffness, and unteachableness of temper.' It would, on such a view, be necessary to prescribe other disciplines to rectify the products of discipline and so *ad infinitum*.   The escape from this infinite regress is to provide studies which, by their appeal *to the whole mind*, engage the will and do something to sweeten the temper and mend the heart.   On the whole this is Watts' position. But in his *Discourse* [3] he is led, through the figure of the uneducated mind as ' the uncultivated field, barren and fruitless or productive of weeds and briers instead of herbs and corn,' to speak of the *cultivation* of the understanding, of the memory, of the judgment,

---

[1] That is, Dr. Cheyne.   The quotation is from the Preface to Cheyne's *Essay on Health and Long Life*.

[2] i. 20. 11. pp. 185-6.   [3] *Discourse*, Sect. ii. pp. 270 ff.

of reasoning, and of conscience.   Now cultivation of faculties is a
more doubtful process than ' use,' or ' exercise,' or ' application,' or
the ' improvement ' of which Locke speaks ; it may, or may not,
assume as great possibilities of ' transfer ' as the term ' extension '
employed by Cheyne.   It is probable, however, that Watts uses the
term as a variant for ' exercise ' and that he does not attach to it
the misleading notion of finally reaping results ' out of all proportion
to the efforts expended.'   Although his analytical tendencies lead
him to place the ' cultivation ' of faculties in the foreground, he
hastens to show that the main point is not discipline but the allure-
ment of the child to learning by appealing to his curiosity, by the
use of illustrations and pictures, by attempting to give clear ideas,
by emphasizing utility, by appealing to his reason.   Here we may
point out that Watts appeals fairly consistently to children's own
reasoning powers ; he is much more consistent than Locke is on this
point.   ' By calling their young reason thus into exercise you will
teach them wisdom betimes : you will awaken manly thoughts
within them, and so lead them to a rational and manly conduct in
their childish years ; by this means also you will always have a
handle to take hold of, in order to persuade them to their duty, and
to save them from mischief.   But if their reasoning powers be
neglected you will train them up like the horse and the mule who
have no understanding : they will grow like brutes in the shape of
men, and reason will have but little power over them in the following
parts of life.'   This is the training of reason through its actual
exercise, and it is fairly representative of Watts' general point of
view.   In several places he speaks of the cultivation and *improvement* of faculties—a combination which gives some ground for
restricting the term cultivation to ' use ' or ' exercise.'

CHAPTER XII

A SATIRICAL VIEW OF FREEDOM

EDUCATIONAL theory, and especially a theory of freedom in education, is often accused of being ' in the air.' Its advocates are popularly supposed to formulate their views either with one eye closed to the conditions of current practice or with both eyes open to certain defects which point a moral or adorn a theoretical principle. Few have attempted to join to their reasoned expositions of what educational theory *ought* to be, a plain statement of what it actually would be if they were to begin with practice as it is and with the real wishes of parents regarding the functions of education, and attempt to systematize what they actually found. Both types of exposition appear in the works of J. P. de Crousaz, Professor of Philosophy and Mathematics at Lausanne and afterwards at Gröningen. The serious side of his work may be illustrated by reference to his *Traité de l'Education des Enfants*,[1] his satire by an English translation of a work concerning the education of a youth.[2]

The first shows the writer's discriminating adherence to Locke's views. There is a keener appreciation of the value of curiosity and of the presentation of ideas within the pupil's mental grasp.[3] The secret of education is to place the pupil in such a position as will enable him to give himself lessons, the opportunities and the materials only being supplied by the teacher. The older views, says the writer, realizing man's need of direction and his dislike of rules, turned education into the appearance of amusement. However artificial they may seem, they are still the best means of education. They fix attention,

---

[1] Published in 1722, and dedicated to the Princess of Wales.

[2] *New Maxims concerning the Education of Youth.* Translated into English by Rev. G. S. Tacheron, London, 1740. The present writer has not been able to trace the original.

[3] Lib. i. pp. 247-250 (Ed. 1722).

make sustained effort possible, and encourage pupils to sur-
mount difficulties. But superficiality must be avoided. One
cannot do a greater wrong than to give children the idea that
they know a thing when they do not know it. A clear analysis
of the results of severe methods is followed by a plea for wiser
measures, which will necessarily demand greater intelligence,
reasoning power and imagination from teachers.[1]

In this chapter we shall limit ourselves to de Crousaz's
satirical views, so that we may the better understand popular
ideas of the meaning and function of education at the beginning of the eighteenth century. As our author reminds
us, the best way to inspire any one with a hatred of vice is
to set before his eyes the irregularities of his acquaintances.
This makes as great an impression upon him as a death in a
neighbouring house makes upon the minds of the sick. They
are all afraid to die.

In the first two years, says de Crousaz, a child is a plaything
for his parents. He is sent to school. Why? Because it is
the custom. It is very important to be sure that the school
keeps the right end in view. The end is determined by the
fact that the boy is destined to shine in society, to take his
share in the government of his country, and so to make others
love and fear him. Indolence is out of the question as a means
to this end, therefore activity must be forthcoming. There are
two principal causes of human activity, envy and malice. To
keep these active is a difficult task, but let us take courage.
Nature will assist all the precautions we may take to settle
these dispositions firmly in the minds of children. How can
we excite envy? In the first place, we can refuse to take
notice of anything that a child possesses, and talk at length of
what other people have. In this way the pupil will learn never
to be satisfied with what he has, and he will be encouraged to
form plans for getting everything that he sees in the possession
of others. Secondly, if we think fit to give him anything,
we can show an extreme reluctance in parting with it,
or signify our intention of giving it to some one else. Thirdly,
we may excite envy and covetousness towards inferiors by
speaking of them as mean persons who have this or that possession. Thus we shall early give the impression that the rich

---

[1] *Ibid.* pp. 390-1.

man becomes rich by always trying to secure what he has not got ; that others have their hearts divided by the demands of selfishness and a mistaken generosity, the failures of education being due to our tardiness in making the selfish or right inclinations predominant. It must be remembered that Nature can seldom triumph over the ill effects of imperfect education ; we must therefore emphasize actions rather than words. Words made the cheese fall from the crow's bill : we make a man a philosopher so that he may part with his money for a trifle. If a pupil shows any reluctance in learning these lessons ' take him up short ' with the impatience of a zealous divine dealing with a heretic.

Every day will afford opportunities for teaching the distinction between a downright honest man who is not rich and a fool or a rogue who is rich. The former is an odd kind of man apt to be ridiculed when he does as others do. If he goes to a feast and eats like other men, a skilful and prudent tutor will explain to the pupil : ' That honest man eats for twice, he is not accustomed to these delicacies.' Thus the fact will be impressed upon the pupil that the most venerable character cannot escape ridicule if he is not rich, and the pupil will draw his own conclusions. We should blame rather than praise men's actions, for the human mind is better pleased to hear scandal than recommendation.

Morality *must* be placed first in education. Some bright geniuses have thoroughly examined the nature of virtue and discovered that it is grounded on ' utibility '—that it is nothing but the art of procuring for ourselves what may give us the highest pleasure. The same geniuses warn us against the prejudices which blind other men. We should attempt to view all things as a man from the moon would, a man with a soul like white paper, entirely new, and free from prejudice. Yet one principle shines through all life's contradictions, *the application of every man to what concerns himself*. Everybody follows this, but some people have not the intelligence to see what concerns themselves. The tears of joy which angels shed on a man's conversion are due to their delight in seeing him begin to act in accordance with his own interest. Be serviceable then to all men when you cannot help doing so ; do not neglect others when your negligence would be prejudicial to yourself. Study to *appear generous* when you find that generosity will be a profitable usury. A strong desire for that which is useful and profitable is the foundation of all probity and the blossom of virtue, but cunning and craftiness to procure it is the ornament thereof.

After morality learning ! Now learning *is* useful because of the reputation it gives. Do but zealously defend ancient errors, on a subject with which you are not well acquainted, and you shall be honoured. Try to dispel inveterate darkness and you will be taken for an ignoramus. Hence it plainly follows that a tutor *must* teach his pupil *Latin*. A man who speaks no language but his own will always be thought vulgar, for people do not admire what they understand. But express yourself in Latin, quote now and then some Greek author in his own words and the most proud and haughty will be obliged to strike the flag before you and own your superiority. Were there no coxcombs in Rome ? you ask. Did not common labourers and porters swear in Latin ? To answer questions like these, the first thing to do is to put the questioners out of countenance with a loud laugh, then gravely add that though a man be perfectly master of Geography, History, etc., etc., yet if he does not understand Latin he is not worth a rush. You cannot imagine the effect of words like these pronounced with all the gravity of a professor !

Are there no discreet men who distinguish appearance from reality, who do not see the difference between a silly fellow who speaks Latin and a knowing and wise man ? Yes ; but such men have no fortunes to dispose of. Very often they are compelled by their interest, and consequently by their duty, to follow the crowd. All *wise* tutors make Latin their main subject. They do this for many reasons.

They can begin by dictating a long exercise to a child. He will spend two or three hours in turning it into very bad Latin. This gives leisure to the tutor. Besides, the pupil is not fatigued, and he does not complain if the tutor is wise enough not to reprimand him for his faults. He makes two or three lines at his ease, then rests ; two or three more, plays ; tries the exercise again ; eats some fruit ; prattles with a servant ; fights with a school-fellow ; at last comes to the end. When by chance he translates some lines with a semblance of accuracy they can be rewritten and shown to his father, the tutor taking care to extol the son to the skies. The howlers will make the father laugh ; the corrections will show the tutor's care. When the whole exercise is fairly written, the father will see in it the work of the hand that transcribed it, will see the child pass the same road that he himself passed—will be pleased to think of what he now escapes, will be born again and grow young with pleasure in that dear image. But if Latin *must* be understood the grammar must be learned in Latin. For experience shows that seven out of every ten scholars remember no Latin other than the rules which they have repeated a thousand times.

This practice, moreover, of learning by heart what they do not understand will keep your pupils docile—an excellent habit —for if they are docile there is no fear that they will become reasoners, or that they will be indisposed to learn religion which, after Latin, ought to be the main concern of tutors. No good tutor would think of inculcating any religion but that which he thinks the true one. The true one is that established by law, and the most short and certain way of teaching it is by authority. To have views on religion is dangerous, so do not allow children to reason on other matters. And be sure to propose everything to them in their younger years with a definite air and voice. If they begin to ask questions or raise objections ' take them up short more than for a lie, and much more than for an oath.' Tell them they are in pains for their salvation, and that the devil transforms himself into an angel of light who always loves to inspire them, as he did our first parents, with the desire of knowing too much. If you find it easy to solve their objections do so with a morose and scornful look, so that they may not desire to raise objections again.

All this is not really hard to carry out : follow nature and help her a little. Man's mind is naturally slothful. Inspire the pupils little by little with love for the established religion. A holy disregard for reason must also be cultivated in their tender breasts. Nothing is more easy in those young years than to hinder its taking root. It is the time to make them understand that the best way of reasoning is to make no use of reason at all. He who makes the best use of his reason is he who, reasoning, concludes that it is not necessary to reason.[1]

---

[1] Cf. Rousseau's view of habit.

Some would have us teach religion according to the capacity of the pupil. They tell us to begin with historical facts and then to explain the commandments, and instead of being satisfied with repetition they would employ the understanding. They think that men have greater affection for truths which they have the pleasure of finding out ; such truths captivate the heart whence they spring, instead of remaining in the memory. But this is a dangerous method, for it accustoms youth to see, and to desire to see, and to understand ; whereas if one begins with the profound and obscure, young minds will very soon be accustomed to submission and dependence. ' We are born in ignorance : we are bred in darkness, errors and prejudices. As soon as we begin to make some use of our eyes and ears we are seduced by a thousand false examples and a thousand contagious speeches ; being a prey to our whims and passions, which are reciprocally at variance with one another . . . we pass a short life in useless projects, in a long repentance, and in vainful efforts. . . .' [1] The safe way of religion is the only way, so we should hold fast to it and keep a grave countenance.

In science be content with superficial notions : this will save time, give less trouble, free you from difficult questions, and give a greater appearance of learning. Do not teach mathematics, save the common rules and necessary practical operations. In the old days ninety-seven out of every hundred pupils gave up this study in the first and second month, but now it will soon be the study of old women. This will be fatal to morality. Too great accuracy is pernicious : famous mathematicians have been known to criticise Homer and from Homer to Holy Writ is but one short step. Encourage play. The man who plays does not need amusements, and he saves the money usually spent on books. He may even win money. And play gives all the exactness, penetration, vivacity, attention that men really need. It has also social advantages. A man without principles or religion is very well received by men who have principles or religion, provided that he plays. So let children play ; but be sure that they do play. Keep them from playing when they play carelessly and so make their amusements a serious affair. Teach social sciences, so that the

[1] P. 98. Cf. the opening sentences of *Emile*.

pupil may see the danger of too great love for his fellow-man and so that he may see how to advance his own interests without shame. Travel is also an excellent thing for young noblemen too old to be considered children and not old enough to be treated as men.

Even if Rousseau was not influenced by this amusing presentation of common prejudices it must have prepared the minds of some for the paradoxes of *Emile*.

CHAPTER XIII

A FREE ACADEMY

In the little known writings of David Fordyce [1] there is a discussion of freedom which anticipates both in phrase and in substance the central views of Rousseau's *Émile*, and at the same time crystallizes the main doctrines of Erasmus, Vives, Comenius, and Locke. The *Dialogues* sketch the proceedings of an academy guided by *Euphranor*, a man of superior talents who unites a profound knowledge of philosophy and mathematics and an admirable proficiency in both the ancient and the modern languages—an array of learning that surely harmonized the claims of the ancient and the modern subjects of education, struggling as they were at the moment for supremacy in the public and the private institutions of academical learning. *Euphranor*, though fitted to shine in any sphere of life, prefers to ' tincture the youth of his country with the truest principles of learning and good manners and a deep sense of obligation to all social and religious duties.' [2] He is as conversant with books as with men and has travelled the world with a gentleman of fortune. Though, like Rousseau, he believes that ' a man of the world must wear a mask,' [3] he speaks only what he thinks true, and does only what he thinks right. He loves to discern the thirst after knowledge in youthful minds, to enter into their studies and to lead them step by step in their inquiries. The society which he has founded is as free and philosophical as one can imagine ; his pupils are taught by conversational rather than by formal or didactic methods and are encouraged to grapple with the master in debate. To hear this eighteenth-century Socrates surrounded

---

[1] Professor of philosophy in the Marischal College, Aberdeen. His *Dialogues concerning Education* (vol. i. 1745, vol. ii. 1748) and *Elements of Moral Philosophy* (published in 1754, three years after his death) are his main works. The *Dialogues* were read in some of the dissenting Academies of the 18th century. *Vide* The Works of the Rev. P. Doddridge, D.D., vol. iv.

[2] *Dialogues*, i. p. 15.   [3] *Dialogues*, ii. p. 9.

by his disciples is to hear the old Academicians at Athens. ' Here you may see a resemblance of their suspense of judgment, of their freedom of enquiry, that patience of debate and contradiction, that caution not to be deceived, and that noble facility of confessing and retracting when one has been in the wrong.   Here every one may follow his own genius and the method of study he finds most congenial.' [1]   No respect is paid to mere authority, no embargoes are laid upon any branches of knowledge.   Reading and writing, riding, swimming, running, and skating, history and fables, geography and chronology, dead languages, and living practical arts like surveying and architecture, Aristotle, Locke, and Bacon, the experimental sciences and the study of the moralists, conversation and travel—all are accepted by Euphranor as liberal and educative.[2] His academy splits up into companies and clubs and the clash of their opinions—real not scholastic disputation—is freedom in education.   What is more natural than that one of the pupils, Eugenio, should bring up the paradox of freedom as a suitable subject for discussion ? [3]

What a mighty pother, says he, is made over *Education*— over the instilling of fit principles into youth, of forming their minds by culture, of furnishing them with notions and languages, of anticipating and aiding their genius by the restraints of discipline !   Would it not be better to ' leave the mind open and trust to the dictates of Nature and good sense, which will teach a truer and more useful knowledge than most masters have themselves ' ?   Is not one half of our life spent in unlearning the prejudices and errors acquired in the other part, and planted with so much care and appearance of wisdom ? Instead, therefore, of putting the mind into a mould and hampering it with the trammels of education it would be better to give unlimited scope to Nature, to lay no bias on judgment and genius, to infuse no positive opinions, but to let the young adventurer, like the bee, wander about in quest of intellectual food, rifle every flower, pick up materials from every quarter, and later range and digest them into a well-compacted and useful body.   This is the only education that safeguards originality and leaves the mind free to take its flights in regions

---

[1] *Dialogues*, i. p. 21.   [2] Cf. *Dialogues*, ii. No. 18.

[3] *Dialogues*, i. No. 6, pp. 108-140.

hitherto unexplored. Homer would never have painted men so boldly had he been forced to submit to the discipline of colleges. Shakespeare's portrayal of human passion would have been a mere echo of life had the native spring of his genius been cramped with systems of learning. Reading and writing may have to be learnt in childhood, but there should be no instruction in the ' peculiarities of any trade or profession or in the badges and singularities of any party.'

Constant rejects these views of Eugenio. He believes that it is of the utmost consequence to season young minds with an early tincture of knowledge as well as of virtue. Thinking, perhaps, of the efforts to educate *Peter, the Wild Boy*,[1] he cites the case of an infant brought up in the woods and allowed to live the life of a savage. Even if such a child were gifted with language by some supernatural means, could he be expected to excel those who had the ' sinews of genius hamstringed by the culture of schools and academies '? Moreover, we are assured by eminent philosophers that the mind is a *tabula rasa* —that it owes its characters to the impressions made upon the senses and to custom, habit, education, and the like. Even if, urges *Constant*, you leave a young child free and let Nature do all, will he form no habits ? He will see and hear and become conversant with a variety of things. Will he remain un-influenced by them ? Will nothing that he sees, or hears, or reads, lead him into false opinion and popular error ? You must really choose between the alternatives of leaving him free to absorb such notions as the accidents of life throw in his way or of sowing early in his mind the seeds of knowledge and virtue and improving his talents by the arts of a liberal educa-tion. For the mind is uneasy till it takes some side or other, and if it is not prepossessed with truth it will embrace error.

Philander, in turn, will not accept the view of the child's mind as a sheet of white paper. Here we have the characteristic contribution of Fordyce to our subject, for *Philander's* views are those of Fordyce's *Elements of Moral Philosophy*. There he insists that every age has a peculiar genius and set of passions corresponding to it and most conducive to the prosperity of all

[1] Peter was caught some twenty years previously in the Hanoverian woods. An account of his life is given in the *Annual Register* of 1784-5, and the educational significance of his case is discussed at length by Lord Monboddo in his *Antient Metaphysics*, vol. iii. bk. 2, ch. i.

the rest.   He distinguishes with great care the characteristics
of infancy, childhood, youth, manhood, and old age, and states
the *permanent* and the more or less *ambulatory* passions of each
of them.[1]   ' By these simple but powerful springs whether
periodical or fixed, the life of man, weak and indigent as he
is, is preserved and secured, and the creature is prompted to
a constant round of action.'   The enumeration of these forces
shows clearly that Fordyce was groping towards a theory of
instinct as the source of the ' springs to action,' and his statement through *Philander* of their gradual unfolding, suggests
Vives' theory of ' premonitions ' of nature.   *Philander's* argument brings together so many anticipations of *Émile* as well as
so many divergences from Rousseau's main doctrines that it
must be quoted at length :

' I would rather,' he says, ' compare the mind to a seed which
contains all the stamina of the future plant, and all those principles
of perfection to which it aspires in its after-growth and regularly
arrives by gradual stages unless it is obstructed in its progress by
external violence.   Our minds, in like manner, are completely
organized if I may say so at first ;   they want no powers, no capacities of perception, no instincts or affections [2] that are essential to
our nature ;   but these are, in a manner, locked up, and are purposely
left rude and unfinished, that Prudence, Industry and Virtue, may
have full scope in unfolding, raising them up, and bringing them to
Maturity.   'Tis the business of Education, therefore, like a second
creation, to improve Nature, to give form and proportion and come-
liness to those unwrought materials.   And, in my opinion, we have
as much need of the hand of culture to call forth our latent powers,
to direct their exercise ;   in fine to shape and polish us into men, as
the unformed block has of the carver or statuary's skill, to draw it
out of the rude state ;   into the form and proportions of a Venus of
Medicis, or an Olympian Jupiter.   But he had need to be a very
nice and skilful artificer who would undertake this creating, this
forming task, and hope to succeed in it.   'Tis an easy matter to say
you must prepossess the mind with right opinions, and accustom it
to good habits.   But the difficulty lies in doing it on a rational

[1] *Op. cit.* pp. 15-20.

[2] Compare this view with Rousseau's doctrine of the development of faculties in a definite order.   Fordyce assumes the functioning of reason in childhood, and emphasizes the appeal to imagination.   On both points Rousseau
differs.   In other respects, and particularly in the use made of the mental
powers—their positive functioning as well as their ' exorbitancies ' (*Dialog.*
ii. p. 86)—and in the idea of ' letting the mind lie fallow ' (iii. p. 64) the germs
of Rousseau's doctrines may be clearly seen.

foundation ; that is to say, in giving it just opinions without weakening its capacity of thinking, and inuring it to the best of habits, without impairing its vigour of acting. Now 'tis certain that opinions which the mind receives from others upon their bare authority without perceiving their reasons and connections may take fast hold of the judgment, especially of the young and inexperienced ; but all such opinions fill the mind without enlightening it, they give no exercise to the mental faculties, but rather teach them to rely on the activity of others, and consequently lull the mind into a stupid indolence, and inapplication of its own powers ; a state the most dangerous and unproductive of real improvement, we can well suppose. Opinions so infused, are early imbibed in the open and unsuspicious season of life ; but let them once have taken root, and been naturalized to the soil, no effort shall make them quit their hold ever after. What shall we do then ? Shall the mind be left to the tutorage of chance, or to pick up its opinions, while it is incapable of judging for itself ? By no means. Would you not form its judgment then, and season it with right principles, to fortify it against the infection of the bad ? Doubtless. But take care how you proceed in the *seasoning* business, lest while you seek an Antidote, you prepare Poison, and render it more susceptible of errors by making it lean upon a guide which may possibly, and we find often does, lead it into them ; I mean the judgment and authority of others. On the whole of this affair, therefore, I would not anticipate but follow Nature. No discreet nurse would give a child nourishment till it craved it, nor continue cramming it when its hunger was allayed ; but patiently await the return of appetite. The mind, too, has its cravings and capacities. I would not give it intellectual food till it showed some desire of it, nor bid it judge till it discovered a capacity of judging. We find that the appetites and capacities always go together, so that Nature never stings with the former till it has bestowed the latter. Whenever, therefore, curiosity and the love of enquiry begin to disclose themselves, it is a natural indication that reason is now in a capacity to act and digest such nourishment as is proper for it. Wherefore to teach the pupil words, to which he can affix no ideas, or to prepossess him with opinions, of which he is incapable to judge, is to cram him with food which cannot nourish, but may, nay must, turn into crudities and ill-humours. But, say some, first teach him the Things and he will understand the reasons afterwards. Can that be called knowledge where the mind discerns no connection, or agreement of ideas ? And if no knowledge is conveyed what is taught but words ? If so, how much wiser is your pupil made than a parrot ? But how is it possible to communicate truth to the open and credulous mind without secretly and insensibly influencing its judgment of the authority of the teacher ? Nothing more practicable or easy, if you will let it teach itself. Strange chimera! What, teach itself before it has got any principles, and become at once its own tutor and pupil! The mind soon begins to compare things, and in proportion to the extent of its observation, judges wherein they differ or agree; it deduces one thing from another, and seldom makes a wrong conclusion if the premises are fairly set before. Let therefore such objects as are proportioned to the stretch of the intellectual eye be presented to it, and placed in the proper point of view and it will by a sudden and instantaneous glance comprehend them truly. All therefore we have to do, or which is fit to do, is to furnish materials, and store the mind with plenty of ideas; it will range and combine them itself and by a natural kind of instinct, cleave to truth while it rejects error. Whereas, if you anticipate its judgment, lay down principles for it, and draw conclusions from thence, though ever so pretty, between which it has perceived no connection, the mind in all this process, having exerted no act of its own, sees nothing, judges nothing, and like one led in the dark or blindfold, trusts only its guide. Now, gentlemen, I appeal to you, whether it bids fairest for going right by thus blindly following the conduct of every guide whom chance throws in its way; or by taking nothing upon trust but by seeing and examining itself with all the sagacity it is master of. Such exercise must naturally strengthen the mind, and enable it to see farther, and judge more surely of things; but the servile way of authority hoodwinks the mind, enervates the powers of thinking, and makes one the dupe of every impostor who has art or impudence enough to set up his judgment as the standard of truth, and impugn his opinions, as the unerring dictates of reason. 'Tis easy to see that it is only the principles and opinions which he has imbibed in the rational way, whose foundations and connections he has seen, or which he has, in a manner, discovered himself, that can secure him effectually against the seductions of error and pre-judices of company and books. For those opinions which he owes to authority may be easily supplanted by other, or greater authority, and where he has no other standard by which to judge he must for ever fluctuate amidst contending authorities without any stable bottom on which to rest. It might be easy to show in like manner, that it is with habits as with opinions; unless they are raised up on a rational and just foundation and cemented with the original principles of our constitution they will never acquire a proper firm-ness and stability, or be secure against the counter-workings of contrary habits and impressions. I mean, gentlemen, that unless the mind see the reason of its actions, and be accustomed to observe the nature and tendency of the course to which it is habituated, and unless that course be agreeable to its original feelings and affections it will never act with vigour and complacence, and though it may contract a strong propensity to a certain object, or scheme of action,

yet the habit, wanting its main basis and support will be easily dis-
placed, when the particular influence, whether of example, or of
bribes or terrors, ceases to act ; or when a better scheme of conduct
which approves itself to its genuine and uncorrupted feelings is
proposed.'

In the subsequent discussion of systematized *versus* incidental
instruction *Sophron* refers to the danger of leading pupils to
venerate unduly the class to which they belong.   He offers an
expedient that will give education more freedom and compass
and be less liable to the criticisms urged against it in debate.
Let the pupil be made acquainted with the history of the world,
the state and revolutions of human affairs in different ages and
nations.   Party-names and interests will appear mean and
despicable to a mind enlarged with extensive views.   Nothing
enlarges it more than a knowledge of men, and history places
facts before us, allows us to estimate and deduce their consequences : it sets men in every light and reveals their interests
and passions.   Past ages appeal to no bias in the mind.   But,
objects another member of the club, where shall we find the
unbiased historian ?   Roman writers give us panegyrics, now
of the patricians, now of the plebeians ; Greeks favour the ruling
aristocracy.   Modern historians defend their own views rather
than present us with simple narratives of fact.   History is
therefore a dangerous study, a kind of opium that lulls the
mind asleep, while a writer dresses up his facts in colours that
disguise and deceive.   The more interesting it is, the more it
is dangerous.   If we really wish to elevate youth and keep it
free from parties and prejudices we should teach mathematics
and philosophy.   The principles of geometry are abstract
truths.   They attach to no party, interfere with no interest,
and lead to no secular or religious system.   They accustom the
mind to a close method of reasoning ; they enlarge its views.
Every new discovery which they offer is a new acquisition and
fully repairs the labour of the search.

In winding up the debate *Philander* gleans many points of
interest for our subject.   (1) The keenest curiosity needs some
guidance.   (2) The inexperienced traveller should not be led
too far from the beaten track.   (3) He should not be kept in
leading strings.   (4) His understanding must be opened yet
not unduly influenced by any particular view of life.   (5) It

is possible for him to be acquainted with the history of systems and sects without being tinctured with their partial differences. (6) Mathematics and philosophy, rightly considered, are histories and may be united with historical studies. (7) The pupil must be taught to be ready to embrace truth wherever he finds it.

Philander also gives one important word of caution. No studies will completely emancipate the pupil from the sway of passion. Man is governed not so much by speculative principles as by *taste*, which may be influenced but cannot be controlled by education. After the pupil has seen the grandeur and the fickleness of the world he has to take his place in the din and parade of life. He has to descend into the little circle of folly, and be ' unphilosophized ' into all the cares and factions of ordinary mortals. Educational speculations sink, finally, into ' schemes for meeting the urgent necessities of a feeble nature.' On this rather pessimistic note the discussion of freedom ends. But the subsequent dialogues [1] draw attention to two laws of human progress that are full of hope. The inferior powers come almost fully into play before the higher ones, and the ' exorbitancies ' of one stage of life are the foundations of success and progress in the succeeding ones. It is Rousseau's main concern to show how the weaknesses and the exuberances may be made the vitally controlling forces of education.

[1] Especially ii. pp. 86 ff.

CHAPTER XIV

ROUSSEAU'S ' WELL-REGULATED LIBERTY '

A GLANCE at one of the numerous refutations of the *Emile* may, perhaps, help us to understand the educational prejudices which Rousseau set himself to uproot ; it may also enable us to estimate more accurately the contribution of his great ' seminal book ' to the meaning of liberty in education. A year after its appearance M. Formey published a small treatise, *Anti-Emile*, the title page of which bore the significant motto : *Tais-toi, Jean Jacques*.[1] It was a running commentary on some of Rousseau's well-known passages. One of Formey's criticisms places Jean Jacques in very clear contrast with even the enlightened advocates of freedom prior to 1762. Commenting [2] on Rousseau's remark that we often punish children before they understand the nature of their mistakes, and, indeed, before they can really be guilty of wrong-doing, he insists that what Rousseau condemns is, perhaps, the great secret of education, and a fundamental point of practice both in the moral and physical education of infancy. If we wait until we are able to speak to a child's reason we may be sure that we shall never succeed in making him listen to reason. The young child is an automaton, a little animal, and it is necessary to conquer and, if possible, to destroy everything in his life that might prove prejudicial to health, education, and good manners. This cannot be accomplished without severity, nor, indeed, without punishment skilfully and prudently administered. Nothing is more pleasant than to see the growth of docility. Let there be no fear of corrupting the child or of blunting his faculties : education, on the contrary, will set the natural forces free and give them exercise. There is no discipline apart from docility.

Before discussing this contrast it may be well to illustrate Rousseau's points of agreement with previous thinkers. Here,

---

[1] From *Emile*, I. 255.   [2] *Op. cit.* p. 31.

again, the views of a contemporary critic are of interest.   In
1766 there was published at Paris a book entitled *Les Plagiats
de M. J. J. R. de Genève sur l'éducation* par D.J.C.B.[1]   The
writer, in his Preface,[2] shows that Rousseau's eloquent portrayal of primitive man had been anticipated by Gyraldi and
Buffier, and hints that a confession of Jean Jacques' indebted-
ness to Hobbes, la Bruyère, Nicole, Bossuet and Locke (to cite
only a few ' sources ') would have included all that Rousseau
had written and that there would have been no occasion to
speak of J. J. Rousseau.   In the text the Benedictine confines
his thesis to *Emile*.   He notes in detail Rousseau's plagiarisms from Plato, Aristotle, Seneca, Quintilian, Plutarch, from
modern writers like Montaigne, de Crousaz,[3] Morelli, Fénelon,
and from contemporaries like Desessarts.[4]   He even quarrels
with the artistry of the patchwork and accuses Rousseau
of emulating the painter who united the head of a man to
the lower parts of a marine monster.

It would be strange that a book which embodied twenty
years' meditation and three years' labour should not bear traces
of ideas assimilated from ancient and modern writers.   Elements are undoubtedly borrowed from the most various sources:
even the emphasis of nature, the postponement of the appeal
to reason and the recognition of liberty in education—three
cardinal ideas of Rousseau—are not completely original.   The
first, as we have seen, appears now in one form, now in another
in previous writers, and notably in Erasmus and Comenius.
Within the decade immediately preceding *Emile* we are told
of an English boy who was able, at the age of five years, to
read and construe one of the Gospels in Latin and in Greek,
and, at six, to show a working knowledge of Hebrew.   The
author, in dedicating his pamphlet to Charles II, urges that if
' children were taught the Latin and Greek tongues so as to be
able familiarly to read ancient authors the gravity and authority
of their sentiments would fashion men to more prudence in
their converse . . . than is now seen amongst us.'[5]   In de-

---

[1] D(om) J. C(ajot) B(énédictin).   [2] Pref. iv.-xiv.

[3] *I.e.* from de Crousaz, *Logique* (1737).   The *Traité d'éducation* is also
mentioned.

[4] Author of *Traité de l'éducation corporelle*, Paris 1760.

[5] *An Essay on the Education of Children in the First Rudiments of Learning*,
by Henry Wotton, London 1753.

scribing his methods he affirms that he will not propose anything *ex cathedra* save as the ' schoolmaster and the capacity
of the scholar concur,' and fondly takes to his bosom the idea
that learning might be a *ludus literarius*. Yet Rousseau himself was not more insistent than this writer that all his proposals
' immediately flowed from the consideration of Nature itself,'
that ' Nature is the best guide,' and that ' if you take not
Nature along with you, if you go before it, or oppress it your
whole endeavour is lost.' How unlike Rousseau, on the other
hand, is the conclusion that the ' rudiments of learning in
children of the first years of education are to be laid in the
knowledge of languages, the Latin, Greek, and Hebrew,
wherein both the fountain of learning as well as Philology and
Philosophy and the principal streams and rivers thereof are to
be had.'

We have seen that the basic ideas of ' negative education '
do not appear for the first time in Rousseau. Forty years
before *Emile*, de Crousaz had stated the ' great art of education ' to consist in the choice of suitable matter of instruction.
In amplifying this idea he had mentioned curiosity, justice,
deepened understanding, refinement of feeling as some of the
ends to be attained by lessons which were *à la portée des enfans*,
lessons which they could appropriate and appreciate. He had
urged as the most subtle secret of education the putting of the
pupil into the position of teaching himself through materials
and arrangements furnished by the teacher.[1] L'abbé de
Fleury had reminded us that the desire to see a young child
acquire a habit of reflection was as sensible as to wish to see a
sapling grow a solid trunk and deep roots in a single night.[2]
Fénelon and others had expressed in their own ways Morelli's
admonition : *Qu'il faut avec les enfans faire prendre à la raison
une robe d'enfant*. And, finally, Locke, Fordyce and Watts had
definitely stated freedom to be an important factor in efficient
educational practice.

What, then, is the *distinctive* note of the *Emile* ? It is,
among other things, an apotheosis of the ' noble savage,' the
creature of splendid isolation, so glowingly characterized by the

---

[1] De Crousaz, *Traité*, vol. i. p. 247.

[2] *Choix des Etudes*, (1686) p. 129. Chapter xvii of this work has many
suggestions for the religious education of children.

magnificent negations of Rousseau's early Essays.[1]   It is a
polemic against the values of modern civilization : it is, if we
are to take the *Confessions* seriously, a lyric in which Rousseau
attempts to harmonize life's medley of discords.   It is, at
many points, a protest against the ' senseless education which
adorns our minds and corrupts our judgments from our tender
years.' [2]   It is an educational romance tinged with the ' profound and delicious solitude . . . the singing of birds and the
perfume of orange flowers ' in which, as the author tells us, he
composed in a continual ecstasy, the whole of the fifth book.[3]
In the words of an early reviewer, ' it is a motley mixture . . . a
medley of obscurity and perspicuity, subtlety and simplicity,
extravagance and good sense, infidelity and piety, good faith
and bad faith, wit and folly, philanthropy and malignity,
prudence and temerity.' [4]   Despite the plagiarisms, the patchwork, the inconsistencies, the sentimentalism, the dreams, and
the paradoxes it has a distinctive point of view and it makes a
distinctive contribution to education.   Out of ideas drawn from
a hundred sources it makes a whole so exquisitely original that,
were all its exceptionable parts deleted, the book would still
have a ' sufficiency of original matter and striking observation
to enable a dozen ordinary authors to divide the remainder
among them and figure away on the subject.' [5]

Are we, then, to find the educational secret of the *Emile* in
Rousseau's way of presenting other people's ideas ?   Buffon [6]
is said to have agreed that certain fine pages of the book contained nothing that he himself had not long ago written, but
he hastened to add that Rousseau was the only writer who
could ensure that such views would be read.   Desessarts,[7] in
the second edition of his *Traité de l'éducation corporelle*, instead
of accusing Rousseau of plagiarism, rejoiced that the master's
plume enchanteresse had disseminated the doctrines of an
obscure author.   The *Emile* is, in construction, a *Traumbuch*,

[1] Cf. *Discours sur l'inégalité*, Coll. comp. de 1782, vol. i. p. 111.
[2] *Prize Essay* (of 1750), Ed. Philibert, Genève, p. 42.
[3] *Confessions*, trans. *Masterpieces of Foreign Authors*, 1891, vol. ii. p. 197.
[4] *London Chronicle*, 1762, vol. xi. p. 590.
[5] *Monthly Review*, vol. 27, Aug. 1762, p. 153.
[6] Cf. *Pestalozzi, élève de J.J.R.* (Hérisson), footnote p. 41.
[7] *Traité* (2nd Edition), pp. ix. and x. (Avertissement).   Cf. also the criticisms of Madame de Genlis in *Adèle et Théodore*, vol. i. Letter xxiv.

but it is a dream book in the Freudian sense. It is concrete
and pictorial, dramatic and suggestive. A great measure of
its success lies in its presenting ideas upon education in such a
way as to educate. But this does not exhaust its claims to
originality. It enunciates in a new form three principles of
first importance. In order to understand Rousseau's concept
of liberty we must briefly consider the three.

I

The first brings us back to the contrast suggested by M.
Formey's criticism. Before Rousseau educationalists had
looked upon nature as tendencies more or less defective which
education had to convert, as chained powers and faculties
which training had to liberate, as dormant human values which
education had to arouse. A passive principle may have lip
service but practically it is a mere *pis aller* ; hence Formey's
concern for those who would wait for the awakening of reason.
But Rousseau frees himself from such shackles, and proclaims
his faith in the child's nature. He does more than this. He
shows how the supposed defects of the child's nature enclose
the germs of later development, and is at pains to teach us how
the very helplessness of childhood is a positive factor in forming the man of strength and independent judgment. Others,
like Basedow,[1] might devote themselves to merely concrete and
often far-fetched efforts to instruct the pupil by amusing him ;
others, like la Chalotais, might emphasize the importance of the
transition from abstract to concrete studies and speak of the
importance of self-instruction, of curiosity, of giving *du ressort
à l'âme* [2] and of providing useful studies. Rousseau incor-
porates these ideas but he makes them subordinate to a general
principle of ' following nature,' *i.e.* of utilizing the inner urge
towards growth of organs and of faculties, and he sets himself
the task of showing that this conception is not only ' intelligible
and feasible in itself,' but ' adapted to the nature of things '
and capable of being ' modified or specially applied to one
country or another, to this class or that.[3] So clearly does he

[1] As in the *Methodenbuch* of 1752 and the *Elementarwerk* of 1774. See also
Chapter xv.

[2] *Essai d'éducation nationale*, 1763. Cf. p. 43.

[3] Author's Preface to *Emile* (trans. B. Foxley, Everyman Ed.).

appreciate the novelty of his idea that he contrasts it with all the theories of the wisest writers that have preceded him. They ' devoted themselves to what a man ought to know without asking what a child is capable of learning.' [1]   The antithesis of the ' child ' and the ' is ' on one hand, and the ' man ' and the ' ought ' on the other, is by no means new, but the attempt to build up an educational scheme solely upon the foundation of the first set of terms and values is distinctly new.   It is also difficult and it is peculiarly liable to error.   It involves an observation and an interpretation of the facts of child life and of the stages in the transition to manhood which are likely to be coloured by personal tastes and prejudices.   Rousseau does not escape the pit into which his predecessors fell.   He fixes his eyes on the child, and advises us to study him for assuredly we do not know him, but his attention wanders to the childhood of the race and his pen takes up the subject of primitive man. As Emile blossoms into manhood he shows little or no enthusiasm for the values of civilization.   The burden of the whole book is civilized man born and dying a slave.   But these are incidents and accidents of the main exposition.   The *Emile* is, in appearance, a method of education where, as in a dream, we behold the condensed and dramatic presentations of the child's primitive ' nature,' and get a glimpse of ways in which these can be utilized in practice, and made subservient to the formation of a happy, ' common-sense '·life.

Only a few of Rousseau's landmarks can be noticed here. The early education of Emile is, in effect, a directed exercise of the senses through concrete life situations designed to bring into play the pupil's powers of judgment and of rudimentary reasoning.   The later chapters deal with the training of the sixth sense [2]—common sense—which Rousseau conceives to be the well-regulated use of the other five.   Strength, vigour, health, exercise, happy activity, keenness, intelligence, truthfulness (without vanity, extravagance, or ornament), precision and clearness of ideas, confidence, knowledge of abilities and limitations, these are Rousseau's conceptions of the ' perfection of childhood,' and the aims of the ' negative education ' of Emile's first dozen years.   Then begin ' work, instruction, inquiry.'   The pupil having learnt something about his own

---

[1] Preface, p. 1.   [2] *Emile*, p. 122.

powers turns to explore his environment. Rousseau fits the
'useful' studies to the requirements of the boy's nature. The
conflict of appearance and reality provokes reflection. The
early lessons in science make Emile see the wisdom of the
warnings so carefully eliminated from the early education.
Emile becomes an explorer and an inventor, re-lives the scenes
of Robinson Crusoe, learns a trade, studies the arts and manu-
factures, and gains an acquaintance with rudimentary economic
laws. Adolescence approaches and Rousseau, confronted by
it, turns poet. The first seeds of humanity are sown through
a study of the weaknesses of mankind revealed in the pages of
history. Religious enlightenment follows. Rousseau, in the
guise of the Savoyard priest, endeavours to unite the principles
of a sceptic with the practice of a devotee. Emile travels and
studies literature and art. He falls in love, sympathetically
guided by his tutor, and wins a young lady carefully educated in accordance with the requirements of *her* nature. The
tutor and the wife are the *ne plus ultra* of Emile's education.

II

The extreme emphasis of facts of 'nature' leads, in turn, to
another new principle—the rigidly scientific determination of
the pupil's curriculum and of his entire environment by the
'data' and 'hard' facts of his 'nature.' Previous advocates
of nature, like Comenius, had placed first the 'all things' to
be taught to 'all men'; instead of 'following nature' they
dragged it along with them like a dog on a leash. Rousseau
has still got his pupil on the lead but the collar and the cord
are gone and control is exercised through the very things
that the boy himself wants to do. Obsessed with the idea of a
normal development of the pupil's 'nature' relatively apart
from, and uninfluenced by, the *social* values of his environment,
the tutor hastens to evaluate every external influence in the
pupil's life and to harmonize it with the active tendencies of
the organs and faculties. If any influence is incapable of rigid
control it is eliminated. 'Nature,' 'men,' and 'things'—the
three catchwords of his analysis of the educative process—must
be harmonized, for it is only when all three agree that the pupil
'lives at peace with himself and is well-educated.'[1]   But it is

[1] *Emile*, p. 7.

clear that Rousseau has little faith in the inner efforts of the individual towards peace. His extreme anxiety to *give* the pupil peace with himself and to *follow* nature leads him to ignore the self which is to enjoy the peace and to suspect the ' nature ' which is to be the dominating force of the whole system of education. . . . *Corruptio optimi pessima*. The attempt to place ' nature ' in the forefront results in a system of educational activities chosen largely because of their amen-ability to the tutor's manipulation.

The social environment is the most plastic of the three sources and it is, therefore, the distinctive feature of Rousseau's system. Some critics, relying on isolated sentences of the *Emile*, would have us believe that the pupil is banished from society and made to renounce all its works. But in reality the tutor uses social influences on a grand scale. Emile's first idea is of property,[1] his first recorded lesson [2] makes use of a gar-dener, his first lesson in science is given by a conjurer.[3] There are hints of the co-operation of a whole village in the treatment of a naughty child, and passages in which the train-ing of Emile ' in the midst of society ' [4] is specifically mentioned. An extensive social environment is assumed in the later stages.[5] Simplification of social relationships so that they are trans-parent to the pupil's judgment, and inflexibility and uniformity of each person's behaviour are Rousseau's main aims.

The reason is found in a supposed fact of the chfld's nature. Childhood is a period of ' imperfect liberty,' [6] designed to make the child realize his *weakness* towards—both ' men ' and ' things.' Necessity, undeviating, immutable, and inviolable, is the great teacher of the early years : the pupil must find ' early on his proud neck the heavy yoke of necessity, under which every finite creature must bow.' So, urges Rousseau, ' let him find this necessity in things, not in the caprices of men ; let the curb be force not authority.' [7] Emile must not be spoiled by the fondness of parents, nor by the caprice of his equals, nor by the submission of his inferiors. He must, wherever he turns, meet a ' wall of brass ' against which he

[1] *Emile*, p. 62.   [2] P. 63.   [3] P. 135.   [4] P. 61. Cf. pp. 64 ; 88 ff. ; 217.

[5] The necessity for social and national education is specifically argued in the *Considérations sur le Gouvernement de Pologne*, especially chap. iv., but Rousseau is there pleading a special case.

[6] *Emile*, p: 49.   [7] *Emile*, p. 55.

may try his strength some five or six times, but in the end learn the futility of his attempts. Every person must be under the control of the tutor, and every word and every social relation-ship must teach a simple, invariable, concrete, practical lesson, in harmony with the demands of Emile's own nature and the nature of ' things.' It is in the harmonizing of the pupil's own powers of control with the control exercised by the tutor that the difficulty of Rousseau's scheme lies. ' No doubt Emile ought to do only what he wants, but he ought to want to do nothing but what you want him to do. He should never take a step you have not foreseen, nor utter a word you could not foretell.' [1]

In the second stage *utility* makes a powerful appeal to the pupil : it affords a means of control less stern and inflexible but very much more efficient. In the pre-adolescent stage almost every social relationship is determined by its utility for the boy's life, and Emile is encouraged to bend natural and physical forces to his own use. Now the sun is not merely the cause of a headache but a means of exploring, and escaping from a forest : fire does not merely burn but helps man to extract metals from ores. The social environment is less artificial, but, relatively speaking, social influences and the tutor's ministrations take a second place. The appeal to the senses and especially to ' common sense ' comes first. Useful ideas are to be gained through personal contact with life situa-tions and useful concrete relationships are to be investigated by the method of discovery. Rousseau desires clear ideas and convincing notions, but his main point is to avoid a ' slavish submission to authority ' and to encourage ingenuity in the discovery of relations, in the connection of ideas, and in the invention of apparatus.[2] To this admirable presentation of the claims of personal investigation Rousseau adds the contrast of the person who is enfeebled by being waited upon and served by others, but he forgets that in his carefully selected and artificially controlled environment Emile has no opportunity of testing his real impulses on persons. By confining the pupil's freedom to the investigation of the physical environ-ment the tutor sets up the very conditions of social enfeeble-ment from which he desires to set Emile free. Extreme

---

[1] *Emile*, p. 85.   [2] Cf. *Emile*, p. 139.

concern for independence results in an extreme dependence upon the few persons who make up the artificially selected and partially misleading social environment of the pupil.

In the third stage, where Rousseau aims at directing the course of the tempestuous passions, a reasonable and reasoned conception of right and wrong is supposed to function.   Here the notion of personal adjustment is practically ignored. Emile is introduced to the follies of mankind through the medium of history and gains acquaintance with God through a discussion of the wrong methods of man's approach to Him. ' Nothing is better fitted to make one wise than the sight of follies one does not share.' [1]   It may be granted that the leisurely functioning of reason in the period of ' negative education ' will probably have done a great deal to produce a reasoning Emile, and that gradually he has gained possession of those standards of value which, in Rousseau's pages, seem to descend upon him, like manna from heaven, when he reaches the desert of human wrong-doing.   But Rousseau is surely not consistent in employing the mistakes of others *pour encourager* Emile.   The earlier training is so formal that a process of disillusionment is seen to be necessary, but the process, whether it is natural or not to youth, is in itself so formal that it cannot be said to make any active use of the personal sense of right and wrong.   Once more, the earlier efforts to ensure free play for the child's ' nature,' lead finally to forms of education which ignore its native exercise and functions.   The methods of educating the passions, the conscience, and the taste are highly verbal, formal, and fantastic.   The ideas acquired are relatively foreign to the pupil's life ; in their acquisition there are few signs of real spontaneity.   Reason is supposed to be supreme, but there is little place for the operation of the active principle, which, in Rousseau's opinion, became really active only when the mind had received its ideas.   Judged by its final results, Rousseau's method is a failure.

The over-emphasis of certain ' facts ' of nature leads Rousseau into extravagances almost as serious as those which he seeks to avoid.   Nevertheless the way of paradox, and even of extravagance has its compensations.   After the *Emile* no apology was necessary for the scientific and orderly presentation of

[1] *Emile*, p. 217.

educational material, and only a ruthless disregard of the subjects and sequences of the orthodox education could have prepared the way for the wider view of an education which would develop the inner and active tendencies in and through their very activity. It matters comparatively little that Rousseau was unable to work out his idea fully or consistently : his concrete presentation of the idea itself was more important and more in keeping with the nerve of his argument than any detailed prescription could ever be. In his *Confessions* [1] he frankly records his failure as a practical teacher. Sentiment had failed him, passion had made him feel helpless in controlling his pupils, reasoning as well as rage had convinced him that often it is the child who is the philosopher and the tutor who is the child. He had studied his pupil, but was unable to apply the results of his study. Others may undoubtedly gain much from his general idea of control through ' nature ' even though they are impatient of the ' *pouvoir occulte du précepteur.*'

III

It is, however, in a third principle that one rightly finds the originality and power of the *Emile.* *For the first time a principle of freedom is enunciated as the basic principle of education.* ' *L'homme vraiment libre ne veut que ce qu'il peut et fait ce qu'il lui plaît.*' ' That man is truly free who desires *only* what he is able to perform and who does what he desires. This is my fundamental maxim. Apply it to childhood and all the rules of education spring from it.' [2] It is, in effect, a reiteration of the desires and capacities of nature as the starting point of education, and its *application* to childhood is a recognition of a certain imperfection in childhood and of a consequently imperfect liberty. It is upon this ' imperfect ' or ' well-regulated ' liberty that Rousseau bases his whole argument and indeed his whole system of education. Unfortunately, many of his critics have chosen to ignore his qualifications, and

---

[1] *Confessions*, p. 280 (vol. i.). Rousseau must have been often irritated by superficial criticisms like those of Madame de Créqui : ' J'ai lu votre *roman* sur l'éducation. Je l'appelle ainsi parce qu'il me paraît impossible de réaliser votre méthode.' Quoted from *J. J. R. d'après les Derniers Travaux* par l'abbé Delmont, p. 129.

[2] Cf. *Emile*, p. 48. *Italics* and translation mine.

indeed his definition, of liberty, and have characterized his system as *absolutely* anarchical or tyrannical.[1]

If we are to take the *Confessions* [2] as something more than an ' explanation after the event,' Rousseau was sincere in his advocacy of well-regulated liberty in the education of childhood. His own sense of justice had been outraged in his early days. The agitation of that time would, he assures us, be fresh in his memory could he live a hundred thousand years. Any act of oppression roused his ' innate characteristic ' of rallying to the weaker side. As an apprentice he had learned to see clearly the difference between filial dependence and abject slavery, between a ' reasonable liberty ' and the extreme prohibitions which made everything an object of desire for no other reason than that he was not permitted to enjoy anything. Even at the age of eleven he had noted the distinction between being ' merely obedient ' and ' entirely submissive '—a distinction of first importance for the understanding of the *Emile*. His slowness of thought and vivacity of feeling, his morbid tendency to introspection, and his intense self-consciousness must have formed the inner springs of his doctrine of ' negative education.' In an interesting passage,[3] he tells us, that thoughtful as he was,[4] he could never learn much except from his father and one of his tutors, and he immediately connects the fact with his consciousness of lack of liberty. ' My spirit, impatient of every species of constraint, cannot submit to the law of the moment ; even the fear of not learning prevents my being attentive and a dread of wearying those who teach makes me feign to understand them ; thus they proceed faster than I can comprehend and the result is that I learn nothing. My understanding must take its own time and cannot submit to that of another.' Here there is a twofold view of submission (1) of the judgment and understanding, (2) of the personality to the wishes of another. Rousseau's chief concern is to give freedom, real and unqualified, for the judgment. He is not much concerned about freedom in the second sense and, indeed, takes for granted, all through the *Emile*, the fact of submission, whether

---

[1] Cf. *La vie et les œuvres de J. J. R.* par. Henri Beaudouin, vol. ii. p. 44.

[2] Cf. *Confessions*, vol. i. pp. 16, 29.   [3] *Confessions*, i. p. 118.

[4] Cf. p. 62. ' I am persuaded that I was never really a child. I always felt and thought as a man.'

it appears in the form of mere obedience, or of whole-hearted abnegation. ' It is easy to be good,' he insists, ' when one possesses a sound judgment.' [1] Everything must yield place to this, the central element of freedom. Desires which conflict with good judgment must be conquered by exposing them to the discipline of the natural consequences of actions—the only guarantee of their being brought before the bar of *individual* judgment and intelligence. Vain desires for power must be thwarted by giving the child a clear perception of his weakness. Even ' interest ' must be subordinated to the demands of a cool examination of objects. One of the errors of the *Emile* to which Rousseau explicitly refers in the *Confessions* was the common one of attempting to secure attention and reasoning by presenting some highly interesting object to the young mind. ' The young pupil, struck with the object presented to him is occupied only with that, and leaping lightly over your preliminary discourses, lights at once on the point to which, in his idea, you lead him too tediously. To render him attentive he must be prevented from seeing the whole of your design.' [2] The machinations of the tutor, clumsy as they are, were designed to bring into play the ' common-sense ' which formed the basis of intelligent action.

In the *Contrat Social*,[3] Rousseau urges that every free act has two causes which co-operate in its production : one moral —the will which determines the act ; the other physical—the power to execute it. The second clause of the definition of liberty in the *Emile*—doing what one desires—covers the whole physical aspects of education. It is not, as we have seen, a new idea, but what a world of difference there is between this concrete presentation of the child's activity and Locke's philosophy! What it did towards securing healthful and happy conditions of education is sometimes forgotten by those who emphasize the meticulous precautions taken to ensure the negative aspect of freedom—desiring only what one is able to perform. The latter aspect, the harmonization of desires and abilities, must, of necessity, be the most critical part of the formula when applied to a creature whose abilities and capacities are subject to the laws of inner growth and to the effects

---

[1] *Confessions*, vol. i. p. 64. [2] *Confessions*, i. p. 199.
[3] *Op. cit.* III. 1. Trans. R. M. Harrington, p. 84.

of external control.   From the very nature of the case, liberty must be imperfect, must be well-regulated, in order that desires may be only commensurate with the capacities : once this is secured a perfect and unimpeded freedom will harmonize both of them with the activities.   The equilibrating of capacities, desires, and activities may, in the *Emile,* lead to a succession of *coups de théâtre pédagogiques,* and to a *système faux et bâtard,* but the conception of liberty which it embodies is none the less alluring and suggestive.

Let us begin by removing the stumbling block of the tutor's prescience, omnipotence, and infallibility.   He is, indeed, a pre-Laplacean calculator infatuated, like many another school-master, with the findings of a genetic psychology, but Rousseau may be forgiven for insisting on a life study of education and on high pedagogical and professional qualifications.   In the *Gouvernement de Pologne* [1] he warns us against making pedagogy a trade, and even artificiality may be preferred to automatism. The tutor may, in the early stages, be apt to change the colour of his dress according to the changes in his environment and in the boy's ' nature,' but a chameleon is not necessarily a bad symbol of a successful schoolmaster.   The tutor is, in short, a lynx-eyed and rather stern and inflexible representative of the grand undeviating uniformity of the physical environment, gifted with a genius for making Emile feel his weakness towards ' men ' and ' things.'   Not an entirely unknown type of school-master, perhaps, but more disposed than others of his kind to rely upon his brain rather than upon his birch for the in-duction of that entire and perfect submission which Rousseau contrasts with ' mere obedience.'   In theory he adopts the definition of liberty in the *Contrat Social* [2]—' obedience to self-prescribed law.'   In practice the ' self ' of the pupil is expanded until it coincides with the ' self ' of the tutor, just as in the *Contrat Social* the will of the individual ideally merges into the universal will.   And just as in the social contract there was a tacit engagement that, in the event of the individual refusing to obey the general will, constraint would be exercised by the whole social body, which would thus ' force the individual to be free,' [3] so in the tutor's mind there was no hesitation in

---

[1] Chap. iv. p. 32. (Ed. Londres, 1782).

[2] *Op. cit.* I. viii. p. 28.   [3] *Op. cit.* i. 7. (p. 26).

forcing Emile to submit himself to the necessity of the physical environment and to the necessity of his own nature. In effect, the *Emile* is a recognition of submission to some form of authority as a fundamental feature of freedom in education. Rousseau is, therefore, in the true line of educational development from Plato to Kant and Hegel. Plato's worship of the state is gone ; gone also are the mediaeval schoolmaster, the authority of the church, and the prestige of learning. In their place is the necessity of Nature, a new kind of pope, infallible and inviolable, with the tutor as his immediate and visible representative.

Well-regulated liberty becomes, then, in practice a method of control without the appearance of authority. It means, in the first place, the recognition of the importance of individual differences in education. ' Every mind,' insists Rousseau, ' has its own form in accordance with which it must be controlled.' [1] Success comes from controlling it in this and in no other way. It means, secondly, control through some internal value or aspect of life which varies according to the stage of development. In the early stages Emile is controlled, urged on, held back by the hand of necessity alone.[2] Later, utility gives an additional means of control, provided the meaning is relative to his age.[3] When the passions appear they are further reins to control his movements.[4] At twenty he is completely under control because he obeys of his own free-will.[5] When reason enters the heart the tutor changes the ' semblance of liberty, the precarious liberty of the slave who has not received his orders,' into real freedom and admonishes the young man to control his heart.[6] Finally, as the above quotations show, all external control is to harmonize with internal control and, in the last resort, to be identical with it. Rousseau does not shrink from assuring us, early in his treatment of Emile, that ' no subjection is so complete as that which preserves the form of freedom ' [7] ; he seems to see no danger in first taking the will captive, in regulating and curbing the pupil's desires, in gradually relaxing the leading strings, and finally in asking the pupil to take control of his own heart. The attunement of the desires to the capacities, and the harmonization of both

[1] *Emile*, p. 58.　　[2] *Emile*, p. 56.　　[3] *Emile*, p. 141.　　[4] *Emile*, p. 194.
[5] *Emile*, p. 298.　　[6] *Emile*, p. 408.　　[7] *Emile*, p. 84.

with the activities, has been theoretically attained, yet few would maintain that Emile has been educated in the light of a concept of liberty.   Wherein does Rousseau err ?

The cardinal error of the *Emile* lies in the view taken of the faculty of reason.   Childhood is the sleep of reason.   The mind is to be left undisturbed until its faculties develop ;[1] consequently until the appearance of reason nothing is to be done to promote any real activity of the mind.   It is most important that the child should be actively engaged in sense exercises, but the mind itself is passive in sensation.   It is important that percepts should be received, experienced, connected, and arranged in an order truly representative of the external world, but any union or fusion of concepts is to be avoided until the mind has a full store of ideas.   In the moral sphere also the child, before the advent of reason, does good or evil without knowing it.   He may note the connections of his conduct with its natural consequences, but no ideas of right and wrong are to be introduced and no standards of value are to be applied to his actions.   This view leads naturally to the idea of controlling the order and nature of the sensory stimuli that play upon the pupil, and this in turn to the control of Emile himself, to the over-emphasis of his mental passivity, to the idea of a simplified yet distorted and artificial social environment, and to the notion that all the means usually taken to encourage and to hasten development are intrinsically harmful.   The educator is to lose time rather than gain it :   to guard the heart from vice rather than to force it to virtue :   to keep the mind from error rather than surfeit it with knowledge.   Rousseau has, it is true, a glimpse of the truth that reasoning may take place at different psychological levels, but the rudimentary reasoning involved in the ' associated experience of several sensations ' differs, in his pages, from the ' reasoning of the intellect,' not merely in complexity but in nature.   His perception of the fact that children ' reason very well with regard to things that affect their actual and sensible well-being,'[2] should have led him to infer that in a very real sense the mind and the reasoning powers are active in childhood.   Instead of this inference he draws the conclusion that because reason, in its complex functioning is absent in childhood, the child's mind is essentially

[1] *Emile*, p. 57   [2] *Emile*, p. 72.

passive and its reason asleep. No doubt he looks upon reason with some suspicion and therefore wishes to keep it inactive, but his point of view is primarily coloured by the prevalent faculty psychology, with its emphasis of independent entities, like memory, perception, etc., which appear suddenly at given points of development, and become stronger through some specific type of exercise. Rousseau has too much sympathy with childhood to fall into the errors of a disciplinary education, and his adherence to the faculty psychology has little *specific* influence upon his aims and methods of education. It gives, however, a very natural and easy psychological basis for a view of development that is essentially biological, serves well his plan of demonstrating definite stages of development in successive chapters of his book, and, above all, it supports his postponement of the appeal to reason. But, as it works out in the *Emile*, it gives a fanciful equilibrium of the desires and capacities attained by controlling some of the vital impulses and starving some of the fundamental abilities. This we shall now illustrate.

(*a*) First, in order of importance, we may consider Emile's social tendencies. In the tutor's anxiety to reflect the order, permanence, and necessity of ' things,' he excludes from Emile's society all real companionship. This over-emphasis of necessity is likely to give the pupil a wrong impression of the plasticity of the physical environment and to teach too powerfully the lesson of absolute, inevitable law before which the individual must lie prostrate. The later stage of utility does something to correct this impression by showing the flexibility of laws for a race of beings not content to find freedom in a slavish submission to physical forces. It gives some opportunity for the operation of self-assertive efforts, for the circumvention of necessity, for the perception of the strength as well as the weakness of the individual. But the transference of this false idea of dependence to the social environment undoubtedly gives erroneous notions of social relationships, and of the boy's social powers and impulses. Its portrayal of a commonwealth in which all the members are absolutely submissive to a chain of laws which they are powerless to break is the negation of social life. Even if it is not so, it is the negation of education and of freedom in education, for it gives the individual no opportunity of finding for himself where

necessity begins and ends.   Real freedom demands the adjustment of the social impulses to inferiors and equals as well as to
superiors.   But Rousseau will have none of this : he will not
even permit any expression of the tutor's approval or disapproval of the boy's early actions.   The later formal training
would certainly make the pupil the ' dupe of his follies.'   Kept
ignorant of all adjustment to creatures weaker than himself he
would assuredly enter society with a mistaken idea of his
powers, and at a time when the expedition of his violent love
would be likely to ' outrun the pauser reason.'

(b) In stating the conditions of intellectual development
Rousseau adds little to Socrates' plea for the very gradual presentation of abstract ideas.   But he is more ingenious in
actually presenting them.   He sees that some abstract ideas
can be readily enough grasped by young children if the
methods of presentation are suitably concrete.   His lesson on
the idea of property is a model combination of sensory appeal,
concrete activity and purposiveness.   An extension of the
method would have ensured the successful introduction of the
' utility ' lessons into the earlier period of negative education.
But Rousseau underrates the pupil's integrative and active
mental tendencies.   His distrust of the ' active principle ' leads
him to limit seriously the most important of all opportunities
for reasoning—the pupil's *native* efforts to equalize desires
and capacities.

(c) Even in the method of discovery there seems to be little
activity that is *really* purposeful from the child's point of view.
Emile seldom or never comes face to face with a problem of
his own.   The tutor ' puts the problems ' and suggests the
vital steps in their solution.   The lessons give the impression
of elaborate and artificial ' preparation ' in the Herbartian
sense, followed by the wholesale ' giving away ' of vital points
through leading suggestions.   The pupil, for example, is in-
trigued over the behaviour of a ' duck ' that feeds from a
conjurer's hand.   He goes home and discusses his problem.
' We try to imitate it.   We take a needle thoroughly magne-
tized. . . .   Another time we may notice the direction assumed
by the duck.' [1]   From whom do these suggestions come ?
Emile is lost in the forest in order that he may become

[1] *Emile*, p. 136.

acquainted with certain geographical facts. Here, again, the tutor cannot refrain from making the suggestion, ' If only we could see the position of Montmorency.' [1] The real activity of the ' active principle ' is in the elaborate preparations of the tutor. On nearly every page there is evidence of Rousseau's failure to distinguish the curiosity of the active mind from the mere caprice of the vacant mind. Legitimate curiosity is stifled and real purposiveness banished in the effort to avoid a premature exercise of the faculty of reason.

(*d*) In the sphere of moral education there is even greater timidity. The root idea of learning from natural consequences is *relevancy* to the child's life, and by this criterion its value should be estimated. It is unfair to argue, as Monroe [2] does, that moral education through the discipline of natural consequences [3] is impossible owing to the child's lack of reasoning power. As we have seen, Rousseau admits that children reason very well about matters that affect them personally, and the reasoning connected with the personal consequences of one's own actions admirably fulfils the condition. In any scheme of education Rousseau's method must play a large and honourable part. The beginning of the moral life must be found in a clear perception of the consequences of one's own acts and here, as elsewhere, one learns most from experience. But Rousseau errs in making it the sole method of moral training. He seems to assume that there is something intrinsically wrong in learning from others : that lack of permanence and uniformity in the moral judgments of our fellows will give a chaotic and distorted view of right and wrong. Here, again, one has to balance the disadvantages of an egocentric education against those which may arise out of our intercourse with society. If there is any real loss of freedom in social intercourse it is the result, not of learning from another but of failing to comprehend the bearing of another's judgment upon ourselves. And what can be more effective in giving a balanced and thoughtful appreciation of moral values than our own early perception of the different forces which they exert in the lives of others ?

[1] *Emile*, p. 144.   [2] *History of Education*, p. 559.

[3] As Professor Adamson notes (Edition of Locke's *Thoughts*, p. 39 *n*.), Rousseau and Herbert Spencer pervert Locke's ' real discipline of *moral* consequences.'

In his attempt to make the consequences of his actions directly and completely transparent to Emile, Rousseau at times over-rates and at other times under-rates the boy's reasoning powers. If he is naturally self-centred, and if he is kept apart from others, and is not encouraged to reason, it is clear that he will often fail to distinguish the consequences of his own action from other consequences over which he has no control. He leaves his window open and suffers from cold, but all colds are not caused by open windows. Why should the tutor not ensure that the lesson is learnt ? Warning would be less prejudicial to the success of nature's teaching than the shielding of the boy from the consequences of his actions, or than the ensuring of his punishment, is likely to be. And, as the fortunes of war may make the tutor catch cold on the next occasion, it would seem prudent to add, as Herbert Spencer does, the tutor's expostulations to the list of natural consequences. A certain reserve and aloofness on such occasions may, of course, do much to retain the pupil's confidence, and the removal of personal antagonisms may lead to more natural and frank relations between him and his teacher. But the tutor's extreme self-abnegation may tend to establish undesirable habits, the consequences of which are trivial or unnoticed at the time. It may thus lead to recklessness of conduct, or if that is avoided by the tutor's care, to a false feeling of security and of ability to manage one's affairs. Apart from Rousseau's contention that vices are instilled by prohibiting them, it does not seem possible to state a single indisputable advantage of the doctrine of moral training through the purely natural consequences of one's actions. Even if this point be conceded it might still be more profitable to deepen some vices than to allow many to have opportunities for free growth. And the possibility of instilling evil brings with it at least some hope of effectively influencing the pupil for good through direct and sympathetic forms of moral training.

Indirect training of this kind, while affording a basis for morality, has no really moral effect. It has little contact with the more subtle motives of a child's actions. It does not tend to encourage the intelligent forecasting of consequences likely to arise from action, and it gives no opportunity of learning from the frank reactions of others. It gives a misleading notion of the self and its world.

(e) There is the same distrust of self-activity in Rousseau's treatment of the imagination and in his education of taste. Although feeling is the very citadel of selfhood, taste is finally declared to be the ' power of judging what is pleasing or displeasing to most people.' [1] The imagination awakes the other ' faculties,' overpowers them, enlarges the possibilities of the individual life, stimulates and feeds desires. *Therefore* its acts must be restricted, and it must be kept asleep until law and order are established among the passions.[2] In the education of the feelings where almost complete freedom might be expected Rousseau pays extreme deference to the opinion of others. He attempts to control both the intellectual and emotional expressions of the imagination, a power which, like reason, re-arranges and combines ideas, establishes new connections among mental contents, suggests new possibilities of activity, sets old ideas in a new light, and, generally, keeps the individual alive to the demands of an inner life which refuses to be fettered and bound by the hardest and most brutal necessity. The distrust of the passions and the egocentricity of Emile's earlier education lead Rousseau to state the theory of adolescence as a second birth. To feelings so bound and passions so egoistic, to reasoning confined to a book knowledge of the impulses of others, the influx of feelings and emotions, characteristic of adolescence, must indeed have seemed a ' second birth,' but the term is a witness to the fact that Emile was denied his true educational birthright.

Rousseau's great book is, after all, a work of science and not a romance. The test is found in the writer's statement of the results of his educational experiment. Few educators are so candid. The distrust of reason, the starving of the feelings, the neglect of the motives of action, the curbing of the social impulses, the stifling of imagination, and the rigid direction of the inventive and exploratory powers produce a youth devoid of vital, personal interests in the ' storm and stress ' period. His first ideal is sketched for him by his tutor. It takes the form of Sophie's portrait, and it is intended to ' repress the senses by means of the imagination.' [3] The first powers

Emile, p. 305. [2] Cf. *Emile*, pp. 44, 45, 180. 191, 192, 284. [3] Cf. p. 294.

developed with such care must now have their period of negative education and be disciplined by a faculty which they themselves long tried to keep in slumber! And just as the extreme efforts to give an egocentric education lead finally to a complete acceptance of the opinions and tastes of others, so in the sphere of personal ideals, the long-awaited reason pays continual deference to the suggestions of the tutor. With the ideal of personal freedom in his heart Emile continually asks : ' What must I do ? ' The tutor is ubiquitous ; he interferes continually, and always with marked effect. Emile is entirely submissive, although in many cases he can scarcely be supposed to see necessity, utility, or right in the tutor's advice. He yields, notwithstanding the promptings of reason, conscience, sentiments, passions, imagination, and all the other natural qualities of the youth of twenty-one! The tutor's final testimonial is : ' Emile is easily guided by the voice of a friend.' [1]

What, then, is the permanent contribution of the *Emile* to the meaning and function of freedom in education ? We have seen that Rousseau professed to follow ' nature,' and that although he introduced a new conception of discipleship, he interpreted the facts of nature in the light, and at the level, of the man-in-himself. We have seen that he professed to determine the tutor's activity and the curriculum of education by a careful balancing of internal and external values, and that although he illuminated the problem of the right relationship of the teacher to the pupil, he overstepped the limits of reasonable and helpful control. We have also seen that he was courageous enough to base education upon a carefully defined concept of freedom, and that in working out his definition he aimed at a sterile balancing of the desires, capacities and activities, placing in each pan such desires and capacities as put a minimum stress on the beam.

Rousseau's permanent contribution to freedom lies in provoking us to ask a pertinent question and in giving us a certain insight into the facts required to answer it. The writer probably intended to bring us face to face with the realities of education much in the same way as the tutor introduced Emile to the conjurer's duck or lost him in the forest at Montmorency.

[1] My typist's re-interpretation of this sentence is suggestive. It reads : ' Emile is easily guided by the vice of a friend ' !

We can imagine Jean Jacques reading de Crousaz' satirical re-interpretation of the appeal to nature in education, wondering whether he might safely develop the same idea in his own concrete and inimitable way, and finally deciding on a portrait of an imaginary pupil, controlled at every point, and yet presumed to be free. That picture might force us to ask two questions : Can we give freedom to our children now that we have secured it for ourselves ? If we can give freedom is it to express the view of the pupil who enjoys it or that of the tutor who enjoins it ? These are the questions that the *Emile* asks. Whether Rousseau shelves them or answers them wrongly he emphasizes four truths. First, that wise internal control has educative possibilities which have neither been realized nor exploited. Secondly, that the internal values provided by the growth of organs and powers are for all stages of education the most effective of educational forces. Thirdly, that indirect attempts to thwart or stifle the desires are likely to be abortive and, in the long run, to bring about an undue submission to the values and behests of others. Fourthly, that no system of education is on sound lines which seeks to determine pedagogical activities *solely* by the natural values functional at a given moment in the pupil's life. The artificialities of the *Emile* are due to the lack of a guiding value for the natural tendencies and desires that are craving opportunities of development. Growth, in other words, is dependent on a glimpse of something to which the individual has not attained, rather than upon the enjoyment of something which he possesses. To foster growth we must surround him with values that beckon to his inner life yet lie partially beyond it. The moral of the *Emile* is that the safest way of providing spiritual nourishment is to present to the pupil the great values deliberately chosen by the race in its continued, if not in its continual, advance towards civilization. With all his hesitation, this is what Rousseau does. If he teaches us anything it is that freedom is not to be found in any mere equilibrium of purely individual and purely natural values. Real freedom never states any condition of merely internal equilibrium ; the free spirit vibrates in sympathy with forces outside it.

CHAPTER XV

EVALUATIONS OF 'WELL-REGULATED LIBERTY'

In his later years Rousseau disclaimed any intention of prescribing a *practical* method of education. *Emile*, he avowed,
was a philosophical work dealing with the natural goodness of
man and with the causes of his decadence in society. 'I
merely wanted to prevent the harm that was being done in
education,' he wrote. But, whether he wished it or not, he
was taken seriously both as an educator and as a philosopher ;
so seriously, indeed, that one of his recent biographers, in
denying that Rousseau solved the problem of education, hopes
that he did not hinder its solution.[1] The immediate effect of
Emile was to stimulate an interest in the *possibility* of freedom.
In this chapter we shall consider its influence upon the experimental work of Basedow, Williams, and the Edgeworths,
and review the criticisms of Priestley and Godwin on certain
sections of the book. Rousseau's influence on subsequent
writers will be discussed in the following chapters, for it is no
exaggeration to say that the history of the idea of freedom
after Rousseau is the history of Rousseau's direct or indirect
influence upon all writers of repute who came after him.

I

Basedow's *Philanthropinum* owed much to Rousseau. A
teacher who could take advantage of a carriage ride to make
his pupil observe the nature and utility of a circle might be
expected to turn the *Emile* to good pedagogical account, and
skilfully to adjust its views to the notions of religious toleration
then current in Germany. Yet what a contrast there is between some of the rules of the *Philanthropinum* and Rousseau's
attempt to keep Emile out of the world ! Education, in Basedow's opinion, must prepare the pupil for the risks of everyday

[1] *La vie et les œuvres de J. J. Rousseau*, Henri Beaudouin, p. 148.

life. Hence his occasional appeal to luck and chance, his acknowledgment of the trappings as well as the privations of life ; his *jours de mérite, de richesse et d'élévation* ; his distinctions between mechanical and reasoned obedience ; his attempts to instruct through amusement ; his ' dosing ' of troublesome boys with medicine, a form of ' purgation ' which would surely have made Plato and Aristotle smile. What a strange medley of concreteness, of work and play, of conversation and dialogue, of frivolity and gravity is the *Elementarwerk* of 1774 !

It shows very plainly the fallacy into which enthusiastic advocates of realistic methods are prone to fall. Rousseau's early environment exemplified the laudable principle of allowing nothing to strike Emile's eye which the boy could not understand, and gave examples of the practical working out of the principle in the usual school subjects. The concrete setting of some of these lessons is so striking that it is likely to captivate the attention of a teacher and incite him to continual effort to present ideas in a concrete, sensory form. Long persistence in this pedagogical exercise is apt to lead unconsciously to the conclusion that what can be made sensory is *ipso facto* educational. A glance at Basedow's *Elementarwerk* will convince one of the fallacy.[1]

II

Priestley agrees with the main contention of the *Emile*—that education demands a measure of freedom. He does so because he believes that it is an art which can be developed only through experiment and research.[2] ' We can never expect to see human nature . . . brought to perfection but in consequence of indulging unbounded liberty and caprice.' [3] But he dissents from Rousseau's view of the function of authority and the

---

[1] Thus (Pinloche, *Basedow et le Philanthropinisme*, p. 75) : ' C'est sur une gravure ou même au tableau noir que Wolke (one of Basedow's assistants) . . . expliquera tous les détails de l'accouchement à ses élèves,' etc., etc. And compare, *e.g.*, the following account of *La morale enseignée par les images* (*Man. Elem.* i. p. 124), Planche V. 'Sur cette gravure, des garcons et des filles dansent et sautent. O la sotte fille, qui lève la jambe plus haut qu'il ne convient à une demoiselle. Sans doute on le lui a dit, mais elle n'y pense plus la vilaine ! Que va dire son grand-père qui l'a regardée sans qu'elle s'en doute ? '

[2] Priestley, An Essay on the *First Principles of Government* (2nd Ed. 1771, pp. 78 ff).

[3] *Ibid.* p. 86.

teaching of religion.   Religious duties should be the educator's first concern, and the child should be early taught to submit to whatever is his duty to God and man.[1]

Priestley's arguments for the child's submission to authority are similar to Rousseau's views of his submission to necessity. The inflexible rule, the efficient functioning of habit, and the association of ideas are the chief points of the argument. The last point is worthy of note.   Like Hartley, Priestley held the principle of association to be as important for the explanation of mental phenomena as the principle of gravity is in physics.   Many of his educational arguments are based on it.[2]   Thus, moderate severity is justified on the ground that merely pleasurable ideas soon pass into oblivion, whereas a degree of pain ensures remembrance.   The efficient forces of education are found in uniform, well-established associations.   The conjunction, rather than the affinity, of ideas is the point of importance.   It matters little that the elements are themselves active, or indeed that their association is itself an active process, although the author's concern for activity is shown in his advocacy of pain as a stamper-in of otherwise inert and colourless associations.

Accordingly, Priestley condemns the maxim ' hastily adopted and with great plausibility supported by some men of genius that nothing should be inculcated upon children which they cannot perfectly understand and see the reason of.'   He points out that, in practice, the maxim is applied only to the teaching of religion and that the attempt to make it universally applicable would soon convince us of its absurdity.   In reality we act on the exactly contrary maxim in everything that affects young children, and, from the nature of things, there is no

---

[1] Cf. *Miscellaneous Observations Relating to Education* (1778), 2nd edition, particularly pp. 13, 72, 75 ff., 149.   In his *Essay on a Course of Liberal Education* Priestley, at that time a tutor in an academy at Warrington and responsible for the teaching of Latin, Greek, French, Italian, Theory of Language and Universal Grammar, Oratory, Civil Law, and History, gives a glimpse of his general methods.   He advocates a ' proper mixture of dignity and freedom.' An eye-witness describes him at a later period of his life as modest and courteous, unassuming and candid, pouring out with the simplicity of a child the stores of his capacious mind, inviting questions, and considering objections to his point of view.   Cf. *Life and Correspondence of Joseph Priestley* by J. T. Rutt (1831); vol. ii. p. 162, vol. i. pp. 22, 50, etc.

[2] Cf. *Memoirs*, vol. i. p. 304, where he refers to the great use made of the doctrine of Association in the *Observations*.

possibility of our doing otherwise. We accustom them to words the meaning of which is unknown to them. Adults have to learn the lessons of life in much the same way. Divine Providence continually presents appearances to their view and they have to search for reality. The gradual deciphering of things which we have long contemplated without understanding, contributes greatly to the pleasure of discovery. So with children. It matters little that no determinate ideas are communicated. They can be accustomed to the outward forms of religion, to keep silence and to kneel when others pray, for example ; they can be impressed with the notion that reverence is due to a power they do not see, and that there is an authority to which all mankind must submit. Mechanical habits will keep these notions active until children enter into their meaning with understanding and pleasure. The process is psychologically similar to the habit of bowing when we enter a room or to the practice of lighting fires on the fifth of November.[1]

This argument pre-supposes (1) that religion is compounded from religious ideas or elements which exist before they are unified, (2) that the parts or elements have only to be brought by some means into association in order to make the whole, (3) that the elements enter into new combinations without themselves undergoing transformation in the process. These points may be further discussed.

The first gains a certain plausibility by Priestley's insistence on the ease with which ' useful notions of religion ' can be given to children. They can easily be taught that there is a being called God. Even if the verbal ' explanations ' lead them to conclude that God is a man who lives above the clouds, no harm will be done. There is, as Priestley says, nothing in this instruction that a child who can use the mother tongue may not be made to understand, but to see, as Priestley suggests, in this ' nothing ' the substance of all that is most important in religion is to confuse actions and words, and to make religion synonymous with ideas *about* religion. The *general* argument, however, is that simple ideas such as these ' grow,' that they become associated in a great variety of ways, and that reason and understanding illuminate and expand them. It is, there-

[1] *Miscellaneous Observations, Works* (Ed. Rutt), vol. xxv. p. 44.

fore, possible that they may later become effective forces of the life and become influential in forming character.

How they do this is not made clear in Priestley's exposition. He insists upon the necessity for religious ' habits,' which are later referred to as ' devotional feelings.' He argues that the impression which ideas make upon the mind does not depend upon *definitions*, but upon *sensations*, and upon the extent and variety of association. The idea of God entertained by a man who has not had a previous religious training must be very different from that of a person accustomed to think and speak of God from infancy. In the former case, the masses of ideas are fixed and stabilized and devotional feelings cannot be awakened ; in the latter, even, though as an adult, he may become profligate, there are hopes of reform if the religious impressions have not been too early effaced. And if religious ideas and principles *could* be introduced into the later life they would be foreign and dissimilar to all the other impressions with which the mind has been hitherto stored and they could not make their presence felt effectively. What is lacking is ' a proper set of *associated feelings* arising from *actual impressions*, the season for which is over and will never return.'

Everything, then, seems to depend upon these feelings and impressions. Here Priestley's exposition is confused and unsatisfactory. His theory requires the association of kinaesthetic sensations with verbal impressions of the Deity. But he does not explain how they produce ' a proper set of associated feelings.' They may, of course, do so, but Priestley seems to have doubts which appear from time to time. He cautions us against rigorous religious exercises. He dismisses the idea of the child's intuitive attraction towards virtue. Those who attempt to make children love virtue for its own sake do not know much about childhood. They do not consider the origin of our affections. ' For the most disinterested of them become so by degrees only, and are far otherwise at their first formation. Except the mere gratification of our corporeal senses, we at first value and pursue everything for some other end than itself, and afterwards come to value it for its own sake. A child has no love or affection for any persons whatever till he has felt their importance for himself.' . . . Yet he does not see that if this observation is true, his previous argument that early learning proceeds through the imposition of adult values is probably fallacious.

Priestley's discussion, however, emphasizes truths neglected by Rousseau. He shows that simple ideas about religion are easily grasped by a child. He sees clearly that religious teaching may give a breadth of view to lessons in history, literature, and, indeed, to all the ' secular ' subjects. He is right in reminding us that the teacher's aloofness from religious instruction would mean that he yielded place to other influences which might be irreligious. He is probably right in arguing that no life and no education can be considered full or rich which has no place for God. He is also probably right in supposing that an atmosphere of sincere devotion to religion will powerfully affect the religious development of the child. But all these truths give no support to the idea of instilling religion through the exercise of authority, and they are inconsistent with the view that education is an experimental science. It is along these lines that experiment is most needed.

III

Many experiments based on Emile's education were made in the closing decades of the eighteenth century. The most detailed, and certainly the most critical, is described in David Williams' *Lectures on Education*.[1] He shows at length the ' pantomimical prettiness ' of Rousseau's methods, and by actual experiment endeavours to sift the wheat from the chaff. An account is given of its application to a child of six years of age, whose education was approached through various phases of natural history. The first excursions and conversations with rustics and gardeners were discouraging : but the child soon busied himself in studying the methods by which natural products were converted into artificial conveniences. The smith's occupation led naturally to a study of stones, earths, and the extraction of ores ; the carpenter's to a study of timber, and to the furnishing of houses, a subject which he pursued at odd moments and in wet weather. The novelty of converting one substance into another by the crucible excited his admiration. The necessity for making and distinguishing objects led to drawing. Collections of various objects were

[1] *Treatise on Education*, 1774, and *Lectures on Education*, 1789.

made and a system of barter introduced. Arithmetic soon appeared. Williams was astounded at his pupil's progress. ' The rapidity with which he actually comprehended or converted to his purpose the four general rules of arithmetic was beyond any example I had seen in the progress of learning ; and I am convinced no such effect is possible by the menaces of authority, or the punishments of tyranny. . . . I could not avoid, on the occasion, reflecting with wonder on that undefinable faculty, by which I had obeyed the hand of authority, and waded in wretchedness through volumes of arithmetical calculations without comprehending or annexing an idea of utility to any of its operations.' [1] The boy's further education is not described, but we are told that parental jealousy put an end to the experiment.

Although Williams does not think that *Emile* was directly helpful in his experiment, his later observations on the development of youths, educated in his boarding school, ' many of whom had been at the most celebrated universities or schools of Europe,' show a discriminating adherence to Rousseau. He insists on social life, refusing to follow Rousseau in disposing of the family by the wand of poetic imagination. A very frank account of his difficulties in adapting Rousseau's ideas to boarding-school life is given. Nothing analogous to ' savage ' life makes its appearance, and Williams finds no support for the idea of a merely vegetative or negative education. The idea of a stage when the faculties exceed the desires is characterized as fanciful. He referred this doubt to Rousseau, who remarked that Williams was conversant only with artificial children. Like a man of science Williams waited patiently for the opportunity to examine a true ' child of nature.' At last a boy of twelve who had been educated strictly in accordance with Rousseau's principles was brought under his notice. There were no signs of superfluous faculties ! He saw ' a little emaciated figure, his countenance betraying marks of premature decay or depraved passions ; his teeth discoloured and his hearing almost gone.' [2] His parents had been patiently waiting for the appearance of curiosity and the other mental qualities which flit across Rousseau's educational stage. They waited for a year after the predicted time. They brought the

[1] *Lectures on Education*, vol. i. pp. 139 ff.   [2] *Op. cit.* vol. iii. p. 5.

boy to Williams, who describes him as so diseased in body and mind that had he been invested with the powers of the Spartan inspectors he would have doomed him to death on the spot.

Williams dissented from Rousseau's views regarding the birth of curiosity. He saw evidence of it in early years. The birth of love he believed to be as gradual as the advent of spring. Some of his pupils out-rivalled Emile in their philosophical and scientific enquiries. They formed a little association of scientists—the eldest was under fifteen—and being disappointed at the ' puerile, improbable, and foolish papers ' of the Royal Society, they drew up a number of problems of their own for investigation.

The most interesting aspects of Williams' experiment relate to moral development. It was known that he professed to instruct youth without punishment, and the fact was turned to good account by some of his pupils. One boy never failed to say that his father had assured him that Williams had pledged his honour not to punish. ' It seems,' he remarks, ' to have been the study of that boy to try the extent of my patience.' A juvenile court was formed to deal with misdemeanours. His greatest task was to deal effectively with lying. He tried Rousseau's *suites naturelles*—not to believe the liar even when he spoke the truth, and to accept as true all accusations of falsehood made against persistent offenders. Lying flourished. Falsehood was then made a problem of the court. The hardened offender dodged all the traps that were set for him by his companions. At length Williams took the bold step of bringing to his school in the capacity of a servant one of the most accomplished liars and cheats he could find. Very soon the court had its hands full. Williams left matters to the boys, stipulating only that their actions should establish precedents applicable to all the members of the school. They debated ways and means. Punishments failed. Williams brought to their aid all the pedagogical authorities that he knew. They consulted together Xenophon's *Institutions of Cyrus*, Plutarch's *Morals*, Locke's *Thoughts*, and Rousseau's *Emile*. The pupil who gave trouble was ultimately withdrawn because Williams would not promise to ' attend to his learning without harassing him on peccadillos in morals.' The servant disappeared. The lesson was learnt : the pupils had been given an insight into the nature of lying and its effects, and they had been taught to purge their own society.   Williams adds the note : ' I own I have not succeeded with others.'

On one important point Williams agrees with Rousseau. On the whole, he has faith in the good nature of children.   ' I have observed them attentively and do not recollect anything like a vicious child in the period to which these *Lectures* are confined.   Little humours, caprices, and perversities are ob- servable ; but far from being injurious they might be improved into means of information or advantage.   It is by the obliqui- ties of the mind as by the disorder of the body, we arrive at the knowledge of its constitution.' [1]

The following paragraph summarizes Williams' observations :

' That in domestic as in political life, order, harmony, and obedience ever accompany freedom, that children may be induced to the utmost exertions of body or mind without tyranny, punish- ment, or reward, that the great instruments furnished by nature, activity and curiosity, may be directed in extensive and rapid pursuits of natural history, natural philosophy, etc. . . . with- out obliging the pupils to sit down or commit books to memory, these truths rest on actual knowledge ; not on the inferences of imagination.   I do not say I have seen all these truths exemplified in one pupil : but I have known children at the age of seven, eight, nine, or ten who understood more natural history, chemistry, and mechanics than I did at five and twenty, though I had endured with good repute the distress and horror of the general mode of forming a scholar.   They could draw from nature ; they understood the practice, though not the rules, of arithmetic.   Not one of them had been " taught to read."   All, however, could read, and acquired the art before it had been expected or desired.'

All that is best in Rousseau is put to the practical test in Williams' experiment.   The acuteness of his criticism contrasts favourably with the adulations of writers like Mrs. Macaulay,[2] and the sanity of his methods with many foolish attempts to imitate the education of Emile.   Lord Kames, who antici- pated Rousseau in urging that man is so fond of liberty that

---

[1] *Op cit*. vol. i. p. 186.   Williams' contribution to education is to attempt ' what no school has yet been instituted to do,' to train children by simple and natural means into intelligent, honest, truthful and just men—aims ' reducible to lessons and practicable as those of languages, doctrines and maxims. Cf. vol. i. p. 60.

[2] *Letters on Education*, Dublin Ed. 1790.

restraint [1] from anything, however indifferent, is sufficient to make it an object of desire, gives examples of the badly regulated liberty of some experiments suggested by Rousseau's ideas.

IV

In his *Memoirs*, Richard Lovell Edgeworth describes at some length the education of his eldest son. *Emile* had made a great impression on him, and he determined to make a fair trial of Rousseau's system. The father himself was but twenty-three years old, and steadily followed his plan for several years, despite the ridicule of relatives and friends. The effects of the education from the third to the eighth year are thus described :

' I dressed my son without stockings, with his arms bare, in a jacket and trousers such as are quite common at present, but which were at that time novel and extraordinary. I succeeded in making him fearless in danger, and what is more difficult, capable of bearing privation of every sort. He had all the virtues of a child bred in the hut of a savage, and all the knowledge of *things*, which could well be acquired at an early stage by a boy bred in civilized society. I say knowledge of *things*, for of books he had less knowledge at seven or eight years old, than most children have at four or five. Of mechanics he had a clearer conception, and in the application of what he knew more invention than any child I had then seen. He was bold, free, fearless, generous ; he had a ready and keen use of all his senses and of his judgment. But he was not disposed to *obey* : his exertions generally arose from his own will, and though he was what is commonly called good-tempered and good-natured, though he generally pleased by his looks, demeanour, and conversation, he had little deference for others, and he showed an invincible dislike to control. With me he was always what I wished ; with others, he was never anything but what he wished to be himself.' [2]

[1] *Loose Hints upon Education* (1761). In his *Art of Thinking*, 1782, the author tells us that he was acquainted with a very respectable couple, whose method of dealing with their child consisted in promises and entreaties. The boy of four years of age compelled his father to give him an apple before he would consent to return a piece he had taken from his father's chess-board. The apple was soon devoured and another chess man seized. The game had to be suspended until the boy was led away to supper. A guest, on another occasion, heard weeping and wailing in a downstairs room and asked the terrified mother if he could be of any assistance. He was told that Master Dickie wanted to ride up to table on the roast beef, that cook objected, that mother would have liked Dickie to have his will, but that father reflected that the sirloin would probably prove too hot a seat !

[2] *Memoirs of R. L. Edgeworth* (second edn. 1821), vol. i. p. 174. The first edition of 1820 (p. 179) has ' four or five years old ' instead of ' seven or eight as given above.

Unable to superintend the boy's education, Edgeworth engaged a tutor, who was apparently unequal to the task. Rousseau himself had the pleasure of examining this product of his literary labours and pronounced him of good abilities. He was struck with the boy's answers to history, and, contrary to the teaching of *Emile*, admitted that history could be advantageously taught to children. Rousseau, being apparently unacquainted with Ireland's peculiar adherence to the past, can hardly be accused of prejudice in finding traces in this young Irishman of a ' propensity to party prejudice,' which the father admitted.[1] A year later, at the age of nine, the boy possessed considerable abilities of mind and of body, was independent in thought and action, but he was difficult in temper, self-willed, and, indeed, scarcely to be controlled. Edgeworth frankly writes now of ' the mistaken principles of Rousseau,'[2] and acknowledges with deep regret not only the error of a theory adopted in his youth when ' older and wiser persons had been dazzled by Rousseau's eloquence,' but also his own failure to prevent habits which could never afterwards be eradicated.[3]

If Rousseau was surprised to find that fathers were taking the *Emile* seriously, he would surely have been astonished to hear of a bachelor who found in it a means of selecting and winning a wife. Mr. Edgeworth's sketch of his friend, Thomas Day, is a combination of reserve and humour. One can catch

[1] *Memoirs of R. L. Edgeworth* (second edn. 1821), vol. i. p. 254.

[2] *Ibid.* vol. i. p. 269.

[3] It seems the irony of fate that this ' child of nature ' should later have been entrusted to a Jesuit institution ; but Rousseau and the Jesuits share equally the honours of one episode recorded in Mr. Edgeworth's memoirs. It is worthy of quotation because of the light it throws upon the ease with which children are sometimes said to imbibe simple religious ideas. Edgeworth, before committing his son to the Catholic seminary, had required and had received an assurance that there would be no interference with the child's religious principles. A month afterwards the Superior informed him that one of the masters had endeavoured to teach his son the doctrines necessary for his salvation, and had taken particular care to mingle his instructions with bonbons. The following conversation had been reported :

' My little man,' said he, ' did you ever hear of God ? '

' Yes.'

' You know, that, before he made the world, his spirit brooded over the vast deep, which was a great sea without shores, and *without bottom*. Then he made this world out of earth.'

' Where did he find the *earth* ? ' asked the boy.

' At the bottom of the sea,' replied Father Jerome.

' But,' said the boy, ' you told me just now that the sea had no bottom ! '

(*Memoirs*, i. p. 274.)

the twinkle of his eye as he penned some of his apparently colourless sentences. Mr. Day's view of feminine 'nature' led him to take the precaution of choosing *two* young ladies as the objects of his experiment, which by a slight extension of Jean Jacques' plan, was to culminate in matrimonial relations. Edgeworth's sober presentation of the facts acquits his friend of any bigamous intent, and as we have no historical grounds for supposing that Day hit upon a limiting case of the 'method of equal groups,' or that he was desirous of adding to Rousseau's means of education that subtle type of 'control' which one feminine mind seems to exercise over another, it seems fair enough to find in Day's own imperfect sensory education the reason of his early inability to discriminate fairly between a brunette and a blonde! Regarded as an early experiment on formal training, the results are against the idea of 'transfer' from one form of sensory training to another. For although Miss Sabrina Sidney 'knew how to make a circle and an equilateral triangle, and the causes of day and night and of winter and summer,' she did not, in Mr. Day's opinion, know how to choose the proper length of sleeve or the right colour of handkerchief on one critical and eventful occasion. It may be that the lack of 'transfer' was due to the absence of an ideal tinged with really feminine aspiration. With the failure came the rupture of Mr. Day's matrimonial intentions— one of the few certain results on record of a course of formal training—and the search for a bride whose previous education had not been so complete.

The chief contribution of the Edgeworths is to be found in the two volumes of *Practical Education*,[1] a work that blends the newer ideas then mooted in education and attempts to put them to the test of experiment.[2] The first chapter on 'Toys,'

---

[1] Published in 1798. The quotations are from the new (third) edition of 1845.

[2] Miss Edgeworth claims for her father the merit of having been the first to recommend both by example and precept the *experimental* method in education. The preface to the first edition insists that if the art of teaching is to make any progress it must be patiently reduced to an experimental science. Many applications of the ideas of Locke, Condillac, Stewart, Reid, and Rousseau are to be found in its pages. Edgeworth's *Harry and Lucy* inspired Day's *Sandford and Merton*. He supervised the translation of Mme. de Genlis' *Adèle et Théodore*, encouraged his family to make a notable contribution to the educational literature of his day, found time to make projects for the establishment of an Irish national system of education, and to build a school of his own in the village called by his name.

however, anticipates the Froebelian theory of education [1]
through play. It places first in order of importance the effect
of toys upon the inventive and enquiring propensities. Occupation should be their first object ; they should provoke
comparison and activity. Here the Edgeworths strike a Mon-
tessorian note. Their view of play occupations which put
the pupil ' in situations where he can make useful observations,
and acquire that experience which cannot be bought, and which
no masters can communicate,' [2] introduces some of the essential
ideas of Professor Dewey. Everything that we now think of
as necessary apparatus or as illustration is included in this
chapter. The general idea is to give a taste for science by
directing the pupil's attention to every object which surrounds
him. Some of the experiments of members of the Royal
Society are noted as being suitable to children : the blowing
of soap bubbles, the colouring of glass windows, shadows,
etc. Instead of showing young pupils the steps of a discovery
we should frequently pause to see if they can offer suggestions.
In this, say our authors, pupils will succeed beyond our ex-
pectations. The book, as a whole, is a remarkable presentation
of the method of discovery ; a method that avoids all the dodges
and artificialities of Rousseau's exposition.[3] Edgeworth's main
aim is to concentrate the attention. To do this without
doing too much for the pupil—a greater danger than that of

[1] *Practical Education*, vol. i. pp. 6-12.   [2] *Ibid.* i. p. 24.

[3] A single illustration from many equally instructive in the text may be
given (vol. i. p. 70). The appendix is a treasury of suggestions for the use of
the method. A boy of nine years, seemingly idle, looks at ' a rainbow on the
floor ' ; wonders what made it and how it came there. He notices the sun
and begins to experiment upon the relation of the things in the room to it.
As he moves one thing after another into the sun's rays and out again into a
corner, he says, ' This is not it,'; ' this has'nt anything to do with it.' At
last he moves a tumbler of water : his rainbow vanishes. Some violets in the
tumbler suggest a cause for the colour. He takes the violets out : the colours
remain. Then he thinks of the water and empties the glass. The colours remain but are fainter. He concludes that the water and the glass together
make the rainbow. He remembers that there is no glass in the sky, yet
rainbows usually appear there. The water alone may be the cause, but
how is he to eliminate the glass ? A bright idea comes into his mind. He
pours the water slowly out of the tumbler into a basin, placed in a suitable
position and, to his delight, sees the colour twinkling behind the water as it
falls. He proceeds to investigate what happens when the sun is hidden, and
forms two interesting hypotheses to account for the colour—the thickness of
the glass and the clearness or muddiness of the drops of water. The authors
remark that we may call this *play* if we please and, if so, then Descartes was
at play when he verified a former theory of the rainbow.

doing too little—is, in his opinion, the most difficult task of education.

The best method is that which appeals to the child's powers of reason. Miss Edgeworth tells us that in later life her father admitted that he laid too much stress on this appeal : he supposed that if reason were really convinced, conduct would necessarily be virtuous. In *Practical Education,* he is by no means an extreme advocate of liberty. He insists that a false idea of its pleasures misled Rousseau. Children are not moved by an idea of the pleasures of freedom : liberty is for them the liberty of doing specific things which they have found to be agreeable. Those who are unduly restrained in infancy may feel a strong desire for exercising their free-will *as* free will : the normal child is absorbed in his tasks. But liberty is certainly compatible with willing obedience, which should be made habitual in childhood. Edgeworth is not content, as many others had been, to state this maxim and to assume that the statement is sufficient.[1] He insists that in the actual formation of the habit we should begin by exacting obedience in the things which children naturally wish to do.

'Bid her wear your necklace rowed with pearl,
You'll find your Fanny an obedient girl.'

Bid a hungry boy eat apple pie, a shivering urchin warm himself, a tired child to go to bed. Give your commands in a gentle, yet decided, tone of voice suggestive of pleasure rather than of penalty. When it is necessary to make a child do a disagreeable thing let the command be a ' wall of brass.' When a habit of obedience to necessity has been formed engraft upon it obedience to the voice of authority. But when you desire a child to do anything you must be certain that he can do it and that you can force him to do it, if necessary. If you can give reasons you should appeal to reason ; if reasons cannot be given you should point out that your demands will be seen to be reasonable in later life. But bodily activity and the gratification of the senses should not be unnecessarily restrained. Like Herbert Spencer, Edgeworth would have children perceive that we wish them to be happy, and he would try to make them see that they are happier through obedience. The obedience which we usually term ' paying attention ' should be gradu-

[1] Chapter vii. vol. i.

ally exacted : ' When sympathy fails, try curiosity ; when curiosity fails, try praise ;. when praise begins to lose its effect, try blame ; and when you go back again to sympathy, you will find that after this interval, it will have recovered all its original power.' [1] The general principle underlying the whole education is to associate pleasure with whatever you wish your pupils to pursue, and pain with whatever you wish that they should avoid. [2] Despite these principles, Edgeworth's works have a strong flavour of disciplinary training which, as it shows itself mainly in the reasons given for the inclusion of certain subjects in the curriculum, does not seriously affect his general scheme and methods of education. [3]

V

Godwin's *Enquiry concerning Political Justice* and his later work, the *Enquirer*, are, like Priestley's *Remarks on a Proposed Code of Education*, a direct challenge to views such as those of John Brown's *Thoughts on Civil Liberty*. Brown, discounting the operation of human reason, and making the appetites and passions the fountain of human action, would hand over to the State the task of regulating them through education, and of giving the individual that best freedom which adopts a system of thought and action founded on the wisdom of the

[1] *Op. cit.* vol. i. p. 110.   [2] Cf. vol. ii. p. 410.

[3] In a Letter to the Lord Primate which appears in the Appendix to the Fourteenth Report of the Commissioners of the Board of Education in Ireland (quoted in *Memoirs*, ii. pp. 438 ff.), Edgeworth controverts Dr. Bell's idea that arithmetic is not a necessary part of early education. He would dispense with reading and writing rather than with arithmetic, and quotes Swift's opinion that what the Irish nation needed most for its improvement was to learn that two and two are four—an opinion, which if it was ever given, was surely not based upon his experiences in Kilroot (near Belfast). The remark was probably intended as nothing more than a hint that some nations do not act upon what they have *learnt* while others undoubtedly do ! Or the Dean may have been really doubting the value of the formal training given in arithmetic, a value which is stated by Edgeworth in extreme terms. It is, in his opinion, the first occupation of the youthful mind that disciplines it to think with accuracy. Advance in accurate reasoning cannot be so easily or so certainly attained by any other process. It is a perfect system of induction : whoever has once acquired a clear notion of this mode of reasoning may advance gradually to the most difficult problems in every human science. It is not to our purpose to consider further the problem of formal training in its bearing upon freedom. Few of its advocates have been content to base their arguments solely upon its efficacy, and probably no schoolmaster has relied *solely* upon it during a single hour of satisfactory or inspiring teaching. That some attention should be paid to the *type* of mental process exercised by school subjects is reasonable in the interests of a well-equipped mind and in view of

agreeing society, rather than that which is tainted with the vague and random conceptions of untutored infancy.[1] Godwin, disclaiming all artifices such as those of Rousseau's system (a puppet-show of which the tutor holds the wires), appeals frankly and directly to the pupil's sense of reason and truth. If the teacher can show that his demands are reasonable and conducive to the pupil's interest, if he regards the human mind as an intelligent agent guided by motives presented to the understanding, he need have no doubt of the efficacy of direct and simple methods of appeal. Children are a sort of ' ductile and yielding substance.' If we cannot mould them as we wish, it is because we foolishly use the power, which we may exert upon their reason.[2]

Reason is the first and best source of authority. Confidence in the superior knowledge of another is a second, but a very inferior and dangerous source, for the voluntary surrender of understanding and conscience is the annihilation of individuality, of fortitude, and of integrity.[3] The third source of authority rests upon sanction and has power to inflict penalties. Such authority is necessary in early education, but children should be educated as if they were one day to be men,[4] not as if life is an eternal childhood.[5] Youth should have a

the diverse functions and methods of the various bodies of human knowledge. But this aspect of the ' full life ' implies *specific* not *formal* training and has to be evaluated in the light of the depth and intensity of the whole life when subjected to a particular type of discipline. This is the final test of discipline as Herbert Spencer (at least partially) recognized. The recent experimental work on ' transfer of training ' has brought to the surface contradictions latent in the minds of many early advocates of formal discipline, contradictions now asserted by some writers to exist only in the imaginations of experimenters. Edgeworth is a good instance of their undoubted presence. Immediately following the claims for a gradual advance from arithmetical training to the most difficult problems in every human science he deals with the advantages of the ' combined literary and separate religious instruction,' which the Irish Commissioners later adopted as their basal principle of a State system. Edgeworth weighs the objection that such a system will foster suspicion and jealousy, and explains it away by saying that the separation can last *but a few hours* daily, and that the children will converse and play together ! What a pity for Ireland that religious instruction could not be based on the principle that ' two and two make four ' ! What a pity that it could not be approached through conversation and play methods !

[1] John Brown, *Thoughts on Civil Liberty* (1765), cf. pp. 19, 23, 26 ff. Cf. Priestley, *An Essay on the First Principles of Government* (2nd edition, 1771, pp. 78 ff.).

[2] Godwin, *Enquiry* (2nd edition corrected 1796), vol. i. pp. 48, 80.

[3] *Enquiry*, i. p. 233.　[4] *Enquirer* (ed. 1823), p. 102.　[5] *Enquirer*, pp. 112 ff.

large measure of independence. It should be curbed only in
moments of real and pressing necessity. Its boundaries should
be clear, evident, and unequivocal. Liberty is to be real, so
far as it goes ; the show and appearance of freedom are to be
deprecated. A system, like Rousseau's, ' of incessant hypocrisy
and lying ' would produce contention, mutiny, sophistry, and
continual argument. Yet, Godwin insists, no person is ripe
for participating in a benefit the advantages of which he does
not understand, and no one is competent to enjoy a state of
freedom who is not already imbued with a love of it. The
general tenor of his argument is that too much may be claimed
both for external and for internal freedom. ' *To be free is a
circumstance of little value, if we could suppose men in a state of
external freedom without the magnanimity, energy, and firmness
that constitute all that is valuable in a state of freedom.*' ¹ If
these qualities are present a man can be neither useless, nor
unhappy, nor inactive.

The main purpose as well as the chief weapon of education
is the appeal to the pupil's reason, and by far the most useful
part of Godwin's discussion is the statement of the means that
he would take to utilize the pupil's reasoning powers. In the
Enquirer ² he affirms that liberty is one of the most desirable
of all advantages ; knowledge should, therefore, be communicated without infringing the volition and individual judgment
of the pupil, or with as little violence to them as possible. Education may be more or less a despotism.³ It may be necessary
to introduce the ' tyranny of implicit obedience.' But the only
way in which a sensitive being can be excited to the performance of a voluntary action is by the exhibition of a motive,
and intrinsic motives are unquestionably the most educative.
To be governed by them is to enjoy the pure and genuine conviction of a rational being. They give a sense of independence and
individuality.

If we cannot demonstrate the excellence of an educational
task we ought to doubt the sanity and propriety of prescribing
it. ' It is probable that there is no one thing that it is of
eminent importance for a child to learn. *The true object of
juvenile education is to provide against the age of five and twenty,*

---

¹ *Enquiry*, i. pp. 260-1. (*Italics* mine.)   ² *Enquirer*, pp. 67 ff.
³ Cf. *Enquirer*, p. 53, where education is stated to be a despotism.

a mind well regulated, active, and prepared to learn. Whatever will inspire habits of industry and observation will sufficiently answer this purpose. Is it not possible to find something that will fulfil these conditions, the benefit of which a child shall understand, and the acquisition of which he may be taught to desire ? Study with desire is real activity : without desire it is but the semblance and mockery of activity. Let us not in the eagerness of our haste to educate, forget all the ends of education.'[1] Three types of educational motive are distinguished : the best is a perception of the value of the thing learned, the worst is constraint and fear. Between these two lie motives arising from incidental attractions annexed to a task by a teacher.

This clear statement of truths, afterwards dimly grasped and vaguely expressed in Pestalozzi's *Anschauungs-Prinzip*, is followed by a direct affirmation of the principle that the pupil, not the teacher, is the leader in education. The boy should be consulted by the man unaffectedly and sincerely. Here, in our opinion, is the first direct recognition in education of what has been called a *genuine and well-regulated liberty*.[2] Godwin states the advantages of his idea at some length. The giving of leadership to the pupil would ' change the face of education.' The boy would study because he desires to learn : he would proceed on a plan either of his own invention or on one which, by adoption, he would make his own. He would consider for himself whether he understood what he read. If he passed over difficulties he would be forced to re-consider his plan of work. He would be *mentally* active. The horse that goes round in a mill and the boy that is led by the hand are not active.

Godwin urges these points in the interest of the teacher as well as of the pupil. He sees that teaching, rightly regarded, is the work of a freeman and that, as it is usually carried on, it is not a man's job. The teacher is condemned to spend his life in handling and re-handling the foundations of science. Like the unfortunate wretch upon whom the lot has fallen in a city reduced to extremities, he is destroyed that others may live. His only consolation is the recollection that

[1] *Enquirer*, p. 69.
[2] The translation of Milton's phrase (*Works*, i. p. 294). See Ch. IX. p. 164.

his office is useful and patriotic. ' His usefulness and patriotism have some resemblance to those of a chimney-sweeper and a scavenger, who if their existence is of any benefit to mankind are rather tolerated in the world than thought entitled to testimonies of gratitude and esteem.'

The true teacher would treat the child as he would treat an adult. He would know that to inspire hatred to himself and distaste to his lessons was not the most promising road to instruction. He would endeavour to do justice to the pupil's views of the subject ; he would communicate his own with all practicable perspicuity and with every mark of conciliation and friendly attention, avoiding tones of acrimony and airs of lofty command. He would strive to give real happiness to youth, not the fanciful happiness, which boys are said to enjoy when deprived of every opportunity of feeling that they are of some importance in the world. Godwin confesses that when, as a boy, he was told of the superior felicity of youth his heart revolted from the assertion. ' *The principal sources of manly pleasure probably are the feeling that we also are of some importance and account, the conscious power of conforming our actions to the dictates of our own understanding, an approving sense of the rectitude of our own determinations, and an affectionate and heroical sympathy in the welfare of others. To every one of these, young persons are almost uniformly strangers.* ' [1] A good teacher will endeavour to render his pupil wise, virtuous, active, independent, self-approving, and contented. This is probably the fullest and frankest view of liberty which we have yet discussed.

Godwin's view of confidence is no doubt influenced by the artificiality of the tutor's behaviour in *Emile* : it misses the essential factors of the frank, simple, relationship of teacher to pupil which Godwin himself recommends. In this relationship at its best there is a unity of aspiration and of aim which reason may approve but which reason very often does not directly determine. It is the consciousness of this unity rather than the possession of superior knowledge on the part of the teacher that begets confidence. His sound judgment and his learning may strengthen it, but sympathy, particularly with the pupil's difficulties, sustains it. Godwin ignores the receptive attitude

[1] *Enquirer*, pp. 63-4.

of the personality to values presented by others with whom we are in sympathetic accord. There would be no place in his conception for Macaulay's ' *cheerful* confidence in the mercy of God,' a phrase suggestive of that sympathetic union of the aims of a more perfect and a less perfect creature which is an essential condition of freedom in education.

Godwin's timidity in recognizing the function of the relatively external determinants of conduct is perhaps connected with, or dependent upon, his psychological view of freedom as rigid *self*-determination. He refuses to admit that voluntary actions are free. To say so is a contradiction in terms. Nothing is voluntary further than it is accompanied with intention and design and flows from the apprehension of an end to be accomplished. He points out very truly that the ' most considerable actions of our lives are necessary actions, actions which may be foreseen and predicted.' The indeterminate actions and indeterminate acts of will, if they exist, lie practically outside the scope of education. The man who possessed the power of capriciously resisting the most powerful arguments would be one to whom the most perfect system of education would be useless.

It follows from such a view that freedom in education cannot be defined by reference either to indeterminate acts of will (such as, for example, we find in Watts), or to ' indifferent '. actions as defined by Locke. Acts of will or actions which *might* or *might not* equally result from certain antecedents can never be the outcome of vital processes of growth. A doctrine of necessity, whether emphasizing determination by the self, or by some agency partly external to it is not necessarily in contradiction to the idea of freedom in education. Why then, it may be asked, have human beings the *sense* of freedom to act or to refrain from action, to will or not to will an act ? The sense of freedom is, we suggest, the teacher within a man's own breast. The past is gone beyond recall and its acts cannot be differently performed. But the future remains and with it there remains the *possibility* of a more active self—a self continually striving to bring determinants, hitherto inoperative or ineffective, into the sphere of daily life and conduct. It is the prospective possibility of a more active self that gives us the illusion of having had the power in the past to act differently. But that power is ours in the future : we may summon to our aid values from the past, and we can bring into consciousness forces that have been submerged in the depths of our personality.   Education, by the introduction of new ideas and the arousal of old forces, can help us to do this.   It can give the greatest service when it presents powers and values, dormant in our lives, as active forces in the life of someone else who is in sympathy with our aspirations.

The discussion in this chapter establishes freedom as a genuine and well-regulated form of the pupil's self-activity, and not as a mere substitute for control.   It emphasizes, perhaps unduly, the importance of the pupil's *reasoning* powers. It suggests that liberty is consonant with obedience and that it is fostered by those feelings of confidence which a frank recognition of the pupil as a human being inevitably brings.

NOTE ON THE DOCTRINE OF PHILOSOPHICAL NECESSITY.

In his *Doctrine of Philosophical Necessity* Priestley contrasts the probable influence of rewards, punishments, and other means of education upon two children, one of whom he supposes to be directed by a principle of necessity, and the other by a principle of liberty (of indifference),   In the first, he argues, every influence judiciously administered would work towards a virtuous and happy type of stabilized conduct.   In the second, the chances of successful and unsuccessful determination of the child's conduct would be equal, and there would be no possibility of forming habits.   (Cf. *Works*, Ed. Rutt, Vol. III., pp. 492 ff.)   He further argues (*Works*, III., p. 482) that the consciousness of freedom ' when rightly understood appears to decide in favour of the doctrine of necessity, or the necessary influence of motives to determine the choice.'

CHAPTER XVI

KANT'S FREEDOM THROUGH OBEDIENCE

SOMEONE has said that it is Rousseau's Baby that sits in the chair of the elderly bachelor philosopher of Königsberg, and hears strange things about his freedom. It is, however, somewhat difficult to believe that *Emile* really inspired the lectures on Pedagogy which seemed occasionally to form part of the duties of Kant's chair. The worship of natural man has disappeared. In its place we find a strong plea for a discipline which will counteract man's natural unruliness,[1] and place him in subjection to the laws of humanity. Gone, too, is the idea of control *solely* through the internal forces. The child is sent to school, not so much to learn as to become accustomed to sit still and to do as he is told. If he is allowed to follow his own will in his youth a certain lawlessness will cling to him throughout life. The strength of the natural impulse towards freedom is the main reason for subjecting it to discipline. The worship of the individual has little place. He must be so trained that ' he shall choose none but good ends—good ends being those which are necessarily approved by everyone and which may at the same time be the aim of everyone.'[2] In the first period of childhood, therefore, the child must learn submission and positive obedience[3]; in the next, he should be allowed to think for himself and to enjoy a certain amount of freedom, although he is still obliged to follow certain prescriptions. Kant thus agrees with Plato and Aristotle that the child should be restrained until he is capable of guiding his own conduct.

Yet Rousseau's influence is clearly present. Practical and

---

[1] *Über Pädagogik*, c. 4.   [2] *Op. cit.* Trans. by A. Churton, ch. 18.

[3] Rink and Schubert read ' passive.' Both ideas seem to agree equally well with Kant's exposition. Positive submission (ch. 28) is defined as being obliged to do what one is told because one cannot judge for oneself : negative submission is being allowed to do what others wish in order to receive from them certain advantages.

stern as Kant's general doctrine is, it is by no means conservative. He regards the prospect of a true theory of education as a glorious ideal; its immediate realization is comparatively unimportant. One principle is particularly emphasized. Children should be educated not for the present but for a possibly improved condition of man in the future—that is, in a manner which is adapted to the *idea of humanity* and the whole destiny of man.[1] Discipline is not conceived in any merely ascetic terms, but is inspired by a sense of the highest values. Its purpose is to develop all the natural gifts. Providence has willed that man shall bring forth *for himself* the good that lies hidden in his nature. In doing this he can learn much from the history of the race.[2] These phrases show the fluidity of Kant's idea of education. His general view recognizes freedom, in some sense, as its central concept. ' One of the greatest problems of education is how to unite submission to the necessary restraint with the child's capability of exercising his free-will—for restraint is necessary. How am I to develop the sense of freedom in spite of the restraint ? I am to accustom my pupil to endure a restraint of his freedom and at the same time I am to guide him to use his freedom aright. Without this all education is merely mechanical, and the child, when his education is over, will never be able to make a proper use of his freedom. He should be made to feel early the inevitable opposition of society that he may learn how difficult it is to support himself, to endure privation, and to acquire those things which are necessary to make him independent.' [3]

Kant himself answers his question. He will allow ' perfect liberty in every respect ' from earliest childhood provided that the child is prevented from doing himself an injury, and that he is not allowed to interfere with the liberty of others. He will teach the child that aims can be attained only by allowing others to attain theirs. He will make clear to him that restraint is exercised so that one day he may be able to use his liberty aright, and be free and independent of the help of others.[4] Kant's view of freedom, then, has for its object to make the pupil aware of his own powers, to lead him to recognize the rights

---

[1] Cf. ch. 15.

[2] Kant raises the question of education through Recapitulation.

[3] Ch. 29.   [4] Ch. 30.

and powers of others, and to teach him to adjust his wishes to the opposition which the realization of his aims is likely to arouse. Although the school is a place of *compulsory* culture, [1] education need not therefore be slavish. Although the pupil must meet with opposition there should be no attempt to ' break his will.' The one will make him docile, the other will make him a slave.

The intellectual aspects of education show much the same spirit of compromise. The ascetic note appears in the strengthening and cultivation of the ' faculties,' [2] and in the distinction of ' free ' and ' scholastic ' culture. But even in the restraint and discipline which Kant repeatedly emphasizes there is a clear appreciation of the value of self-activity, a clear enunciation of ' doing ' as the best means to ' understanding,' and even a recognition of the self as the best teacher. *Man lernt das am gründlichsten und behält das am besten, was man gleichsam aus sich selbst lernt.* [3] Children need not exercise their reason continually, nor should they be encouraged to argue about everything. It is not necessary that they should know the principles underlying every part of their education, but ' on the whole we should try to draw out their own ideas, founded on reason, rather than introduce ideas into their minds.' When the question of duty arises its principles should be made clear to the understanding.

Moral culture is considered at length. It must be based upon ' maxims ' and not merely upon the prevention of evil habits, which we call discipline. In another passage [4] Kant distinguishes sharply a maxim from a law. A maxim is a subjective principle of action, and contains the practical rule set by reason as it operates in the subject himself ; it is thus, in effect, reason acting under such limitations as are imposed by the subject's ignorance, inclinations, or propensities. Law is, on the other hand, the objective principle, valid for every rational being, and carrying with it the force and sanction of a categorical

---

[1] 69.   Kant recognizes the value of play, but strongly insists upon the value of the work attitude.   ' It is bad for a child to learn to look upon everything as play.'

[2] Generally, as in 72, the *Gemüthskräfte*.

[3] Cf. *Metaphysics of Morals*, ch. 46.   Cf. also trans. by Abbott, 1879, footnote to p. 54.

[4] Ch. 75.   Cf. chs. 70 and 76.

imperative. Now, although Kant ultimately finds freedom in obedience to law, as thus defined, he very definitely urges that children should learn to act according to ' maxims,' *the reasonableness of which a child is able to see for himself.*[1] He recognizes the extreme difficulty of this requirement, but sets himself deliberately to give young children clear ideas of what is right and wrong. Here he comes face to face with some of the harsher aspects of discipline. He realizes that if we are to establish real morality we must abolish punishment. Morality is so sacred and sublime that we must not degrade it by placing it in the same rank as discipline. Infringements of school discipline must be punished, but the point of *first* importance in the development of morality is readiness to act in accordance with maxims. These will be, at first, mere ' school ' principles, but clear and undeviating obedience to them is the foundation of the moral life. There are many matters of indifference in which children may be allowed to exercise their powers of choice. Once the choice is made, once the rule is recognized and accepted, it must be followed. Obedience, Kant insists, is an essential feature in the character of a child.

Kant's main argument requires the child's obedience to the demands of a will which is recognized by the child himself to be good and reasonable, but he regards ' absolute ' obedience to the command of a master as an equally necessary factor in early education. The *purpose* of this unquestioning submission removes some of its apparent inconsistency. His main concern is to introduce Rousseau's necessity into the moral sphere. There must be an atmosphere of generally accepted maxims pervading the school and the teacher must see that the pupils' rudimentary ' laws ' are respected and obeyed by everyone without favour or predilection. Kant thus assumes that, even in the lives of children, ' maxims ' may be invested with something of the sanction and universality of law and that, when so recognized, they should be obeyed, notwithstanding the presence of counter-impulses and inclinations. He recognizes the problem of the ' fickle ' will and wishes to set it free through a training which reinforces and strengthens its deepest aspirations. In this way he thinks that ideas of duty will be formed : a child will always be able to see that he has certain duties as

[1] Ch. 77.

a child, even if he finds it impossible to form the idea of duties as a *human* being.[1] In a later paragraph, however, this view is apparently re-considered. The obedience of the growing *youth* is stated to consist in submission to the rules of duty, or, in other words, in obedience to reason, while it is argued that the notion of duty is beyond children, who regard it as something which, if not fulfilled, will be followed by punishment.[2] In a still later passage Kant recommends the association of duty with common routine activities, and with examples and rules, but this is followed by reference to such duties as dignity and reverence as well as to cleanliness and truthfulness.[3]

The same vacillation appears in the remarks upon the teaching of religion to young children. If children could never witness a single act of adoration, and never hear God's name spoken, it might, he thinks, be the right order of things to teach first the aims and ends of humanity, and to bring the pupil into contact with the order and beauty of the works of nature, and then to proceed to the ideas of a Supreme Being and a Lawgiver. But this method is evidently impossible, and in presence of man's actual devotion to God, the uninstructed child would either become indifferent to Him or fall into entirely erroneous ways of conceiving His functions and powers. The remarks upon the actual teaching of religion add little to the views already considered.

In the pedagogical aspects of freedom Rousseau's influence upon Kant is clearly perceptible. In both writers the central idea is an appeal to reason, but its function and content are very different in the two treatises. Rousseau regards childhood as the sleep of reason : Kant finds evidence of reason in the first year of life.[4] Rousseau confines its early operation to the circumstances that affect the pupil's sensible well-being : Kant brings some of its transcendental qualities into his

[1] Ch. 82. A boy of fifteen assures me, as I write, that he understood the idea of duty when he was nine years of age.

[2] Ch. 86.   [3] Ch. 95.

[4] Cf. ch. 48. Rink and Schubert read : ' During the first *three* months the sense of sight is not fully developed.' Others read ' eight ' for ' three.' Kant refers to the laughing and crying activities developed at the same time and adds : ' When the child has once reached that stage there is always some reasoning, however vague, connected with his crying.' ' Wenn das Kind nun in diesem Zustande ist, so schreit es mit Reflexion, sie sei auch noch so dunkel, als sie wolle.' (Rink, p. 49).

educational theory. He banishes emulation, for example, and substitutes for it the child's comparison of himself with 'a concept of his reason.'[1] The first *Critique* based, as it was, on the principle that ' we only cognize in things *a priori* that which we ourselves place in them,' was a powerful reinforcement of the creative power of reason, and undoubtedly helped, as Nietzsche suggests, by its emphasis of 'a master pedagogy of the spirit ' to replace Rousseau's ' slave pedagogy of things.'[2]

It would be quite out of place to consider here the philosophical implications of Kant's ' pure will,' or ' pure reason ' or ' transcendental freedom ' in their relation to the question of freedom in education. However important these may be for a theory of knowledge or for a system of metaphysical ethics they can scarcely be considered as important for a practical activity, like education, which has to regard the pupil, not as a creature in whom reason is theoretically irresistible but as a being in whom impulses often dominate reason. It may be profitable, however, to note some of the features of Kant's conception of freedom—unqualified obedience to the moral law—and more particularly the difficulties he finds in reconciling this notion with the hard facts of human life. The greatest difficulty from the educational point of view is shelved by Kant's radical divorce of the free operations of the good will which is determined by the dictates of reason, from the life of inclination, propensity, and instinct which is virtually subject to the rule of rigid necessity. This makes everything really educational and really moral depend upon the dictates of reason. Kant, of course, admits that our most certain, most immediate, knowledge is not derived directly from reason. ' Two things,' he urges, ' fill the mind with ever new and increasing admiration and awe . . . the starry heavens above and the moral law within. I have not to search for them and conjecture them as though they were veiled in darkness or were in the transcendent region beyond my horizon : I see them before me and connect them directly with the consciousness of my existence.'[3] The moral law, beginning from the invisible self, exhibits an infinite world traceable only by the under-

[1] Cf. ch. 99.

[2] Cf. *The Educational Theory of Immanuel Kant*, by E. F. Buchner, p. 38.

[3] *Critique of Practical Reason*, 312, trans. Abbott, p. 260.

standing, a world with which the self is discerned to be in universal and necessary connection. It infinitely elevates the individual's worth as an intelligence, through a personality in which it reveals a life independent of animal nature and impulse and even independent, within certain limits, of the sensible world.[1] But the more clearly we emphasize the immediacy of the moral law, and its identity with the dictates of reason, the less we are entitled to speak of the individual's *obedience* to it, or of his sense of *obligation* or of *duty* to it. If we keep within the sphere of the pure will and the pure reason it is difficult to see how notions of obligation or obedience could ever arise. As Abbott points out : ' A being which gave itself the moral law and whose freedom, therefore, is autonomy, would not be conscious of obligation or duty, since the moral law would coincide with its will.'[2] In effect, then, Kant's theory drives him to admit that even though willing the moral law we resist it.

From the point of view of development it seems more clearly in line with facts to connect the ideas of duty and obligation with the potential presence in the mind of a resisting force, and to regard the possibility of this resistance to the moral law and to duty as being implied in the quality of obedience. This, in turn, would debar us from accepting Kant's ideas of moral law and of duty as absolutely *internal* forces. Resistance implies something external to the self, something which demands from it an adjustment which at the moment is not fully admitted. An external reference of this kind appears in many passages of Kant's writings, and particularly in his discussion of the meaning and function of conscience.[3] There he admits that although the operations of conscience are transactions of a man with himself, yet the individual finds himself compelled by his reason to act as though at the command of *another* person. But Kant sees that to identify the accused with the judge is an absurd representation of a tribunal, for in such a case the complainant would always lose his suit. He therefore argues that conscience, if it is to escape self-contradiction, must in all duties conceive *some other than itself* as the judge of actions. He examines the qualifications necessary in such a judge and concludes that when we examine the ideal or actual judge

[1] *Ibid.*   [2] *Ibid. Memoir of Kant*, p. lv.   [3] *Ibid.* pp. 311, 321.

which reason frames to itself it is clear that he cannot be identified with the pure reason of the individual. The latter has not, and never can have, all power (in heaven and on earth) to give his laws the full effect that belongs to them, which is a necessary part of the office of judge. Finally, he declares that conscience must be conceived as a subjective principle which declares our responsibility to God for our actions. It is to be noted here that reason *compels* the individual to refer a difficult line of action to an external judge who is not subject to limitations in respect of power and universality. Reason in its very act of compulsion submits to something greater than itself and in its act of *obedience* recognizes the possibility of disobedience and of resistance.

It is also worthy of note that Kant's categorical imperative —Act only on a maxim which is at the same time willed as a universal law—begins with the subjective or individual point of view, and that the willing of the ' maxim ' as a ' universal law ' would, in practice, generally necessitate the reference to an external standard. At times Kant writes as if the finding of maxims in agreement with those of our fellows was quite sufficient to elevate them to the rank of ' laws,' but, in general, he emphasizes the fact that mere conformity to the moral law does not make an action moral, and that the real test is action in behalf, and for the sake, of the moral law itself. But the actions which follow upon the mere ' maxim ' are not adequately considered by Kant. He dwells upon the concurrence of ' maxim ' with the ' pure will ' insisting that it marks the triumph of duty and gives freedom. But he has little to say of the function of merely selfish principles of action and of actual violations of the moral law. It seems unsatisfactory to explain all cases of the successful operation of the categorical imperative by a reference to maxims which somehow are harmonized with the pure will, and to evade an explanation of the unsuccessful operations of the imperative by referring them to the region of physical necessity. And although Kant admits that moral defection brings with it a sense of self-humiliation and self-condemnation he gives no explanation of the state of consciousness in such circumstances. It could scarcely be explained on merely psychological grounds. In such a state some inclination or propensity has been gratified ; the individual has apparently asserted his freedom to deny the demands of the moral law, and if this is self-given there seems to be no reason why dejection should follow one rather than another of the aspects of the self. Surely the markedly negative self-feeling associated with these moments is a witness to our inability to meet the *demands* of morality, a witness therefore to a markedly *submissive* attitude to the demands of an *external* standard, just as the consciousness of achievement arising from our recognition of the call of duty is a witness to the reception, the *adoption* and the positive *assertion* of those demands and of values that had hitherto been relatively external to the self.   If this be the true explanation we cannot agree that freedom is *obedience* to the moral law ; it is rather the active acceptance or the assertion of it.

Kant's insistence on the *internal* nature of the moral law has, therefore, dangers as well as great positive value for an education in the light of a concept of liberty.   By making it a self-given principle of determination he really commits the individual irrevocably to a subjective standard of morality.   His insistence upon obedience to a self-given moral law tends to make him forget the processes of reasoning that actually test the relevancy of a moral value to the individual, that lead to its acceptance in the given circumstances of a moment of his life, that result in its adoption as an obligatory principle of action in similar circumstances, and that finally bring about its positive assertion, in a more or less habitual form.   The legitimately assertive aspect of obedience is overlooked, and for it is substituted the activity of a pure will that serves as a corrective to the subjectivity of individual motive.   In short, and again in Abbott's words, Kant treats human nature too abstractly.   In eliminating the matter of experience he has eliminated that on which frequently the whole question turns.[1] His great service, however, is his eloquent presentation of the demands of something—whether we call it morality, or the pure or the good will, or duty, or conscience, or God, matters little—that fashions and directs life.   If there is no room for this there is no function for education.

1 *Memoir of Kant*, p. li.

CHAPTER XVII

PESTALOZZI'S ANSCHAUUNGS-PRINZIP.

PESTALOZZI'S contribution to our subject is to be found neither in any well-knit theory, nor in any really consistent practice, of an education based upon freedom, but in patient self-sacrificing efforts to test the practical value of previously suggested ideas. He was not content to be a merely philosophical advocate of the newer theories, or to test their worth in the education of a single pupil or a selected group of pupils. He set himself the task of studying the laws and limitations of human nature as it actually existed in a section of the community hitherto almost untouched by philanthropic schemes of education. The story of his life is one of apparent failure, but his personal devotion to education inspired many hearts, and out of his difficulties there emerged the conviction that freedom, in some sense of the word, was a practical force of great value in the education of the people. Had Pestalozzi been less of a saint, his experiments might have been superficially more successful, but his very failure was a witness to a faith that refused to abandon an ideal, and his tenacity and conviction did more to inspire a real belief in the humanizing influence of education in the elementary school than any state eulogies or official commendations could ever have done. Pestalozzi's real place in the history of freedom is that of an adventurer intrepid enough to place himself in the position of an impartial observer, and to carry on persistently the work of observation in a sphere of discovery where the rewards were likely to be particularly precarious and the aims of his work to be very largely misunderstood.

In this chapter we propose to ignore the contradictions and confusions of his exposition, and to limit the discussion to one or two directions in which he broke new ground.

Twelve years after the publication of *Emile* we find Pestalozzi keeping a careful record of the development of his three-year-old son.[1] Rousseau's influence is apparent, but Pestalozzi is an independent critic rather than an enthusiastic disciple, a keen observer rather than the framer of a definite system. Freedom is urged again and again, but Pestalozzi is convinced that it must include obedience. He attempts to state and to weigh the arguments in favour of both concepts. Liberty is good ; its curtailment arouses the child's displeasure ; it tends to encourage moderation in later life ; wisely used it induces the child to keep eyes and ears open, and to make him contented, happy, and even-tempered. But this complete liberty is possible only when a child has been taught submission to the nature of things. Without obedience there can be no real education. Unlimited liberty in some things would mean ruin ; it would not stifle or eradicate the passions ; it would not develop the talents and habits required in social life. A childhood passed in entire freedom would mean an adolescence weighed down by fetters and bonds.

The conclusions drawn from these early observations and meditations express very clearly and adequately the point of view which Pestalozzi held all through his pedagogical vicissitudes. Both liberty and obedience must find a place in education. His advice to the teacher is : ' Be thoroughly convinced of the immense value of liberty ; do not let vanity make you anxious to see your efforts producing premature fruit ; let your child be as free as possible, and seek diligently for every means of ensuring his liberty, peace of mind, and good humour. Teach him absolutely nothing by words that you can teach him by the things themselves ; let him see for himself, hear, find out, fall, pick himself up, make mistakes, no word, in short, where action is possible. What he can do for himself let him do ; let him be always occupied ; always active, and let the time you leave him to himself represent by far the greatest part of his childhood. You will then see that nature teaches him far better than men. But when you see the necessity of accustoming him to obedience,

---

[1] Cf. Green, *Life and Work of Pestalozzi*, p. 40. De Guimps, *Pestalozzi, his Life and Work*, pp. 46-7.

prepare yourself with the greatest care for this duty . . .
Make sure of his heart and let him feel that you are necessary
to him. . . . If he often asks for something you do not think
good, tell him what the consequences will be, and leave him
his liberty. But you must take care that the consequences
are such as he will not easily forget. Always show him the
right way. Should he leave it and fall into the mire go to his
rescue, but do not shield him from the unpleasant results of
having enjoyed complete liberty and of not having listened to
your warnings. In this way his trust in you will be so great
that it will not be shaken even when you have to thwart him.
He must obey the wise teacher or the father he has learned to
respect ; but only in cases of necessity must an order be
given.'[1]

This excellent empiricism contains, as we shall endeavour
to show, Pestalozzi's main contribution to the practical meaning and function of freedom, but before considering it a brief
reference may be made to his philosophical conceptions. In
the moments of his exaltation he breathes the rarefied atmosphere of the highest ideals and looks down in pity and sorrow
upon the corruption of primitive human nature. He follows
Kant here rather than Rousseau. ' Primitive natural freedom
and social law are ever at war.'[2] Even social law and the social
state do not bring satisfaction : they are only a step beyond
the sensuousness of primitive nature. The highest form of
human freedom is free human will and the power that goes with
it. The glory and freedom of primitive existence, the purity
of instincts, the aspirations of social life are only partial goods.
They are, indeed, partial illusions. An inner force impels man
' to something nobler than the purely animal and social
creature which is all that nature and sex can produce.'[3] The
individual has to gather experience among the ruins of his
primitive instincts and to break up the rigidity of his social
outlook if he is to be free in the highest sense of the term.
Pestalozzi finds something akin to three stages in development. The child approaches most nearly to the innocence,
the instinctive life, and the sensual enjoyment of the animal.
In youth these delights have to be forfeited ; hence it is a

---

[1] De Guimps, *op. cit.* pp. 47-8.   [2] *Educational Writings* (Green), p. 70.
[3] *Ibid.* pp. 72 and 73.

period of ' demoralization ' like the former period of purely sensual enjoyment. Finally, the adult, as his own master, regards everything from the point of view of his own purposes. Freedom, independence, and personal rights belong exclusively to this period.[1]

But if Pestalozzi denies the highest *type* of freedom to the child and, indeed, to the youth, it is because each of these stages lacks the characteristic experience which gives the highest freedom. This later quality, however, is the *result* of the experience of the earlier stages, which have therefore a very necessary and important bearing upon the later freedom. ' But for the illusions of my childhood and the absence of all rights during my years of apprenticeship I should not have been stimulated to the strong and steadfast effort which is necessary if man is to rise to an independence based on law and justice.'[2] Pestalozzi thus thinks of the experiences of childhood as necessary forms of expression for that inner impulse towards development which continually impels man to something higher than purely animal and social nature. His main task is to discover ways in which the teacher can foster the native forms of expression so that they may be vehicles of that spontaneous effort towards the moral life which is man's deepest aspiration. Here and there we find an ascetic note—the emphasis of pain, the mastery of desire, the ruins of primitive instincts, the rise of morality in our dead selves. But the distinctively Pestalozzian ideal is the positive appeal of moral agencies, closely attached to the animal wants of childhood and clearly relevant to its demands. With many a stumble and many a faltering step Pestalozzi pursued the path of experimental investigation in the hope of giving a concrete and practical embodiment to this empirical view of liberty.

It would, we think, not be unfair to the general spirit of Pestalozzi's entire work to find in it, as in this passage, *a practical attempt to make possible a direct relationship of the self to the formative experiences of real life.* So far from denying freedom and rights to youth, an aim like this gives a broad and useful conception of freedom, and although, in practice, Pestalozzi often departs from ' directness ' and ' reality,' as these would usually be interpreted, he consistently and patiently

[1] *Ibid.* p. 74.   [2] *Ibid.* p. 74.

tries to ascertain for himself the meaning of these terms and to work them out in attractive and practical forms. In his *Wie Gertrud ihre Kinder lehrt* he himself states what he has specially done for the very being of education. He has fixed, he tells us, the highest, the supreme, principle of instruction in the recognition of *Anschauung* as the absolute foundation of all knowledge. He has sought to discover the nature of teaching itself, and the prototype by which nature has determined the instruction of our race.[1]

The *Anschauungs-Prinzip* is the great contribution of Pestalozzi to education, and although he gives no really satisfactory discussion of its meaning its main purpose is scarcely in doubt. Kant had defined *Anschauung* as knowledge directly obtained from an object present to the senses, or as a mental image resulting from the actual presence of the object. These seem the basal meanings of the term for Pestalozzi. But he extends the immediacy and directness of knowledge associated with the term *intuition* to the region of the feelings and particularly to the sphere of the moral feelings. He also seems to use the term to include mental acts and mental faculties as well as the knowledge obtained by direct contemplation of an object, and, further, to include objects which have not been directly present to the senses, but which are the objects of an internal scrutiny or ' observation ' of the mind. The latter use of *Anschauung* seems to include any synthetic function of the mind, such as reasoning, judgment, or induction. No doubt in these functions an actual basis of sense-impression is always present, but Pestalozzi links up the term with the ' changing of the results of sense-impression ' into ' the work of the mind.' [2] Finally, he uses *Anschauungen* for the elements or starting points of moral training (*innere Anschauung*), out of which ' feelings of love, gratitude, trust, sympathy . . . re-

---

[1] Cf. *Päd. Bibliothek*, Albert Richter, p. 161 : Wenn ich jetzt zurück sehe und mich frage : Was habe ich denn eigentlich für das Wesen des menschlichen Unterrichts geleistet ? so finde ich : ich habe den höchsten obersten Grundsatz des Unterrichts in der Anerkennung der Anschauung als dem absoluten Fundamente aller Erkenntniz festgesetzt, und mit Beseitigung aller einzelnen Lehren das Wesen der Lehre selbst und die Urform aufzufinden gesucht, durch welche die Ausbildung unseres Geschlechtes durch die Natur selber bestimmt werden muss.

[2] Cf. Pestalozzi's summary of the ways in which knowledge arises : *How Gertrude Teaches her Children*, 2nd edn. 1820, trans. Holland & Turner, p. 115.

ligion, and morality develop.'[1] It is also extended to cover a person's spontaneous efforts to gain sense-impressions. These efforts and the strong desires and personal interests are the basis of ' moral self-active education.' In effect, then, Pestalozzi uses the term *Anschauung* for any mental process (or the result of any mental process) that engages the subject directly, and that so completely engages him that he identifies himself with the object or result of that process, recognizes in it something of unmistakable relevance to his own life, and experiences a measure of the creative activity which accompanies the incorporation of an idea or value inadequately expressed in his life.[2] The term is particularly well adapted to express that idea of the direct contact of a pedagogical activity with something of intrinsic value for the pupil's life which we have met in previous writers, an idea which has never been placed in such a commanding position as it occupies in Pestalozzi's pages. It may be useful to gather together from various passages some of the specific illustrations and applications of this principle.

They all emphasize the necessity for *personal* experience in education. In the *Denkschrift*[3] of 1800 Pestalozzi considers the means taken by nature herself to bring the world into contact with the individual, and to bring to maturity in his mind the impressions received by the contact. Three factors are specially mentioned. In the first place, nature works through the sensory stimuli of the pupil's specific locality (*Lage*), and through it determines his sensory outlook on the world. The value of education from the natural environment is frequently emphasized ; never have the claims of a real study of nature been more forcibly or truly presented. In his records of the early education of his son,

---

[1] Cf. Green, *Life and Work of Pestalozzi*, p. 231.

[2] The main emphasis is placed on sense-perception. Pestalozzi recognizes quite clearly the error of Rousseau's view that the mind is passive in sensation. Green, in an illuminating criticism of the principle (which he translates as the Principle of Concreteness) remarks that adult perception, being so much a matter of routine, has practically lost the activity which Pestalozzi, with genuine philosophical insight, attributed to the sense perception of children. Children, he says, probably experience the pleasure of such activity frequently, and the greatest pleasure comes with the consciousness of the personal share in the experience. (*Life and Work of Pestalozzi*, p. 131.)

[3] Green, *Life and Work*, p. 293.

Jacobli, Pestalozzi writes of the great open lecture hall of nature, of the teaching of the mountains and valleys, of the child's sensitiveness to nature, of his interest in the bird and the caterpillar. In the presence of these, the language teacher should be dumb. In *Lienhard und Gertrud* he shows how educative the ordinary objects and occupations of everyday life may be. Gertrud knows little more than spinning and sewing and the usual arts of the household, yet she lays the broad foundations of education. She counts with her children how many steps it takes to cross the room, how many panes there are in the window. She teaches them to measure and to compare, to note the action of fire, of water, of air, of wind, of smoke. She draws their attention to common substances like water, makes them note the forms it takes in the tub, in the brook, in ice, rain, hail, She does not, as popular ' education so often does, attempt merely to remove ignorance ' ; she directs eyes and ears and hands towards the objects and occupations of the environment.

In the second place, nature makes use of the individual's necessities (*Bedürfnisse*). This idea is not so fully worked out by Pestalozzi, but in his *innere Anschauungen*, and in his recognition of the individual's own strivings and efforts he anticipates the biological view of education. He would have us remember that all we are, our purposes, and all that we ought to be, have a common centre and that centre is the individual himself. ' Mere sensory experience of the environment is not enough to awaken spiritual existence.' In his general exposition, however, he links up necessities (*Bedürfnisse*) with individual responsibilities (*Verhältnisse*), the third of Nature's methods. Indeed he immediately conjoins the three factors, insisting that Nature lays the foundations of general knowledge, and of morality, in these concrete realities instead of in ' the shifting sand of words.'

He is, on the whole, very close to the Kantian view of the freedom of man's spiritual life, and his ascendancy over nature. ' It is only spiritual and moral nature that is able to bring itself into harmony with the physical—and that can and ought to do so.'[1] But he has little place for the operation of a ' pure reason ' ; the harmonization must be attained through the

---

[1] *Wie Gertrud ihre Kinder lehrt* (trans. Holland and Turner,) p. 160.

responsibilities, needs, and relationships of life itself. ' Every influence,' urges Pestalozzi, ' that in the development of our powers and activities turns us away from the centre point, on which rests the personal responsibility of everything that man is bound throughout his life to do, to bear, to attend, and provide for, must be regarded as an influence opposed to wise, manly education.   Every influence . . . that makes us incapable of serving our fellow-men or our country must be regarded as a deviation from the laws of nature, from the harmony with myself and my surroundings. It is, therefore, a hindrance to my self-culture, to the training for my calling, and to my sense of duty.' [1] The freedom of the spiritual and moral nature is thus to be found through the practical activities, the surroundings, the necessities, and the duties of everyday life.

We shall find a corrective to the subjective limitations of this Pestalozzian conception of ' nearness ' in the works of Hegel, and in the meantime shall reserve criticism. It should be noted, however, that although Pestalozzi's *main* concern is for the education of young children and although he takes the view that the poor should be educated for the duties and relationships of the social class into which they are born, he states his central problem—a far greater one than that which he thinks he has solved—in unmistakably general terms. He states it thus : How can the child, considering the nature of his disposition, and the changeableness of his circumstances and relations, be so trained that whatever is demanded of him in the course of his life by necessity and duty may be easy to him, and may, if possible, become second nature to him ? From his point of view this is simply the problem : what can the teacher do to ensure the child's freedom ? Pestalozzi's suggestions towards its solution are an application of his principle of *Anschauung*, to the sphere of morality.

In one of his early writings Pestalozzi urges that morality is nothing more than the way the pure will is directed to the full measure of the individual's knowledge and responsibilities. It is the way in which father, son, ruler, subject, man, or slave, carries out duties to his own satisfaction and to the satisfaction of those to whom he gives or owes food, shelter, obedience,

[1] *Ibid.* p. 179.

loyalty, and gratitude. ' The more closely nature attaches my *instinctive* existence to a moral object, the more points from which I am touched by my animal weal and woe, the more stimuli I find, the more impulses I feel towards morality. . . . Thus social duties favour my morality in proportion as they concern objects which are in close natural relation to me ; and, conversely, they are favourable to immorality as the motives underlying them are remote from such relations.' [1] This is a noteworthy passage basing, as it does, the higher moral life on instinct, animal weal, and impulse. One of the great contributions of Pestalozzi to education is his attempt to show that the regulation of the child's animal wants and tendencies subserve the purposes of morality.

Here, as in early instruction, Pestalozzi finds the mother the true teacher. Just as ' a mother's instruction requires no art,' [2] so her natural impulses to her child require no direction ; they lead to the stimulation and development of the moral feelings. It will be noted that this is an appeal from the mother's instincts to those of her child. The development of the human race, says Pestalozzi, begins in a strong passionate desire for the satisfaction of physical wants. The mother's breast stills the first storm of physical needs and creates love. It also evokes patience : the child learns that he has to wait until his mother ministers to his needs. Fear is developed : the mother's arm stills it. Love and trust are united and develop the first germ of gratitude. Nature is soon found to be inflexible towards passion ; the mother herself is unmoved by irregular desires. The child rages, the mother is inexorable. He ceases to cry and learns to subject his will to hers. The first germs of obedience are developed. Love, trust, gratitude, and obedience develop the first germ of conscience ; the child has the first faint shadow of the feeling that it is not right to disobey a loving mother ; he begins to feel that the mother is not in the world solely for *his* sake, that the world itself does not exist for *him*, and, slowly he begins to realize that he is not in the world for his own sake. With this the first shadow of duty and right appears. Slowly this grows until it gains the fullness of the good man's impulse to immortalize his being in the higher imperishable being of the

[1] Green, *Pestalozzi's Educational Writings*, p. 77.
[2] Preface to 2nd ed. of *Lienhard und Gertrud*.

whole—*Not oneself but the brethren*—Not the individual but the race.[1]

The central points in this theory of moral development are (1) *obedience*, and (2) the rôle played by primitive instinct in the development of morality. Two remarkable passages in Pestalozzi's writings throw further light on their meaning. The first immediately precedes the theory summarized above. It urges that ' *obedience in its origin is an activity whose driving wheel is opposed to the inclinations of animal nature.*' Its cultivation, says Pestalozzi, depends on art. The *First Edition* claims that it ' is not a simple result of natural instinct, but yet it follows the same course of development ' ; the *Second Edition* that it ' is not a simple result of pure instinct, but it is closely connected with it.' . . . Its first manifestations are further stated to be simply passive ; active obedience develops much later, and later still the consciousness that it is good to obey the mother. There might seem to be some confusion in the idea of a force or activity that is passive, but the general sense of Pestalozzi's discussion is that this force, whatever its origin, is at first inhibitory in function : it succeeds in quelling the instinctive forces of rage which find expression when some physical want remains unsatisfied. Pestalozzi sees its close relationship to the instincts yet hesitates to classify it directly with the expression of animal impulse. In its origin, however, he agrees that it is very similar to instinct. He seems to give to it two marks of instinctive activity ; it is innate, and it is evoked by a specific, yet relatively complex, situation. Thus, for instance, in the mental state there may be desire aroused by physical wants : there may also be incipient pugnacity aroused by the thwarting of the child's primitive impulses. There supervenes a force which thwarts one or both of these and which re-adjusts

---

[1] *Wie Gertrud ihre Kinder lehrt*, pp. 183 ff. Cf. also p. 145 : ' From the moment that a mother takes a child upon her lap she teaches him. She brings nearer to his senses what Nature has scattered afar off over large areas and in confusion, and makes the action of receiving sense-impressions and the knowledge derived from them easy, pleasant, and delightful to him. The mother, weak and untrained, follows Nature without help or guidance and knows not what she is doing. She does not intend to teach, she intends only to quiet the child, to occupy him. But nevertheless in her pure simplicity she follows the high course of Nature without knowing what *Nature* does through *her*, and Nature does very much through her. In this way she opens the world to the child. She makes him ready to use his senses and prepares for the early development of his attention and power of observation.'

the individual to his environment. The rage may be supposed
to be a merely reflex line of discharge opened when other out-
lets are closed, but even on this supposition the ' force of
obedience ' modifies the expression of one or more functional
lines of instinctive activity.

The other passage appears in one of the *Letters to Greaves*,[1]
in which the fundamental differences between the mere animal
and the human being are under discussion. Pestalozzi, after
insisting that animal instinct knows no higher object than self,
points out that in man ' there is something which will not fail,
in due time, to make itself manifest in a series of facts altogether independent of animal life.   While the animal is for ever
actuated by that instinct to which it owes its preservation and
all its powers and enjoyments, a something will assert its right
in man to hold the empire over all his powers and to lead him
to those exertions which will secure for him a place in the scale
of moral being.' Here Pestalozzi is studiously vague, but the
general discussion, as before, speedily connects the ' first tokens
of a spiritual nature in the infant ' with appropriate maternal
treatment of the physical wants of the child.   The functions of
this *assertive* and *controlling* ' something ' are very similar to
the ' opposing ' characteristic of ' obedience ' which we have
previously noted.   It seems, therefore, that in the first edition
of *Wie Gertrud ihre Kinder lehrt* (written 1801), Pestalozzi
thought that obedience followed the same development as
instinct, that in the *Letters to Greaves* (1818) he sharply differentiated the ' something ' (which is strikingly similar in function
to obedience) from animal instinct, and that in the second
edition (1820) he maintained again its close initial connection
with instinct.   In view of the fact that the revised second
edition still contained the statement that active obedience
appeared considerably later than passive obedience we are
probably safe in assuming that in the passage from the *Letters
to Greaves* he is still thinking of the same type of inhibitory force,
but dealing, as he there is, with its strongly positive effect upon
moral development, he particularly emphasizes its assertive and
controlling powers.   And although there are three definitive
assurances that this germ of morality was not ' instinct ' there

[1] Letter xi.   See Green, *Educational Writings*, pp. 212-3, or Letter ix.
London trans. of 1827, p. 39.

are many passages that show Pestalozzi's *appeal* to instinctive
tendencies in his attempt to nourish the incipient moral life.
He seems, indeed, forced to think of morality as developing in
close conjunction with, if not out of, the primitive tendencies
amongst the ruins of which he found the philosophical beginnings of morality. But even if he looked upon morality as
evolved from an obedience rooted in instinct he saw clearly that
obedience was not a purely passive force, but an active and
inhibitory tendency, and that the mother in appealing to it,
was appealing to an ally in her child's own nature.

Obedience is also fully discussed in the *Idee der Elementar-
bildung*, 52-54.[1] Here, again, the mother raises the child
to freedom by exacting obedience. She teaches him to walk
so that he may no longer need her guidance ; she makes him
capable so that he may be able to help himself ; to know so
that he may himself know what he needs. . . . ' The obedience
which she exacts is that which his own nature and his needs
demand. Her will is no other than law, which his own reason
would impose on the child if he were a man, *i.e.* free, and to
which he would submit of his own accord.' Pestalozzi thus
makes all obedience an appeal to either an active or a latent
value of the personality. In exacting obedience, and even in
punishment the mother unconsciously declares the child to be
a free and reasonable being. Here, as in other passages,
Pestalozzi joins necessity with freedom and freedom with
necessity. He sees quite as clearly as Rousseau the value of
the ' wall of brass,' but, unlike Rousseau, he brings it into
the spheres of practical activity (work) and religion. He
very carefully insists that although the mother is the first
Providence the child knows, and although her image becomes
his conscience, and her command brings with it something of
the unvarying and eternal nature of morality, yet the conception of morality must be united at all points with the
child's individuality, and with his sentiments and relations
towards his brothers, sisters, relatives, fellows. ' It is then in
conformity with the progress of the child's development in all
directions, and is in its essence nothing else but the extension
of the activity and of the sphere of his pristine moral nature.'

[1] *Pestalozzi's Ausgewählte Werke.* (Mann), iii. Sections 52-4, or *Pestalozzi's
Sämmtliche Werke.* (Seyffarth), xvii. pp. 219 ff.

And Pestalozzi seems to find in the operation of the maternal instinct the only sure and safe means of preserving morality. ' The germ of morality in so far as it emanates from feelings peculiar to infancy, rapidly decays unless we succeed in attaching the first pulsings of higher moral feelings, as the threads of life, to the golden spindle of Creation.' [1]

This close conjunction of the moral life with instinct seems to be supported by two other characteristics of Pestalozzi's theory and practice—his attempt to introduce the natural unity and purpose of life itself into educational activity, and his appeal to the whole self of the pupil. Both of these exemplify his desire to utilize the pupil's own values, and particularly the active powers of obedience, rather than to prescribe duties or enforce commands by external compulsion. In the face of the most difficult conditions he maintained a happy family atmosphere in all his institutions. No one better than Pestalozzi himself knew the meaning of his maxim : *Life* educates. No passages more eloquently state the true *origin* and the real *unity* of educational agencies than these : ' Do not forget that all you are, your purposes, and all that you ought to be have their origin in yourself.' [2] ' Only that which affects man as an indissoluble unit is educative in our sense of the word. It must reach his hand and his heart as well as his head. No partial approach can be satisfactory. To consider any one capacity exclusively (head or heart or hand) is to undermine and destroy man's native equilibrium. It means unnatural methods of training and produces partial human products. It is as wrong to think only of morality and religion as it is to have the intellect solely in mind.' [3]

We do not propose to estimate the value for freedom of Pestalozzi's methods of intellectual education : they often seem to be in flagrant contradiction to his general principles. But even if he suffered from the delusion of having discovered the three elementary powers, sound, form, number, and even if he yielded to the temptation to substitute meaningless elements for meaningful wholes it must be remembered that he was all the while consistently seeking for that directness and simplicity

---

[1] Green, *Educational Writings*, p. 146.

[2] *The Pamphlet of 1800. Life and Work of Pestalozzi* (Green), p. 296.

[3] *Educational Writings* (Green), pp. 268-9.

of real experience through which nature presented the objects
of the outer world. It must be remembered also that his
method, however uninteresting in some respects, did not fail to
arouse the interest and the effort of his pupils. His own admonition seems to have been observed in much of his work.
' Let the results of your art and your instruction, while you try
to found them upon natural law, by the richness of their charm
and the variety of their free play, bear the impression of freedom and independence.' [1] He was, indeed, as he confessed,
often infatuated with ' a poor invention, crooked and stupid
enough compared with Nature,' and often imagined that because
children did as he wished, his wishes followed Nature's path.
But few experimenters have so sincerely recorded their ' ten-
tative and erring measures ' ; few would have confessed to
prescribing the ' wildest nonsense ' simply because it was
difficult. Even here, however, he was attempting to refer his
' nonsense ' to the child's actual power, and behind it there was
a principle which occupied a cardinal place in later writers.
' All instruction of man is only the art of helping Nature to
develop in her own way ; and this art rests essentially on the
relation and harmony between the impressions received of the
child and the exact degree of his developed powers.' [2]

One might sum up his contribution to education in his own
sentence : *The natural way of teaching is not coercive.* He aimed
at gathering together the haphazard lessons of Nature, and so
uniting them with the happy activities of the family that their
relevance would be apparent to children. He sought to find
for the natural forces of childhood directed and purposeful
modes of expression, simple, and yet so carefully graded in
point of difficulty, that the child's ' inner forces ' might be
strengthened and consolidated into a real unity of moral
endeavour. He realized that teacher and parent can do much
to increase the relevancy of instruction to the child's life, and
that through skill and wisdom they may exert an influence,
which will make the pupil more clearly aware of the ways in
which his spasmodic efforts may be focused and unified. He
also realized that wise influence would enable the pupil to see
a positive value in compulsion, in submission to authority, and
in that obedience to external demands without which little of

---

[1] *Wie Gertrud ihre Kinder lehrt*, p. 79.   [2] *Ibid.* p. 26.

permanent value in education can be accomplished. With great pedagogic insight he first exercised these influences in specific and limited yet ' near ' relationships of life, and sought to extend them gradually until they leavened the pupil's every-day relationships and finally became ideals of duty permeating the whole of his life. Before Pestalozzi no one realized so vividly what the teacher might do in gaining the child's confidence and affection, in extending the range of his interests, in focusing values that might otherwise have been outside the orbit of his life, in encouraging and reinforcing his powers, in leading him to see the value of continued effort, in teaching him to realize that compulsion, accepted and adopted in moments of insight, may prove more expressive of the deeper issues of one's nature than any easy self-chosen path. No one did more than Pestalozzi himself to show the world that the wise exercise of a great teacher's authority need not be incompatible with freedom, and that it may, in fact, do much to reinforce and strengthen the deepest impulses of the heart. And, having done these things, he did much to realize his own aim : ' I will put skill into the hand of the mother, into the hand of the child, and into the hand of the innocent ; and the scorner shall be silenced and shall say no more—It is a dream.'